Praise for The Long Term

"*The Long Term* is a powerful collection of voices, curated and edited by a powerful lineup of veteran organizers and radical thinkers. The writers in this collection make a compelling and eloquent case against 'the prison nation' and give us a glimpse of the resistance and the alternatives that are already in the works."
—Barbara Ransby, author of *Making All Black Lives Matter: Reimagining Freedom in the Twenty-First Century*

"As I read this book, I savor the words of s/heroes with whom I've stood shoulder to shoulder in struggle and new voices that carry me to spirits and spaces that I now know deeply connect to my life and work. As the title tells us, captured lives inside and ongoing resistance are inexorably linked to struggles for freedom wherever we find them. This beautifully textured book offers so many entry points into stories of trauma that give rise to life-breathing resistance; solidarity even across bodily separation that fuels our collective creativity; and reasons not only for despair but for confidence in our combined vision and work. The freedom struggles reflected in the pages of this book and represented by its very publication offer us wisdom and inspiration to keep moving not only against oppression but onward in liberation."
—Mimi Kim, PhD, School of Social Work, California State University, Long Beach and founder of TORCH, Training and Organizing Resources for Community Health

"The essays collected in *The Long Term* address essential questions facing contemporary movements: 'What must be transformed and built to eliminate harm, cultivate strong communities, and create forms of authentic public safety? What are the levers and the mind-sets that make prisons and policing appear logical, necessary, and possible?' This collection pulls together brilliant insights from writers inside and outside prisons, making critical insights and proposals about what it will take to get rid of police and prisons and build real safety and justice. This book is a must-read for anyone fighting against racism and criminalization. *The Long Term* is full of insightful, practical wisdom about how the punishment system is operating, what is fueling it, what reform attempts are inadvertently propping it up, and what kinds of work are actually necessary to abolish it. *The Long Term* is a bold and important contribution to feminist, anti-racist, and anti-punishment scholarship and activism."

—Dean Spade, Associate Professor, Seattle University School of Law, and author of *Normal Life: Administrative Violence, Critical Trans Politics, and the Limits of Law*

The Long Term
Resisting Life Sentences, Working Toward Freedom

Edited by

Alice Kim, Erica R. Meiners, Audrey Petty,
Jill Petty, Beth E. Richie, and Sarah Ross

Published in 2018 by
Haymarket Books
P.O. Box 180165
Chicago, IL 60618
773-583-7884
www.haymarketbooks.org
info@haymarketbooks.org

ISBN: 978-1-60846-899-7

Trade distribution:
In the US, Consortium Book Sales and Distribution, www.cbsd.com
In Canada, Publishers Group Canada, www.pgcbooks.ca
In the UK, Turnaround Publisher Services, www.turnaround-uk.com
All other countries, Ingram Publisher Services International, IPS_Intlsales@ingramcontent.com

Cover artwork by Damon Locks.

This book was published with the generous support of Lannan Foundation and Wallace Action Fund.

Printed in Canada by union labor.

Library of Congress Cataloging-in-Publication data is available.

10 9 8 7 6 5 4 3 2 1

Contents

Section 1: We Are Alive

Section 2: Long-Term Sentencing, Illusions of Safety, and the Pursuit of Toughness

Section 3: For Feminist Freedoms: Confronting Misogyny and White Supremacy through Abolition Politics and Anticapitalist Practices

Section 4: Building Resistance for the Long Term

Section 5: Litanies for Survival

List of Images

Introduction

The Rise of Long-Term Sentences and Teaching Inside as Feminist, Abolitionist Labor

I n 2011, when the Prison + Neighborhood Arts Project (P+NAP)—a group of artists, scholars, organizers, and writers—started teaching arts and humanities classes at Stateville prison in Illinois, our work was organized by the prison administration under a program called "Long-Term Offenders." The abbreviation LTO, casually written on institutional paperwork and used by prison guards, is the prison administration's shorthand for people who are serving long-term sentences, meaning life without parole or virtual life sentences of fifty years or more. For the people we met in our classes at Stateville prison, the term "LTO" signals something profound: it represents the nation's ideological and political commitments to the long-term removal of people from their communities into prisons, a label that condemns many to a continuously controlled life.

In this book we deploy the notion of the long term to show how the impacts of long-term sentencing extend beyond prison walls. The loss of family, community, and resources and the struggle against targeted criminalization are woven into the fabric of our everyday lives. Long-term sentencing is only the most blatant example of the "prison nation," a term provided by activist, scholar, and coauthor Beth E. Richie.[1]

Although Illinois successfully abolished the death penalty in 2011 after a decade-long moratorium on executions, students in our classes are still condemned to die in prison. They are among the nearly 206,000 people serving life or virtual life sentences in the United States, according to 2017 research from the national advocacy

organization the Sentencing Project. Policies implemented in the
1980s and 1990s—particularly life without the possibility of parole,
mandatory minimums, and "three strikes and you're out" laws—
contributed to a prison population increase of more than 1.5 million
people over the last thirty years. As the number of people in prison
has increased, so, too, has the severity of their sentences. Illinois,
our home state, is one of six states where all life sentences are imposed without the possibility of parole. As the Sentencing Project
outlines, of the 5,092 people serving life or virtual life sentences in
Illinois in 2017, 68 percent were Black people while the state's total
Black population was estimated at 14.7 percent.[2]

This engineered pattern is evident throughout the nation. Reflecting the structural racism that is endemic to the criminal legal
system, one in five Black people in prison in the United States is
sentenced to virtual life or life sentences. Young people are not immune either: some twelve thousand people nationwide were sentenced to long terms as juveniles. Almost one-half of women serving
life without parole are survivors of physical or sexual violence, illus-
trating the clear link between gender violence and state violence.
The national advocacy organization Families Against Mandatory
Minimums reports that people released from prison in 2009 served
sentences that were, on average, more than a third longer than those
of prisoners released in 1990. The tally is staggering, a consequence
of the so-called tough-on-crime logic that powered the policies that
lock people up and throw away the key.

This framework to restore "law and order" moved into the conservative lexicon in the 1960s to directly assault Black power and
civil rights movements. From Richard Nixon, whose 1968 presidential campaign focused continually on crime and urban unrest,
to Ronald Reagan's war on drugs, to Bill Clinton's 1994 crime bill,
politicians across the political spectrum evoked the threat of crime
to criminalize nonwhite, particularly Black, communities.[3] Not simply a conservative political agenda, reforms advanced by Democrats,
some in the name of ending racial bias in sentencing, also contributed to the expansion of our carceral state over the last three decades,
as scholar Naomi Murakawa outlines in *The First Civil Right: How
Liberals Built Prison America*.[4]

The massive buildup of carceral control—systems of surveillance, criminalization, and confinement operated by federal, state, and local governments—has earned the United States the distinction of being the world's leader in incarceration.[5] From metal detectors in public schools to Immigration and Customs Enforcement (ICE) raids at work sites, carceral practices are facts of everyday life. Every year eleven million people cycle through local jails around the country, and others are subjected to detention centers, electronic monitoring regimes, and other forms of punitive surveillance and control. As in many other states, the majority of people in Illinois state prisons come from urban areas; Chicago neighborhoods with engineered racial isolation experience grotesquely asymmetrical investment in police rather than in quality and equitable public schools. In 2013 the *Chicago Reporter* calculated that the annual price tag to lock up residents from just one block in Austin, an African American neighborhood on Chicago's West Side, was an estimated $4 million with the cost rising to $644 million for all of Austin.[6]

The shifting of financial resources away from education and into punishment and surveillance also holds true inside prisons, where resources for meaningful programming are scant. Not surprisingly, the rise of long-term sentences coincided with the loss of programs aimed at "rehabilitation." The 1994 Violent Crime Control and Law Enforcement Act, the most expansive crime bill in the nation's history, decimated higher education programs in prison by eliminating Pell Grants that provided federal financial aid for incarcerated students. As a result of this loss, approximately 350 secular college programs in prisons closed. Today, higher education programs inside are slowly being rebuilt through partnerships between colleges, nonprofits, and state departments of correction.[7] Gillian Harkins and coauthor Erica R. Meiners point out that these programs are uneven in their goals, ideological allegiances, and institutional structures.[8] This growth has coincided with increased public scrutiny on the problem of mass incarceration over the last decade.

Yet today, in many states, people with life sentences, those ineligible for parole, or those marked as gang-involved or who have convictions for sexual offenses are often placed at the back of the line for the limited educational or vocational opportunities that are available. These discriminatory practices operationalize the "throw away the key" rhetoric, leaving people inside describing prison as a "living grave." Just as funding for public schools and higher education in the free world has been siphoned away, so too has state support for services and resources in prison. When P+NAP started at Stateville prison, the John Howard Association (JHA) of Illinois, a prison watchdog organization, had disclosed in their 2010 Monitoring Report: "Like all maximum-security prisons in Illinois, Stateville has extremely limited educational or vocational opportunities. The prison offers a small GED program, a barber program, as well as a handful of on-site industries jobs for its approximately 2,550 population," but most people who are incarcerated at Stateville "have nothing to do but sit in their cell."[9] In this same report, JHA noted that the Illinois Department of Corrections' policy dictates that people with shorter sentences take available educational and vocational classes ahead of those with longer sentences, which effectively bars many people with long-term sentences from participating in programming.

Refusing this logic that some are disposable while others are worthy, and framing our work as movement building toward freedom, P+NAP was created to build connections with incarcerated people serving long terms, and to resist their disappearance into the vacuum of prison. Because we are educators who believe in a world without prisons, our learning and teaching is an intentional intervention in the apparatus of the carceral state. All of our classrooms are sites for creating new knowledge about building communities without criminalization and incarceration.

Many of our students in prison have spent much of their life in a cell. One student, Ricky Patterson, described prison as "a dark place physically made to mentally break men by oppressing their bodies and shackling their minds to a sinking place of hopelessness." If, at its best, education is about creating opportunities to ensure that all flourish, prisons are by their very design at odds with this vision. Caged inside a facility constructed and organized to isolate, control, and censor, our students' lives testify to the lie of the still circulating myths of "violent criminal," the "Class X offender," and the "superpredator." Eric Blackmon, another P+NAP student, described the "brilliance" of those behind the wall where "a person stripped of everything survives" by invoking "a different kind of love, a different kind of hope, and a different kind of dream."

P+NAP operates despite the rules and regulations of the prison. The books and courses we teach are subject to approval and internal review by the state and prison administration. Together with visitors coming to see their loved ones, we are "shaken down" or searched by officers when we enter the prison. Lesson plans and homework are checked to prevent any censored material from entering the prison. While we do not teach with officers in the room, they can and do enter our classrooms at any time. "Fraternization" is what the prison watches for and punishes. The list of actions that are forbidden is long and dynamic: Never accept a birthday or a condolence card—usually beautifully handmade in the prison economy. We cannot give a spare pen to a student. Restrictions extend beyond the site of the prison: a condition of being permitted to teach inside in our state is that we agree not to ever communicate, with any of our students outside the classroom, their family members in the free world, or with anyone incarcerated in any other Illinois prison. Interviews with media outlets must first be cleared by the prison.

Even with the extensive list of rules that regulate our access to the prison, the bottom line is: *the prison is always right.* And while the consequences for breaking the rules for us might be removal from this prison (and all other state prisons), the slightest infraction from students may result in solitary confinement, barred access to all programs, transfer to another prison, or denial of privileges (yard time and visits).

We recount our experience of these conditions to illustrate that while we perceive the stakes to be high, they are impossible for our students and their families. And yet we recognize that our classrooms in this prison are similar to other contexts where we, and many of our comrades, teach and work. Some of these restrictions resemble the conditions in Chicago's public school system where "softer" versions of security checks and surveillance are implemented. Teachers face increased scrutiny of course content and materials, students face zero-tolerance policies and metal detectors, and in most educational institutions, police can enter a classroom at any time. Building freedom for all requires naming the profound differences between teaching inside the prison and outside it, but it also requires identifying the similarities in order to build stronger coalitions and alliances.

For many of us, this labor at Stateville is our third or fifth shift; it is labor beyond our paid employment, and our unpaid care work. And like much of the other unpaid labor that sustains our communities, this work is mostly done by women. This reality is acutely spatialized in prisons across the United States: visiting rooms are full of sisters, mothers, lovers, and aunts, while just beyond the doors of the visiting room are incarcerated people. Outside the prison, again, mothers, sisters, grandmothers, lovers, and wives bear the burden of incarceration and take up the fight for their loved ones in courts and on the streets. They are the ones who accept exorbitant fees for collect phone calls from the prison, mail books to their incarcerated loved ones, and add money to commissary accounts.

The overlap of (hetero)gendered, racialized care work and the structures of carceral control brings the movement to end long-term sentences into dialogue, and perhaps into tension, with other feminist facets of our personal and political lives. Alert to the various challenges and possible contradictions of working in a maximum-security prison men—rather, for people the state identifies as men—part of our work is to name and critique how movement work done by women is often geared toward supporting and freeing cisgender men. "The work of the world," the poet Marge Piercy writes, is "as common as mud" and women are often the ones "who strain in the mud and the muck to move things forward" and "do what has to be done, again and again."[10]

As a collective dedicated to ending the nation's reliance on prisons and to building feminist and antiracist struggles for justice, we are critical of how forms of liberal, generally white, feminism continue to play a key role in bolstering and upholding carceral practices. Long-term sentences, more surveillance, and increased criminalization are frequently advanced in the name of "protecting women and children"—a stance often termed "carceral feminism." As Victoria Law explains in her contribution to this anthology, "While its adherents would likely reject the descriptor, carceral feminism describes an approach that sees increased policing, prosecution, and imprisonment as the primary solution to violence against women." Such punitive measures purport to address the harm some women experience, yet criminalization is not a deterrent, nor a preventive tool or response capable of igniting cultural shifts that reduce violence.

In 2001, INCITE!, Women, Gender Non-Conforming and Trans people of Color Against Violence, and Critical Resistance issued a statement on "Gender Violence and the Prison Industrial Complex" calling for "social justice movements to develop strategies and analysis that address both state and interpersonal violence . . . that do not depend on a sexist, racist, classist, and homophobic criminal justice system."[11] From this framework many local groups are creating practices that respond to harm without criminalization. For example, two organizations in Philadelphia—Philly Stands Up and Philly's Pissed—implemented a community-based restorative justice approach to address sexual violence within their communities "through direct involvement of those who have caused harm."[12]

Our feminist politics includes commitments to end gender violence and to build stronger and safer communities without strengthening prison, policing, and borders. While the work inside the prison—teaching, advocacy, learning, support, and attempts at institutional change—continues, and hopefully offers opportunities for new forms of academic and cultural expression, we also challenge feminist practices that feed the carceral state and have created policies that opened doors to incarcerate many of our students. Our courses link feminist movements and analysis to our students' lives.

We stand in the tradition of feminists, often women-of-color queer people, who understood that "there is no such thing as a single-issue struggle, because we do not live single-issue lives," as poet and activist Audre Lorde wrote in 1982. Building from the work of earlier Black feminist organizers, including the Combahee River Collective, legal theorist Kimberlé Crenshaw popularized the term "intersectionality" to refer to the multiple ways that power and privilege intersect and to name how social positions and identities—ethnicity, gender, sexuality, ability, race, class, and others—are mutually constitutive.[13] All of our identities shape our lives and modalities of resistance and refusal. While we coalesced through our teaching at Stateville, we have overlapping and deep stakes in other, concurrent movements: projects to elevate the dignity and rights of people living in public housing, collectives to germinate the analysis and experience of women-of-color writers and thinkers, struggles for queer liberation and against capitalism, mobilizations to end the violence of policing and to build community, and, uniformly, movements to end violence against all women.

An abolitionist feminist praxis is needed now more than ever to challenge the indefinite long-term caging of our communities. To build communities that ensure real safety for all, we invest in the question Angela Davis, a former political prisoner and freedom fighter, posed in 2001: *Are prisons obsolete?* Always imperative, abolition includes movements for decarceration, eliminating punitive drug laws, shrinking—not reforming—police powers and forces, and redirecting public resources from punishment toward communities. Critical Resistance defines prison-industrial-complex abolition as "a political vision with the goal of eliminating imprisonment, policing, and surveillance and creating lasting alternatives to punishment and imprisonment."[14]

A practice and a politic, abolition is working toward the obsolescence of prison, but, as importantly, this paradigm surfaces necessary questions and opportunities for action. What histories of dispossession and displacement must be named and accounted for? What must be transformed and built to eliminate harm, cultivate strong communities, and create forms of authentic public safety? What are the levers and the mind-sets that make prisons and policing appear logical, necessary, and possible? Abolition involves dismantling institutions that reproduce and mask harm, but it also demands the more radical work to imagine and to build up practices, vocabularies, and communities that facilitate self-determination. The work to build up community responses to end sexual violence; the mobilizations to challenge the indefinite caging of our communities; our collective and daily labor inside and outside of prisons to demand other futures—this is decidedly radical feminist work. We are in the struggle, together, to build communities that ensure real safety for all, leaving no one behind—this is an abolitionist practice.

Beyond Reform, Building Freedom

During the Obama era, rhetoric inched away from "tough on crime" to "smart on crime." The Obama administration did support policy changes that freed thousands of incarcerated people, yet these shifts unfolded within a limited and exclusionary reformist framework. While Barack Obama was the first sitting president to visit a federal prison and to release thousands of people serving long prison terms for drug-related convictions, his administration also advanced the largest deportation machine in US history. As some Democrats and Republicans came out against mandatory minimum sentences for "nonviolent crimes" and advocated for other, purportedly more humane forms of control—such as electronic monitoring—to reduce the nation's prison population, headlines touted the "end of mass incarceration." This growing public awareness about the consequences of mass incarceration was complicated, often focusing more on the exorbitant financial cost of housing aging people in prisons and on alternative forms of surveillance and control, but only for people with "non-serious, non-violent, non-sexual" convictions, to use political scientist Marie Gottschalk's phrase.[15] For example, the 2016 Second Chance Pell program restored some previously eliminated federal funding for postsecondary educational opportunities, but only for a finite number of people behind bars who would be released within five years.

In the last decade, smart-on-crime approaches have shifted some sentencing policies. In 2014 the Sentencing Project reported that twenty-nine states had adopted reforms designed to scale back the scope and severity of mandatory sentencing policies, California voters approved a referendum that curbed the state's "notoriously broad 'three strikes and you're out' law," and some judicial sentencing discretion has been restored to federal judges by the US Supreme Court.[16] Legal challenges propelled by family members working with lawyers and activists have also overturned death sentences and mandatory life-without-parole sentences for people convicted as minors. While such actions have meant freedom for some, even these legal wins have resulted in complicated outcomes, with other minors still facing long prison sentences. Largely overlooked in this emerging national conversation are the root causes of crime and targeted criminalization.

Most people serving long-term sentences have not benefited from initiatives intended to shrink the prison population. According to 2017 research by the Prison Policy Initiative, nearly nine hundred thousand people who are incarcerated were convicted on "violent offenses."[17] Our students are among them. Their culpability and "violence" often form the backdrop to justify relief for "nonviolent offenders." Entrenched in white supremacy, America's punishment paradigm relies on racist narratives to justify extreme sentencing practices. "The ideologies that support the prison system demonize those who have been touched by it," says Angela Davis, "but prisoners are like you, and prisoners are like me."[18] This includes "violent" and "nonviolent" offenders alike, categories created by the state that aim to dehumanize.

Our collective labor, engagement, and learning remind us that it is important to make distinctions between reforms that legitimize and strengthen the prison system and those that diminish its power and function. While reforms such as reversing mandatory sentencing policies are necessary, these efforts often exclude half of our nation's state prison population and ignore the fact that long-term sentences were not the norm less than thirty years ago. More importantly, these reforms don't recognize the reality that caging people does not eliminate violence or produce public safety. Though sometimes creating freedom for a small number, these "fixes" often legitimize the system just enough to make it politically palatable to the (whiter, wealthier) public.

Reform without a vision of fundamental change; without a politics that aims to leave no one behind, can give way to new forms of captivity and containment by the state. Take, for example, reforms such as electronic monitoring, house arrest, mandatory drug testing, and other forms of probation. While for some these alternatives might be preferable over prisons, they threaten to extend imprisonment "beyond the walls of the jail or penitentiary" into our homes and neighborhoods, as author and activist Maya Schenwar astutely points out.[19] These "kinder and gentler" forms of punishment create more insidious forms of control and containment by the state and legitimate a carceral logic. As activist and scholar Karlene Faith wrote in 2000, "When appraising whether a project is reformist reform or has revolutionary reform potential, the question to ask is, 'Cui bono?' That is, 'Who benefits?' If the reform benefits women in the long run, strengthens communities, and reduces the numbers of prisoners, it is revolutionary; if it eases conditions for a few women, temporarily, but at the same time reinforces a correctional ideology that benefits the state and a philosophy of retribution, it is reform."[20]

Beyond alterations that simply shore up a system designed to have people disappear and to confer premature death on many, in this political moment the nation is faced with another danger. The Trump administration actively seeks to reverse even these meager reforms. Current attorney general Jeff Sessions not only rescinded the Obama administration's decision to eliminate the use of private prisons in the federal system but also publicly objects to federal government monitoring of local police forces, pushes for tougher penalties for drug-related crimes, and more. Whether the current federal regime can slow down the state-level trickle of bipartisan shifts toward "smart on crime" policies remains to be seen.

The contributions in this book contribute to the ongoing national conversation on prisons and targeted criminalization by applying a long-term lens to help us think more deeply about what it means to be (un)free and to act with more urgency in our collective struggles for freedom. Prior decades of organizing precipitated the nation's recent reform moment. High-profile exonerations of people who had been wrongfully convicted; investigative reports exposing racial bias, corruption, and prosecutorial misconduct in the courts; and activism against capital punishment and the violence of policing were all responses to America's rush to incarcerate. An international campaign to stop the execution of Troy Davis and spontaneous protests across the United States against the murder of Trayvon Martin were the precursors to the current Black Lives Matter movement.[21]

Also fueling this moment was a wealth of publications and research by activists, scholars, incarcerated people, and formerly incarcerated people: Angela Davis's *Are Prisons Obsolete?*; Marc Mauer's *Race to Incarcerate*; Ruth Wilson Gilmore's *Golden Gulag: Prisons, Surplus, Crisis, and Opposition in Globalizing California*; Mumia Abu-Jamal's *Jailhouse Lawyers: Prisoners Defending Prisoners v. the USA*; and anthologies edited by Joy James, including *Imprisoned Intellectuals: America's Political Prisoners Write on Life, Liberation, and Rebellion*, and Bettina Aptheker and Angela Davis's *If They Come in the Morning: Voices of Resistance*. These books amplified the organizing work of germinal, often grassroots, anti-prison organizations, including Justice Now!, All of Us or None, the Sentencing Project, Sylvia Rivera Law Project, Chicago Legal Advocacy for Incarcerated Mothers, and Critical Resistance.[22] Michelle Alexander's book *The New Jim Crow: Mass Incarceration in the Age of Colorblindness* served to popularize a critique of the prison-industrial complex that links the mass incarceration of people of color with the legacy of slavery, an analysis previously made by abolitionists.[23] Alexander's argument that mass incarceration is the new caste system resonated because so many Black, Brown, and poor people had experienced and witnessed the devastating effects of criminalization and incarceration.

As evidenced in this collection, the work to end long-term sentences is multifaceted. The current wave of resistance to the enduring spectacle of Black death at the hand of the state creates opportunities and openings for organizing against new (and old) harsh carceral policies. It will take all of us, and every tool we have and more, to build the movements we know we need. Legal and legislative wins can be valuable. Yet removing bad laws, and even shuttering super-maximum prisons, is not enough—*while necessary, never sufficient.* The work for the long term is to build flourishing and accountable communities. Through a range of creative direct actions, including strikes and marches, the Black Lives Matter movement, particularly Black-, queer-, and feminist-led mobilizations, not only raises the visibility of the violence of policing in Black and Brown communities but also amplifies the need for a radical shift away from targeted criminalization. Policy work can get us in the door, but deeper cultural, ideological and systemic shifts will keep us all free. As educators, we understand our work as one facet of movement building for liberation from the carceral state. If we shift the lens from a narrow focus on sentencing reforms or incarceration rates to a broader understanding of how punishment and carceral logic profoundly and persistently limit freedom *beyond the cages*, we can enable more radical and broad-based resistance movements. As Nelson Mandela said, "To be free is not merely to cast off one's chains, but to live in a way that respects and enhances the freedom of others."[24] Because our freedom is inextricably linked, we must invoke those who have been discarded and condemned to lifelong incarceration as co-strugglers.

Mandela's sentiment informs our work at Stateville and our efforts in collecting the work that is included in this book. In prison, the precariousness of life in a system designed to confer premature death is juxtaposed with the abiding slowness of everyday existence that is the reality for people facing life sentences. This is palpable in our classrooms, but present too is a feeling of vibrancy—an insistence from students that they are alive and living for the long term even as they are locked in a death trap. For those of us who are free and who advocate for people in prison, how do we do the work in ways that address this paradoxical reality? How do we not reproduce or augment the carceral system? How is our work transformative and meaningful for the here and now and for the long term?

Unfinished Labor, Always Messy

The contributors to this anthology invite readers to consider the questions and tensions we encounter in our own families, workplaces, campaigns, and projects and in wider movements. How is our collective work taking up the mantle of leaving no one behind? How are we working toward dismantling or at least shrinking our reliance on punishment and policing? How are we interrupting the "nonviolent vs. violent offender" binary that is so prevalent in criminal legal contexts? In the spirit of abolition, how are we building sustainable, healthy, safe communities? One way to build shared tools and analysis is ensuring that our campaigns, organizations, and actions expose white supremacy, capitalism, and heteropatriarchy—all of which fuels and normalizes the construction of border fences, mandatory drug tests at worksites and shelters, and surveillance cameras in parks and in some schools. In our experience, key to keeping these structures of power exposed is making sure that those who are most impacted by these punishing systems are at the center—of leadership, decision making, and agenda setting. Goals matter, but the process is just as vital—*how* we do our work matters.

This collection asks that readers—including the artists, parents, writers, lovers, organizers, scholars, and sisters who contributed to this project—take stock. Who are the people persistently caged away from the rest of us? What was gained, and lost, during reforms and movements under the "crisis of mass incarceration"? What is needed to practice accountability, to heal and to thrive together? In this not unfamiliar moment, yet another juncture in the "afterlife" of slavery according to historian Saidiya Hartman, what moves us *all* closer to freedom?[25]

Our project is centered not only on lives spent in prison but also on the many forms of harm the carceral state metes out and masks. Punitive immigration as well as unfair educational and employment policies that lock millions of people out of minimum-wage (not living-wage) employment are also part of the prison nation. Numerous research studies, including reports produced by state and federal governments, quantify how children in protective services, particularly those in foster care, have some of the worst life outcomes, such as being less likely to graduate from high school, having higher rates of suicide, and being more likely to end up incarcerated. Many transgender women, particularly women of color, report a lifetime of harassment by policing—being routinely stopped and accused or arrested for theft, "suspicious activity," or sex work—a phenomenon commonly termed "walking while trans." Perhaps because the violence is gauged as less severe, or the bodies affected are marked as disposable or insignificant, or the state is able to cloak and justify its harm, these everyday practices of systemic or state violence are often less recognized as being intimately tethered to our prison-industrial complex. Embodying different dimensions than a prison cell, these cages are not less real. To win freedom for all of us we must share a dynamic analysis that makes visible all forms of cages and at every scale. By naming, describing, and analyzing experiences of these logics of control, the voices in this collection contribute to a body of resistance against the shadow cast by long-term sentencing.

More political education materials are needed—in classrooms, church basements, and kitchen tables—to shift hearts and minds. Contributions to this anthology, including first-person narratives of campaigns to challenge death by incarceration, testimony from people surviving solitary confinement, and interviews with free family members who struggle through their own version of "doing time," are all crucial tools for ongoing political education. As this book documents, the goal of movement work is not only to create more opportunities for people to be seen and heard—both those inside and others most impacted—but also to engage a wider public in analysis and ideas. Dismantling our investments in criminal legal frameworks and associated cages requires opportunities for all to feel, in different ways.

Given this landscape, we urge readers to use the tools and analysis in this collection to build and strengthen relationships—within our families and worksites—and dare ourselves to imagine and practice other ways to seriously engage and address the effects of harm without augmenting punitive criminal legal systems and institutions. For many people an authentic desire to feel safer continues to be hijacked by our carceral state, with tactics such as bathroom bills and surveillance cameras. In an effort to make America "feel safe again," in the words of the current commander in chief, security eerily resembles a police state. In early 2018, New Orleans officials initiated a $40 million "public safety plan" that takes surveillance to a new level, including a proposed city ordinance that would require "every business with an alcohol license to install street-facing security cameras."[26] In October 2017, leaked documents exposed the fabrication of a new "domestic terror" designation by the FBI: the Black Identity Extremist (BIE) movement. With chilling echoes of the FBI's COINTELPRO program of the 1960s and '70s, the BIE movement is marked as a threat to law enforcement officers because of its grievances against police violence.[27]

In Chicago, where Mayor Rahm Emanuel shuttered fifty public elementary and high schools in 2013 (with more on the docket for 2018) and closed six of the city's twelve mental health clinics in 2012, he has the green light to build a brand-new police training facility, with a whopping $95 million price tag, while promising to hire one thousand additional police officers at a cost of approximately $125 million per year.[28] While more police may provide an illusion of safety, Chicago's brutal history reminds of us of how the violence of policing terrorizes and destroys communities. Yet letting go of the feelings of security, however illusory, offered by the carceral state is risky, especially for those of us who have experienced harm. Eliminating the "cops in our hearts" and not just the ones in our heads, as antiviolence organizer Paula X. Rojas writes, can be potentially the more difficult work.[29] Perhaps the intimacy

16

suggested by poetry, art, and storytelling holds the potential for unlocking these investments.

◆

This book invites readers to explore long-term sentencing as an intricate matrix, a force of devastation, a system of extreme deprivation, and a lived experience. Section 1, "We Are Alive," features the voices of people directly affected by incarceration, who convey, in detail, the boundlessness of the long term and enumerate how the long term extends beyond the confines of a cell or a given sentence. These stories foreground struggles in sustaining relationships with loved ones, as well as the challenges of developing critical self-analysis and maintaining emotional health within the extremity of a life sentence. These narratives also illustrate the vibrancy and determination of people who have been locked up and hidden away, marked as expendable and unworthy. Collectively, these contributions proclaim, "We are alive."

Section 2, "Long-Term Sentencing, Illusions of Safety, and the Pursuit of Toughness," sketches an architecture of long-term sentencing, revealing how it serves as an insidious pillar of targeted criminalization. Authors, both incarcerated and in the free world, delve into the histories and mechanisms of long-term sentencing and explore the intersecting, insistent, and violence-producing measures of "toughness" that continue to drive punitive US policies, discourse, and ideology.

In section 3, "For Feminist Freedoms: Confronting Misogyny and White Supremacy through Abolition Politics and Anticapitalist Practices," writers reveal how long-term sentencing—as a product of white supremacy and heteropatriarchy—perpetuates racialized, heterogendered norms. Contributions in this section urge a critical analysis of the carceral state from a feminist, abolitionist lens, as well as reimaginings of justice in the form of community accountability and abolitionist praxis.

Section 4, "Building Resistance for the Long Term," draws on the accumulated wisdom and creativity of organizers—incarcerated, formerly incarcerated, and in the free world—to fashion strategies for resistance and plans for abolitionist work. Centering love and grassroots organizing, these narratives highlight how long-term solidarities and commitments are fundamental to the movement's survival and growth.

Finally, section 5, "Litanies for Survival," offers essays, personal testimonies, and a poem to illustrate how people who are incarcerated and their loved ones endure and resist long sentences while sustaining and nurturing their collective humanity.

The coeditors of *The Long Term: Resisting Life Sentences, Working Toward Freedom* see this collection as a step along the way to building the world we want to live in. Still, even with contributions from a wide range of people who have survived or resisted the long-term sentence, the narratives in this book do not capture the breadth or depth of work on long-term sentences. That is not possible. We are still learning "how to talk about prisons as institutions that collect and hide away the people whom society treats as its refuse," as Angela Davis says.[30] What this collection does represent is a refusal to discard those who are incarcerated and an insistence on growing a shared abolitionist politic and practice. Beyond catalyzing dialogue, we hope these readings deepen already existing work, enable people to build new networks, and provoke other lines of analysis and fresh solidarities.

There is no seminar, rally, checklist, or course to keep us on the path to getting and staying free, but our campaigns and struggles, however intimately they transpire, must be generous, collective, radical, and public.

Section 1

We Are Alive

"There are no criminals here at Rikers Island Correctional Institution for Women."[1] These words from Assata Shakur written from her prison cell in 1978 resonate with the opening contributions of *The Long Term*. There are no criminals here either—just a declaration, a simple yet profound rejection of the state's classification of all incarcerated people. This refusal is compelled by what Assata termed a "fierce determination to move on closer to freedom." Similarly, in this book's first section, the writers and artists on the inside and outside of prison reflect on the resistance strategies they have been forced to devise or improvise, and also insist "We Are Alive."

Contributors ask, What are the costs of "serving the long term"? And how do we bear them? In her essay "On Leaving Prison: A Reflection on Entering and Exiting Communities," Monica Cosby remembers "Survival Day," a day to mark the resilience of the poor and working-class Chicago neighborhood she grew up in. "The whole of Uptown would gather on the mall to celebrate another year of our community's survival," writes Cosby. Other contributors recount events, relationships, activities, and connections that have sustained them while incarcerated and free, including cooking, singing, reading, making art, and writing. And, most urgently, they document their insistence to be seen and heard in spite of the master narratives and master machinery that seek to disappear them.

Lyle May, a student and writer on death row in Raleigh, North Carolina, shares the same sense of supreme urgency with this assembled collective. For May, writing has been an instrument to claim space and recognition. In a 2016 essay published in *Scalawag*, he observes, "Writing is a way of seeing the world and communicating that experience with others. Whether it occurs in a letter to a loved one or an essay in a magazine, writing is an essential tool I use to connect with society and express my humanity." And May says his writing is fueled by his "desire to understand and be understood by others."[2]

Like May, in "We Are Alive" writers and artists press for visibility and connection. Even as the carceral state attempts to engineer their erasure and their removal to the margins, they declare their right to sovereignty, friendship, love, respect, education, and self-expression: every day, every day, every day.

Prison Is Not Just a Place

■ Raul Dorado

The months of October and November 2016 brought sudden and unexpected changes. Approximately one thousand people from behind the walls at Stateville Correctional Center and three hundred from its Northern Reception Center were transferred to various facilities located in the southern region of the state.[1] These moves were mostly a result of the closing of the notorious F House, the country's last operational panopticon-style cell house, also known as the roundhouse. While a few prisoners welcomed change, the redistribution of our brethren was dreaded by the rest of us. None of us knew who was leaving or staying until the day before shipments, when lists were read over the loudspeaker along with the orders "Pack up, you're leaving." Although very impersonal, to us it was as if the ghostly voice of death were holding roll call. With few exceptions, people in prison abhor change. We prefer the hell we know to the one we don't. Decades' worth of friendships are instantly destroyed as fellow prisoners are torn out of our prison community like meat from a carcass. Our crude displacement also strains family ties; the farther south we are transferred, the more difficult it is for our loved ones to visit and support us.

Prison is not just a place; it is our life. A maximum-security facility houses mostly long-term offenders, many of whom have already served twenty years and have no foreseeable release date. Behind these walls we form concrete bonds of brotherhood and just about every other imaginable relationship common to ordinary people. There are even blood relatives here. It's not unusual for a father and son or for brothers to find themselves as cellmates. There have been instances where fathers and sons have met for the first

21

time in prison. More commonly we are coworkers: barbers, cooks, janitors, and so forth. We are classmates in adult basic education, pre-GED, GED, and a variety of educational programs. We are a church and choir members. We work and study side by side, eat and pray together; we coexist. In *The Narrative of the Life of Frederick Douglass*, Douglass describes his closest relationships with those he mentored in Sabbath school and those he labored with, side by side, in wheat fields. Slavery was unaccommodating to family ties; relatives were routinely separated, knowledge and sweat became the bonding agents in the formation of new relationships. These conditions prompted Douglass to write, "I loved them with a love stronger than anything I have ever experienced."[2]

Complete strangers become brothers over the course of ten, fifteen, twenty years of fighting the same fight, wrestling against similar feelings of despair and hopelessness. Time binds us as appeal after appeal for freedom is struck down by panels of black-robed judges slamming their gavels with the same conviction and finality that the reaper swings his scythe. I shared a cell for three years with someone I now consider a brother. On the outside we would have been mortal enemies separated by neighborhood boundaries, colors, and the flash of crooked fingers. On the inside we were joined by ethnicity, culture, and the realization of being very much alike. I knew the name, age, and birth dates of his children and siblings. When I called home, I would hand him the phone and he would speak to my brother. On visits, we would greet each other's family. We collaborated on meals, artwork, and letters to loved ones. When it came to meals, each one of us contributed whatever commissary food items we could. It didn't matter how little it may have been; the other put in the rest and we took turns cooking. He was a better cook and made a prodigy out of me, and now I cook for others. When it came to artwork, I would craft clever greeting cards with moving and pop-out parts, and he would decorate them with colorful designs using pens, markers, and colored pencils. We are both bilingual, but Spanish is his primary language and I am more fluent in English. When writing in our second language, we would help each other better articulate our thoughts. We were each other's Spanish/English dictionary. I can remember a time when this brother received a letter from a reviewing court informing him that his appeal had been denied. Of all the convoluted legal jargon, he mostly understood the word "denied." I was tasked with explaining to him the court's rationale for crushing his hopes and shaking his faith, if not in God then certainly in our judicial system. Having had multiple appeals denied myself, I was able to sympathize with him and knew exactly how he felt. It's a visceral feeling that leaves you in a fog for the next couple of days or so until you are able to shake it off. The level of trust we learned to place in each other is remarkable given that prison is a place where men are purposeful in guarding their innermost thoughts with the mental engineering of an Acropolis wall.

Recently, and for no apparent reason, this brother and I were separated. One afternoon I was on the yard exercising while he was at work in the inmate commissary. A guard approached the fence, called out eight names, and informed us we had to be escorted to our cells to pack our property because we were being moved. Immediately a herd of emotions stampeded inside of me, and muffled voices whispered dark conspiracies in the hallways of my mind. When I got to my cell, my cellmate was already there. The guard rolled the cell bars closed behind me and said, "You got thirty minutes to pack it up!" We soon learned he would be sent one way and I another. We were given half an hour to sort through our belongings and the last three years of our lives. In this regard, plantations and prisons are not much different. They are two forms of the same callous system—a heartless machine that sorts out men the same way the US Postal Service mechanically sorts mail.

The parallels of the slave trade and contemporary mass incarceration are much too similar to be coincidental: both slaves and modern-day prisoners manufacture their own food and clothing and perform many of the services that keep institutions functional. Whereas slaves once harvested wheat for plantations owners, prisoners now fill the barn; where forced labor once generated profits, our idleness now generates hourly wages. People of color are the coal and wood burning in the furnace of greed and hatred. The years of our life fuel this industry of mass incarceration. Am I a slave? If I concede that I am a slave, then I admit to things I am not yet ready to admit to—for instance, that I no longer belong to myself. If I resist the notion of being a slave, I risk misplacing my resistance.

Douglass bewailed separation as being final, as causing unbearable pain. He asserted that he himself was ready for anything other than separation. Indeed, Douglass gave an account of a heartrending event where a fellow slave was sold to a Georgia trader for finding fault with his master: "He was immediately chained and handcuffed; and without a moment's warning, he was snatched away, and forever sundered from his family and friends, by a hand more unrelenting than death."[3]

I'm serving a life sentence without the possibility of parole. I have been ostracized from my family and community. I don't get to decide who I share a cell with or who my neighbors are. At any moment I can be relocated from one place to another like an interchangeable part. Frederick Douglass was eventually able to flee his captor and become the leading abolitionist of his time. For obvious reasons, I can't flee my captors, but I seek freedom from ignorance and psychological slavery through my efforts of self-education and rehabilitation. I'm not sure whether these efforts will ever abolish my life sentence or the parallels of slavery inherent in our justice system; nevertheless, I resist because it is the one thing within my power to do. If I allow myself to become despondent and complacent, I will remain in a state of slavery. However, if I peacefully resist, every book I read and every word I write will work to loosen the grip of the unrelenting hand that snatched me away from my family and community.

Larger Than Life
Building a Movement across Prison Walls to Abolish Death by Incarceration

■ Felix Rosado, David Lee, and Layne Mullett

> *We believe this systemic negation of the human capacity for redemption is a crime against humanity.*
>
> —Right 2 Redemption

Ironically it is common to call death behind bars "life." Why? The truth is, for the more than fifty thousand people in US prisons serving the sentence known as "life without parole" and another forty-four thousand serving "virtual life" (fifty years or more), growing old and dying behind a wall or razor-wire-draped fence is no life at all.

Decades of resistance to racism and state repression, led by formerly and currently incarcerated people, fuels a growing consensus that mass incarceration is a problem. While there are many avenues from which to challenge mass incarceration, we believe there is a particular strategic importance to ending the practice of condemning people to die behind bars.

In 2014 three Philadelphia-based organizations gathered to discuss launching a campaign to end the practice of death by incarceration in Pennsylvania. Comrades who were currently serving death-by-incarceration sentences contributed to the meeting by mail. These organizations—Decarcerate PA, Fight for Lifers, the Human Rights Coalition, and Right 2 Redemption (an organization based inside the Pennsylvania State Correctional Institution [SCI] at Graterford)—went on to become the anchoring organizations of the Coalition to Abolish Death by Incarceration (CADBI), a statewide effort to pass legislation that would retroactively abolish the state's ability to condemn people to die in prison.

CADBI's founding members behind the prison walls insisted on the importance of changing the narrative. Words shape—and reshape—our reality, both as individuals and as a society. Words have power, and we have the power to use words to make change. Because language matters, instead of using the phrase "life without parole," we set out to popularize the phrase "death by incarceration." Using language that names the real nature of a "life" sentence provides an avenue for the listener to understand how the sentence conflicts with a fundamental value. Change starts with us, with the words we use.

Although popularity for state-sanctioned killing in the United States has waned over the years, death by incarceration has skyrocketed, to little fanfare. While the death penalty is supposedly reserved for the "worst of the worst," a life sentence is for the "more deserving." This misnomer places death by incarceration neatly across an imaginary line from death by lethal injection. Compounding the problem, many death penalty abolitionists advocate vigorously for death by incarceration as a viable, more humane alternative to a gurney, needle, and heart-stopping three-drug cocktail. Upon closer examination, however, the boundary between death by injection and death by incarceration withers away. The fact remains: both sentences begin and end with a human being dragged in vertically and carried out horizontally. Today, one in seven incarcerated people will die in prison while serving their sentence.

The Supreme Court has determined that "death is different," which has led to higher levels of scrutiny and constitutional protections for capital punishment: a bifurcated trial with distinct guilt and penalty phases, automatic appeals, lax application of appellate time limits, and so on. Skilled attorneys who believe it's morally wrong for the state to murder as punishment for crime rush to file appeals and pleas for clemency on the eve of death warrant execution dates. These resources and mechanisms are not available to those serving death by incarceration.

Yet dozens of men in one state prison alone—SCI Graterford in Pennsylvania—are killed by decades of incarceration each year. This sentence is not *life*. This is an in-house death sentence. We believe that no human being, whether on death row or in the prison's general population, should be denied the possibility of redemption. Imagine if we were all defined by—and punished for—the worst act we've ever committed, *forever*. Would we want this for ourselves? How about for our children? The idea of "another chance" has always been central to the human condition since the beginning.

Abolition from the Plantation to the Prison Cell

The movement to end death by incarceration did not start with this current campaign. We trace the struggle back to the Underground Railroad, one of the first organized mass movements to end chattel slavery in this country, in addition to the resistance coming from the Maroon rebellions and slave uprisings like the Nat Turner revolt. A vast network to end the barbarous practice of chattel enslavement, the Underground Railroad was one of the earliest attempts to attack slavery with a secretive national movement that included the participation and leadership of both men and women of various racial backgrounds.

Though these movements led to the "official" end to slavery, the dehumanization and exploitation for profit of Black bodies has continued, undergoing some significant mutations to disguise the true intentions of those utilizing and benefiting from such inhumane practices. The Black Codes, the peonage system, and Jim Crow segregation all have elements of legalized dehumanization and enslavement attached to them. The Thirteenth Amendment itself outlaws slavery "except as a punishment for crime," allowing basic human rights to be violated when a conviction is received (and conviction does not necessarily equal guilt).

Incarcerated activists, along with those on the outside, know that our prison state was born in slavery's shadow, founded on white supremacist assumptions and designed to prevent Black people from organizing for political power and self-determination. In the 1960s and 1970s, imprisoned freedom fighters like George Jackson connected with the Black Panther Party to challenge racism both within and outside the prison walls. Similar connections were forged between other incarcerated people and outside organizations associated with dismantling oppressive systems, because conscious activists knew that movements to end oppression must start with the most severely oppressed segment of the population.

In prison, our rights to live as decent human beings have been systematically removed, and most people on the outside have little understanding of what that truly means. Condemning a human to be forever locked inside of cages is a particular kind of oppression. Therefore the movement to end death by incarceration is necessary because prison is ground zero for the struggle for justice and freedom in this country.

This struggle centers education and action, because those in power who benefit from incarceration and enslavement have a vested interest in obscuring the truth. Here in Pennsylvania, approximately five thousand people are serving death-by-incarceration, or DBI, sentences. Sixty-two percent of those serving DBI or virtual life sentences are Black, even though Black people make up less than 12 percent of the state's population. This overwhelming racial disparity shows the enduring legacy of slavery along with the discriminatory nature of the system.

Families and communities alike are being destroyed by mass imprisonment. In our fight against death by incarceration, we are not only building on the legacies of resistance of those who have come before us, but, like the conductors of the Underground Railroad, we are also charting a new path to freedom.

Why Fight Death by Incarceration?

Lawmakers and other political figures have been paying lip service to "criminal justice reform" for many years now. But much of this attention and the small reforms we have seen are focused on people whose convictions are classified as "nonviolent." We believe this emphasis on nonviolent convictions is a mistake, and the idea of "nonviolence" itself is misleading.

Who exactly is a "nonviolent drug offender" (the phrase used ad nauseam in the "reform" discourse)? True, it is clearly politically expedient to separate incarcerated people into two neat, distinct categories and to advocate for some form of relief for those the public fears less and is more sympathetic toward. But will doing so bring about smart policy or meaningful change? Our fear is that a focus on those with minor convictions will not result in a substantial decrease in the prison population. It also runs the risk of reinforcing a broken system by implying that it could work with only a few cosmetic changes when in fact we need to be completely rethinking our ideas about justice and transformation.

Who is to say which among us is most worthy of more humane treatment and redemption? Is it the "nonviolent drug offender," the man in prison for two bags of heroin who was in a fistfight last week? Or is it the woman in prison for killing her abusive boyfriend thirty years ago who hasn't had a single violent infraction since and now teaches nonviolence to hundreds of others each year? To use the crime one has been convicted of as the sole criterion is likely the least accurate way to determine who someone is and how they have transformed. Wouldn't a better use of our labor be to create a system of justice based on healing, redemption, and *real* accountability, a system that empowers people to stand up and put things "more right"?

Critically reconsidering death by incarceration and other long sentences forces us to ask ourselves not "How do we most severely punish someone?" but "What are the roots of the harm that was caused?" and "What are the structures that allow individuals and communities to heal?" In Pennsylvania alone, thousands have died and will die behind bars after decades and decades of living exemplary, nonviolent lives and helping others do the same.

And who is better positioned to help create that system than some of the people who have spent decades behind bars doing that work? There are so many activists, mentors, educators, mediators, and leaders who are already critical parts of the movement and—if given the opportunity to come home—would be an essential part of building up such a system on the outside. Our communities would be stronger and our lives enriched by bringing them home.

The Path Forward

Abolishing death by incarceration in Pennsylvania will be an uphill battle. As of 2016, Pennsylvania has more people sentenced to die in prison than any state in the country except Florida,[1] and our legislative body is conservative and reactionary. Ultimately we'll need thousands of people to join us in exerting political pressure and changing public perception before we see victory. But we are also heartened by the hundreds of people who have already joined us in this fight, and by the organized and strategic efforts and outreach that are already happening both inside and outside of prison.

As the struggle for transformative justice moves forward, we remember those who came before us and the lessons gained from the brave men and women who made enormous sacrifices in the fight for liberation from this carceral monstrosity. We must remember how to grow without compromising the integrity of our movement by forgetting our past or the bigger movement of which we are a part.

At its heart, the struggle to end death by incarceration is about more than just one single issue and more than just a policy change. To really move toward liberatory rather than repressive forms of justice, we must ask ourselves, do we want a system that routinely deems our family, friends, and neighbors forever irredeemable? Do we want a society that deals death to the most vulnerable? Or do we want to live in a world where the inherent dignity of all is respected and upheld?

These questions are not rhetorical; they're a matter of life or death. And we're fighting for life—not the kind of life lived inside a cage but life with space for growth, transformation, redemption, and justice.

Death by incarceration is immoral, and that alone is reason enough to abolish it. But we also believe that challenging this ultimate antihuman sentence can be an important key to challenging the validity of the entire criminal legal system and the flawed assumption that putting people in cages for indefinite periods of time will somehow make us safer.

Successfully defeating lengthy sentencing schemes requires directly addressing harm and violence and speaking the powerful truth that long sentences do nothing to repair the harms caused by an individual act of violence or to address the systemic disenfranchisement of poor people and people of color in this country.

Our struggle to end death by incarceration necessitates not just a change in policy but also the foregrounding of a new vision of what justice could look like—one that centers on compassion, accountability, redemption, and healing.

It Do What It Do
(Me & Homer Talk Poetry)

■ Krista Franklin

How can poetry save him now?

—Patrick Rosal

I.

County blue is not vast,
not bright, but it sucks
you in and swallows
like a bird disappears
into nothing in the distance,
reappears in a new place,
to different eyes.

County blue is dingy,
washed out, overused,
a sharp navy whose edge
has dulled against the cutting
board of time. A blue that's
been buried and brought
back, a little death
still clinging to its hem.

I can't speak for the wearer
of this particular blue.
How does it feel to slip it
on each day? To tug at the slouch

of it as it creeps down your hips
like the hand of someone
you're sleeping with but don't want
anymore, disgust hollowing
you like a cored apple. I'm sure
words can't even approximate it.

2.

Words are bridges. I don't tell
him that. The way we reach
for each other across them is enough.
We say it together, "e-pis-to-lary," then
dig into its heart for meaning
like kids goring the dirt with a stick.

It's here that the blue drops
away from him. We escape it
on words that are really nothing,
but everything. Figuratively,
I hold his hand like I know
the route out when really
I am just as confused as he.
He is the one who guides
us toward the doorway.

3.

There are no coincidences.
His name holds the Odyssey
in it, but I don't tell him
because at his age
I would have stumbled
through those epic pages
like a fugitive in the woods
at night. My eyes would've glazed
over, and I'd be gone.

I want him here.
Cause I like the way his face
unfolds like a letter when he
unravels my tangled stanzas,
and asks me how to find new words.
I like the way his mouth cracks
into pure white light
that helps us see in this dark.

4.

The dictionary is not a body,
it's a book. It doesn't bleed
or breathe or cry in its cell
at night. It doesn't swell
up or jump bad or swing
when someone gets smart.
It's just a book.

But when we open it—me
and him—all the words
tumble like a combination
lock in our minds, and we slip
out through the unguarded exits
they create. Not literally, of course,
cause at the end of this,
I'm the one leaving here.

He goes back to county blue.
But this time when he leaves,
he's clutching a thesaurus in his hand
like a shank.

On Leaving Prison
A Reflection on Entering and Exiting Communities

■ Monica Cosby

eturning from prison after twenty years has been nearly as
traumatizing as being in prison for that length of time. Trying
to rebuild my life and reunite with my family after my long absence from their lives, and to keep my sense of self that I'd managed
to reclaim while in prison, has been daunting and difficult. The community to which I returned was so different; after sixteen months
out of prison, I am still struck by how much changed during the time
I was incarcerated.

I'm from the Uptown neighborhood on the North Side of Chicago. Those of us from the North Side have called it the North Pole
for decades. Most of the families I knew while growing up are gone.
Buildings I knew well are no longer there, and the ones that remain
are largely unaffordable. My own family no longer is in Uptown;
they moved out of state in 1998 just before I was sentenced to prison.
A few of my favorite places are still around. It is a comfort to me that
the Uptown People's Law Center—a nonprofit legal organization
that specializes in prisoners' rights, tenant rights, and social security
benefits—is still in Uptown, and Jake's, a restaurant I'd gone to since
childhood, is right down the street from the law center. So much,
however, is gone. The times when I feel home, when I feel free, are
few and far between.

The Communities I've Lost

I've lost two communities. The first is the one I grew up in, sitting on the lake, walking along "the rocks" just off Montrose Beach,

34

being a student at the long-gone Uptown People's Learning Center, working with the Heart of Uptown Coalition and the Chicago Area Black Lung Association as a teenager, going to the movies with my friends at the Uptown Theater and the Riviera, and buying my favorite music at Topper's, a record store in the midst of what used to be a bustling shopping district. There was Survival Day, when the whole of Uptown would gather on the mall to celebrate another year of our community's survival.

The other community I've lost is the one I was a part of in prison. I was part of that community for so long—almost as long as I lived in Uptown. It was a community composed of deep, abiding, loving, affectionate, mutually beneficial, supportive friendships and kinships. Our solidarity was born of shared sorrows, grief, guilt, shame about our pasts, and regrets for our failings. Together we suffered the indignities of being in prison. Out here I am missing my prison family as much as I missed my biological family while inside.

Prison is a society, a community, as much as any other that exists in the "free world." As with any society, there are communities within the larger community. While in prison, I was in a theater troupe, Acting Out Theatre. The women in that troupe were sisters, friends, and mothers to me. We laughed and cried and argued and comforted one another. This community extended outward—to cellmates and friends who weren't in the troupe but would help me learn my part by running lines with me on the rec yard or in the shower room after lockup time.

One of the women in my troupe had her cell shaken down by correctional officers, and contraband was found in her cell. She and her cellmates were told that if no one claimed the contraband or told whose it was, the four of them would be taken to solitary. One of them took responsibility for the contraband, though it was not hers. She was a friend of many of us in our theater troupe. She knew how important being in the troupe was for all of us, and how the women on the grounds looked forward to the troupe's performances, so she decided to claim responsibility for the contraband in the hope that the troupe would not lose a member. That is community at its best: acts of solidarity and a sense of responsibility and caring for everyone in the community with you.

My membership in the theater troupe gave me more than community and meaningful relationships in prison—it also helped me to be in relationship with my youngest daughter. During my time in prison with my troupe, my youngest daughter was in high school, participating in theater. We had something in common, something to talk about in our few letters and phone calls. We'd compare experiences, talking about troupe dynamics, how we prepared for our roles, and even costuming and set design. At one point she and I were performing in our respective troupes' productions of Shakespeare; my daughter played Helena in *A Midsummer Night's Dream*, and I was Don John in *Much Ado about Nothing*. She sent me pictures of herself in full costume from a couple of the productions she had a role in, which I shared with my troupe with more love and pride than I can ever write about. My baby girl is so talented, intelligent, creative, and beautiful, and our respective theater communities gave us the chance to connect. I always looked forward to our letters and conversations about theater.

Since my release from prison, we do not talk nearly as much as we did during my last few years in prison. My return to "community" has distanced me even further from my youngest daughter. This breaks my heart. I wish and hope to remedy this disconnect, but how? Outside of the context of our theater communities—and with no shared community—what route do we have to build a connection? I have told her that I am here for her whenever she wishes to try to rebuild our relationship, but I want to respect her boundaries, so I will not force myself into her life.

How Prison Separated Me from My Children

My youngest daughter was one year old when I went to prison; she was twenty-one when I was released on parole. It was only in the first couple of years of my incarceration and my last couple of years that I had any steady communication with my family. I was in Cook County Jail from 1995 to 1998. During that time I was able to see my daughters nearly every week—from behind a Plexiglas window, but still I saw them. After my conviction, my family moved out of Illinois, and the strongest connections in my life were suddenly broken.

From September 1998 to December 2015, I saw only one member of my family, one time. My oldest daughter came to see me in August 2013. We'd planned visits several times before and they'd always fallen through; I had all but given up hope.

Then she and I were in the visiting room, along with my two grandchildren, who before that time I'd seen only in a few pictures. I was overjoyed and afraid at once. What if my daughter didn't like me? What if she didn't recognize me? After all, I hadn't seen her since 1998 while in Cook County Jail, when she was ten years old.

She and I now have a fairly solid relationship, though we have had to work hard for it. I am happy to say that we talk on the phone nearly every day. I have spent time with my four grandchildren, and it has been frightening and beautiful. I was afraid to hold my youngest granddaughter for the first time, when she was six months old. I'd forgotten how small babies are.

My children and I have been separated by miles and years. We have been separated by my actions and my failure to act. My daughters have their own feelings about my having been absent so long, and that is their story to tell, not mine. I have never forgiven myself for being gone from my children's lives, nor do I expect that anyone else will. I hope but do not expect. Indeed, no one can or will ever hate me as much as I have hated myself, nor can anyone judge me more harshly than I have judged myself.

Of course, there are those who will continue to judge and condemn me and anyone else who has been in prison. This makes the return to community even harder.

Struggling with Reentry in the Absence of a Caring Community

I have met hundreds of people from many different organizations purporting to be allies of incarcerated and formerly incarcerated people in the sixteen months I have been out of prison. However, the people I can call on for support are few in comparison to the number of people and organizations I've come across. I have come to believe there is a difference between "ally" and "community." The idea of an "ally-ship" to me seems to suggest a temporary connection—once a shared goal is accomplished, all the people involved go their separate ways. It is practical, yes, and necessary to have allies in any movement, but to me an ally-ship feels very dry and dispassionate.

To me, "community" means something different. Within community, there is shared responsibility and accountability, caring and connection. It is understood that the health, happiness, success, security, and stability of the community is directly connected to that of the individuals within it. In community, support is given where it's needed. Solidarity is lived, not just a word spoken.

Returning to Chicago from prison, I quickly discovered what a lack of community feels like and what dangers it poses. I was paroled to a halfway house. Ostensibly, this placement was meant to help me reintegrate into society, but in fact it hindered me greatly. I had no sense of belonging to a community, no feeling of being supported or being able or welcome to ask for guidance to this new world. Neither did I feel that the halfway house was an ally. The process of getting my ID and fulfilling other requirements of parole (which, if left unfulfilled, would mean a parole violation and potentially a return to prison) was overwhelming, nearly impossible to navigate. I received no help from the halfway house.

It was only through the Uptown People's Law Center—still in my life after all these years—and my case manager at Treatment Alternatives for Safe Communities that I was able to get my ID and fulfill those other requirements. While living at the halfway house, I felt constantly under threat because I questioned some of its policies. I was constantly afraid of being sent back to prison. Other residents felt the same way. We did not feel safe or supported there, but we were stuck. Anyone familiar with how parole works knows that one cannot just leave while on parole.

While at the halfway house, I refused to say the Serenity Prayer during Alcoholics Anonymous (AA) meetings. While I understand that AA and the Serenity Prayer may work for some people, it is not for me. I had no significant history of alcohol or drug abuse, and attending AA or any other substance abuse treatment program was not a part of my parole stipulations. I am not religious in any way. I asked why I was required to attend AA. My question was not well received.

Meanwhile, we finally managed to persuade the halfway house to bring in a counselor to run a group for survivors of domestic violence and sexual assault, but it ended abruptly after the counselor refused to hand over all of her notes to the halfway house staff, citing the right of therapist-patient confidentiality. Our group met three times, then it was gone.

While in prison, I was fortunate enough to participate in many groups and classes, earning certificates relating to reentry, domestic violence and healthy relationships, critical thinking, and many others. My achievements were dismissed by the director of the halfway house; she told me they meant nothing.

Rediscovering Community through Restorative Justice

However, a couple of good things happened at the halfway house. Two women, one from the restorative justice community, the other from the Unitarian Universalist Church (a nondenominational church), came to speak with me. This was not arranged by the halfway house but through the Uptown People's Law Center. In talking with them, I found hope, coming to believe maybe I did have a place on the outside. I was invited to attend restorative justice circles, eventually becoming a restorative justice "circle keeper" (a facilitator of restorative justice processes aimed at healing and repairing harms). I felt at home in these spaces, particularly since I'd taken part in peace circle training while at Logan Correctional Center. I was also invited to a meeting with the Unitarian Universalist Prison Ministry of Illinois, where I was asked to help design the restorative justice circles that are now being held weekly in Cook County Jail and soon to be held in Logan Correctional Center. These circles are radically inclusive, welcoming to all regardless of race, sexual orientation, or religious beliefs. They include readings from Starhawk to Kahlil Gibran. In the conversations about choosing readings, I was not condescended to or patronized. My contributions and input were welcomed and respected, and my being and my selfhood were never diminished. These were the spaces in which I finally felt free.

Being a part of these communities has helped me to reintegrate, to belong, to be truly free. Even though there were a few people within each community who questioned whether "violent offenders" (a label that could be applied to me) have a place within said communities, at no point was I made to feel unwelcome. Rather, when this question of "violent offenders" was raised, the larger community reassured those who were raising the question that, yes, people like me belonged in their space. In arguing for my inclusion, they cited two principles of Unitarian Universalism: the inherent worth and dignity of all people and respect for the interdependent web of existence of which we all are a part.

The principles of restorative justice are very similar to the principles of Unitarian Universalism. As much as anything else, these principles are about both accountability and taking responsibility. Restorative justice is about caring for one another and addressing harm in such a way that the heart and humanity of both the victim and offender are affirmed so that there can be true reparation of harm.

A person who has committed a violent crime is not always a "violent person." Too often the criminal legal system ignores the totality of a person's life in deciding who is and is not violent. This happens even in spaces occupied by people claiming solidarity with those who are caught up in the criminal legal system.

Restorative justice understands these truths. Within a restorative justice framework, everyone understands that the health of a community is intricately bound to the health of all its members. And in this frame "health" is defined broadly, meaning emotional and mental well-being, social and economic stability, happiness, solid relationships within the community, a sense of pride in one's self and in the community, and the freedom to live and learn and love without fear of judgment or recrimination.

Within months of being released, I also became involved with the LGBTQ prison abolitionist group Black and Pink, first through speaking at a letter-writing event held by the group along with Love & Protect and Moms United Against Violence and Incarceration. The event was a show of solidarity with Ohio teenager Bresha Meadows and others who are incarcerated. I am proud to say I am now an organizer with Moms United Against Violence and Incarceration. To be in a space where I am welcome, where my thoughts and feelings are not dismissed but heard, and where I can engage in authentic conversation, is such a gift. Since that time, I have become friends with people in Black and Pink, the restorative justice community, and the Unitarian Universalist Church. These are not just allies. They are my radically beautiful community, and I am grateful to have found them.

There are so many of us in prison who have wished and cried and prayed to undo the past, to change things and do them differently. We've done this wishing, crying, and praying even while knowing there is no going back—so we've also wished for the chance to live our lives better, for the chance to make things right. How can we do this if we have no community to help or guide us?

In a true community, all of these concerns can be spoken, addressed, and alleviated, because everyone is valued. No one is thrown away or disposed of. When we talk about the "reentry" and "reintegration" of people coming out of prison, that critical component—real community—must not be forgotten.

Long-Term Separation

■ Efrain Alcaraz

I am an immigrant, born in Mexico, now living in a US prison, and my life has been full of separations. One night when I was six years old, my dad came home after a night of heavy drinking and accused my mother of being unfaithful to him. This led to an argument, which got out of control. My father then began to beat my mother. I tried to stop him, but I was so little, it was no use. My mother told me to run, so I ran next door to my grandparents' home. Later that night, after Dad went to sleep, my mother came to get me and my little sister. She took us away to her parents' home, where I ended up living for the rest of my time in Mexico.

The next big separation in my life came when my mother decided to leave me and my sisters in Mexico. She decided to leave us with our grandparents in August 1993 and go to the United States. I was only six years old. This was a heartbreaking separation, but I understood why she was doing it. My mother was working several jobs but was barely able to support us, so she decided to come to the USA looking for better wages. This separation was not only hard on us kids; it also broke my mother's heart. My grandparents were now burdened with trying to support three children until my mother was able to start sending us money.

Being the oldest of three children and the only male, I felt that it was my job to help support my younger sisters; Sandra was five and Yessica was one. I did not feel as though this responsibility should fall entirely upon my grandparents. They were raising us the best they knew how. Grandma was strict. She kept us truthful and honest. Grandpa taught me how to work for things we needed and how to respect others. They taught me that work was more important than school, because work is what put food on our table and money in our pocket. Now that I am incarcerated, I understand how important an education really is.

The next big separation came when my mom returned home to Mexico. I was fourteen years old, and I remember it like it was yesterday. I was so excited to see her after all those years. After a couple of weeks being home, she told us she was taking us to the United States to live. So now I was going to be separated from my grandparents and great-uncle, who had become a father figure to me. And I would be leaving the only home I really knew.

I felt as though I was being torn in two different directions. On one hand, I wanted to stay in Mexico. I had begun to pave a path for my life to follow. I was making money and had begun to purchase livestock in the form of cattle. My life had direction. On the other hand, I wanted to be with my mother and sisters. There was no way I could disrespect all that my mother had sacrificed by telling her I wanted to stay in Mexico.

Two weeks after she told us we would be leaving, we were on our way. Our journey to the USA began with our meeting a coyote in another small town about thirty minutes from my hometown. We traveled there by car and the coyote escorted us to another part of Mexico. From there we received directions on where we must travel, how to answer questions if stopped, and the basic dos and don'ts. That was this coyote's sole job until we met the next coyote to receive the next set of directions. This transfer of information from coyote to coyote continued until we were all safely across the border. The last coyote was the person my mother had paid to get us safely across the border and to our destination in Chicago. He put us on a bus that took us close to the border. This was a very grueling trip that lasted over twelve hours.

Next we had to wait three days until the right time to cross the border into Texas. We walked three hours during the night to a waiting point. We spent six hours in the dark desert waiting for the okay from the coyote's connection to continue. Afterward, we walked another two hours until we reached a creek. We hid in that creek for about a day and a half. One of the coyotes brought us food and water while we waited for the okay to travel again. We

finally received the green light around four o'clock in the afternoon.
We began walking and were spotted by a border patrolman; he was
about three hundred yards away from us. Everyone began to get very
nervous; I could see fear in my mother's eyes. I could only imagine
that she was seeing all her money, hard work, and dreams being lost
that very instant. The coyote told everyone to calm down and wave
our hats to the border patrolman. When we waved to him, he waved
back, and then we were on our way again. I wondered if the coyote
had paid him to let us pass.

We walked another couple of hours until we reached an ex-
pressway. This was our final and most dangerous waiting point. If
we got caught here, all of our efforts and difficult travels would be
for nothing. Finally our ride showed up, and they took us to a safe
house, where we could eat and shower. We waited there one full day
until the coyote brought us a change of clothes and airline tickets
to Chicago. He took us to the airport and instructed us on how to
answer any questions we would be asked by airport security. Security
was on high alert because of the 9/11 attacks.

We passed through security with no problems and were on our
way to Chicago. When I got off the airplane, I stepped into a whole
different world. It was December and the first time in my life I had
ever seen snow! I had come from a farm in Mexico with wide-open
country to the third-largest city in America. I felt trapped.

We arrived at Mom's apartment, which was very different from
our house in Mexico. She had an indoor toilet and hot running water, two things we did not have in Mexico. Her apartment was very
clean and comfortable.

One of the first things Mom started to insist on was the need
for her children to go to school and learn English. My sisters were
very excited about school, but I had been taught that work was more
important. I decided against school and found myself a job. I became
an employee at McDonald's, unloading supplies from the delivery
trucks. After about eight months, I began a new job doing construction work. I felt like I was finally on my way to a better life. I was
earning more money than ever before and was able to save some for
myself and help my mother too. There was even enough income to
send some home to help my grandparents in Mexico. My goal was

to save enough money to go back to Mexico and live comfortable in my old life.

In October of 2008 I was arrested; four years later I was sentenced to a very lengthy prison term. This was the first time I was away from my sisters. I felt as though I had left them unprotected and with no one to guide them. My mom had focused her attention on me instead of where it should have been: on my sisters. When I was arrested, I felt like I had disrespected all of my mother's hard work and dedication.

Separation from the outside world has left me feeling like an animal in a cage, wanting to be free with the rest of my group. Being separated from my family has been very heartbreaking, but it has also made me be more self-supportive. I have become aware of how much I depended on them. Now that we are not together, I miss the smallest things most. Things like laughing together or eating a family meal. I miss having them to talk to when I've faced trouble, and being there for them when they've needed something. Being locked away has also robbed me of the joy of having children and a family of my own. I can never have that feeling of love that only a father knows.

Today I feel as though I am divided from the person who I really am. Being in this prison, I have to be someone different from myself in order to survive. As a kid, I was responsible for feeding livestock and moving them from pen to pen. Now I feel as though I am the livestock—always waiting for those watching over me to feed me and unlock one door only to lock another.

Time after Time
For Transgender Women, Trauma and Confinement Persist after Sentences End

■ Toshio Meronek, with Cookie Bivens

ookie Bivens was just sixteen when she entered California's juvenile penitentiary system. Finding kinship within a gang in East Los Angeles at a young age, she knew that many of the people around her would end up caged, so it wasn't unexpected to her that she ended up behind bars.

Years into her life sentence, she recognized that the sex assigned to her at birth didn't fit. As a trans woman in an intentionally gender-segregated place, she was highly sexualized and faced physical and sexual abuse. As she had on the outside when she was a teenager in a gang, Bivens sought protection where it was offered: among circles of men within the prison. She learned about the Transgender, Gender Variant, and Intersex Justice Project (TGIJP) from a friend inside the men's prison where she was confined and began writing letters to the organization for advice. TGIJP was founded in 2003 by Alex Lee, a trans man whose intention from the start was to build an organization that both served and was run by incarcerated and formerly incarcerated Black trans women. Under the successive leadership of Black trans directors Miss Major Griffin-Gracy and now Janetta Johnson, the San Francisco–based organization is among the largest and longest-running groups to serve this intensely criminalized population.

Her exchanges with people there helped lead to her parole after having spent thirty years in cell blocks. Released in 2017, Bivens is now part of the reentry program at TGIJP, which aims to make leaders out of formerly incarcerated trans women. After spending most of her life inside, reentering society has come with plenty of issues compounded by being Black, femme, and low-income in a society that does not value those identities—all of this in addition to the psychological anguish she now experiences as a result of the trauma and abuse she faced inside. And the truth is that Bivens's sentence didn't end with her release. She has to regularly report to a state-mandated parole officer and undergo drug tests, plus she can't travel more than 50 miles outside of the county of San Francisco without difficult-to-get permission. She is facing a prolonged sentence on the outside. Making a dollar above minimum wage, Bivens has a semi-stable room-share in a house on the outskirts of San Francisco, but she has also spent nights on the street due to lack of housing. She explains this to me when we meet at a burger restaurant next to one of the city's touristy consumption magnets, Powell Street, as cable cars rumble toward another money pit, the city's mini-Disneyland, Fisherman's Wharf.

Bivens shows me pictures of herself with her niece, now in her tweens, taken at the wharf not long after she left prison. They both look excited to be out on the pier, but it was Cookie's first time, and her facial expressions display some kind of bliss. We talk about some of the things she missed out on during those three decades locked up, and what she still misses.

Cookie Bivens: When I got out, I wasn't sure if I'd be able to transition into a society that had changed, especially with technology. And it still dogs me.

The only computers we were able to use were in the law library—they didn't show us how to navigate the operating systems. I'm learning how to operate it; I still have to learn.

When I got out I didn't know how to use a debit card. When I was in line [at a store] they were like "PIN number, PIN number!" And I felt like a little baby out here. I always had to ask somebody to help me, and sometimes they don't have time, and sometimes it doesn't get done.

Toshio Meronek: *How does the CDCR [California Department of Corrections and Rehabilitation] set up people for getting a job once they get out, if at all?*

Cookie: The only thing that CDCR does is put you in housing; it doesn't teach you the skills you need to work in society. You can go to some classes to get coping skills, like anger management or stress-coping skills, but they had computers inside prison and they could've been teaching us stuff, but I think they're caught up so much in security and risk or whatever that they don't even go there.

They do help you with some trades—like they have [classes in] customer service. I was in coffee; I learned how to grind coffee and the process of roasting coffee, shipping, and handling. I learned some marketable skills. I don't say too many good things about CDC, but you *could* get some marketable skills.

Toshio: *What happens when you add the layer of being trans to that? Did they prepare you for the idea that not only are you going to have this record, but you're also going to deal with the fact that trans people have some of the highest rates of unemployment on the outside?[1]*

Cookie: No, they don't prepare you for levels of discrimination when it comes to gender.

Toshio: *You knew other girls inside; did that make life any easier inside?*

Cookie: I wouldn't particularly say it made life easier. In prison a lot of the girls are divided, because anytime you try to get girls together, it's always some type of division. It doesn't stem from the girls, but they're affected by the manipulations of what the boys do. If we don't have our own [formal] committees, it's hard to get the girls together, and for the most part the boys divide us against each other [so they can keep all the social power]. So you might get some like-minded girls, but it's very difficult in there when you've got a group of men who see a group of trans girls coming together and say, "Let's get at this trans girl," or "Let's get at that one, and let's cause division." A lot of that's going on.

Toshio: *Are you still in a relationship with the man you were with on the inside?*

Cookie: I was with the same man for ten years. We're not together, but we love each other and we support each other. I support him on getting out of prison. He was a juvenile when he went in, like me, and I support him trying to navigate the parole system. He encouraged me to do these things, and I did it, so he also feels inspired. And I support some of the girls, too; we talk on the phone, to try to be prepared coming out here and hopefully transition them into a better situation than they would be, coming outside.

Toshio: *What about other basic needs, like food? It's hard for people with certain felonies to get food stamps, for example.*

Cookie: Getting out in San Francisco, you do have access to [general assistance] or social security if you qualify. But housing here, as you know, it's hard. The time I spent on the street, it was like, "It's not easy out here." Especially when it's cold. But I don't want to be so much of a burden.

Toshio: *But the thing is, the system has set you up with so few opportunities when you come out.*

Cookie: Yes. Especially being trans, because trying to find housing, having a name that fits your gender makes a difference. Say you went online looking for a house, but they want you to use your government name. When they see that you're trans, it kind of messes things up. Same for work, too. Hopefully this thing we worked on [California Senate Bill 310, the Name and Dignity Act, allowing trans people to change their legal gender markers while still inside prison][2] comes to fruition. If I used my government name, they're looking for a male.

Toshio: *Knowing that prisons are created to be violent institutions, how did being trans affect how you survived inside?*

Cookie: It gives you a strength. It builds character because you have to go through so much. To me it gave me a strength of survival; it gave me a strength to stand up for myself. Even outside, you have to deal with so much; when you get knocked down, you have to pick yourself back up. You go through a lot of psychological shit, but trans people have a lot of strength. You have to.

Toshio: *How does parole limit your life, as someone who's been inside long term?*

Cookie: It limits my life because I'm super-controlled. I have to get permission to travel. To do anything. And where would I be with my parole officer if I fucked up? We're not perfect, as people. I'm still fucking up.

Toshio: *Police can take you in for anything, any day.*

Cookie: See, this depresses me a lot, too. Some days I think, "I'm gonna drink, I'm gonna smoke, whatever." There's always this looming threat that hangs over your head. I think that parole should be more flexible coming outside. For us long-termers, [if] we fuck up, give us some chances; don't just lock us back up. We go through a lot.

You can get an asshole parole officer who can be like, "I'm gonna throw you back in the halfway house." They're not actively helping you find housing or giving you subsidies for this housing. I think that parole should help people with subsidies for housing. You've been gone so long, and you've got all these prisoners coming out, and they don't really have a chance except a transitional home, which is gonna run out in a couple months. They should have a hookup to where they give someone who's been in prison a housing priority. But I don't see that.

Toshio: *A lot of people coming out, it seems like the last thing they'd want to do is come to work for an organization that deals with prisons. What made you want to?*

Cookie: It started in prison, through another trans [person] who hooked me up with TGIJP, and I basically felt like, okay, we have an organization that is supportive of the trans [people] coming out of prison [to] transition into society, and that was very interesting to me. It's not perfect, but we do have something, and we can create something that's even more solid for them.

I was advocating in prison for the girls to stay strong, stand together, so we can end discrimination behind these prison bars and attacks happening against us. And I always wanted to help my sisters to come out and have an easier transition, to get on their feet. I know a lot of trans [people] inside that have been down a long time, and they do need help. My passion is basically to help the next girl out and get back on their feet.

Toshio: *What would you say is the single hardest thing getting out as a long-termer?*

Cookie: Some of it's internal. I feel like I'm on the bottom of the totem pole. And we don't have enough girls that's incarcerated or formerly incarcerated [who are interested in helping out]. I could collaborate with some girls that's been in prison, because we understand what we need, but when you approach your average trans girl who's never been inside, they might take a flyer, but 99 percent of the time they drop it on the street. I've seen it happen. And that's usually because they've got their own stuff they're dealing with. If we want something to happen, we've got to do this ourselves, and a lot of the time it feels like we're starting from the ground up.

Toshio: *How can people prepare themselves for coming out from a long-term sentence?*

Cookie: First of all, you have to have built a support network out here on the streets. Get marketable skills for yourself in prison, if you can. Coping skills. Have good parole plans.

Toshio: *What are ways that somebody who's trying to help someone getting out from being inside a long time, how can they help?*

Cookie: Helping with navigating cities, helping with getting a driver's license, getting on general assistance, getting housing, and moral support.

A Living Chance

Adrienne Skye Roberts Interviews
Ellen Richardson, Kelly Savage, Amber Bray,
Rae Harris, Barbara Chavez, Judith Barnett,
Mary Elizabeth Stroder, Stacey Dyer,
Natalie DeMola, and Laverne DeJohnette

A Living Chance: Storytelling to End Life Without Parole is an ongoing project initiated in 2014 by the California Coalition for Women Prisoners (CCWP). This project emerged from conversations with longtime CCWP members serving life without parole (LWOP) at the California Institution for Women in Corona, California, and the Central California Women's Facility in Chowchilla. During this time, the mainstream anti–death penalty movement authored two pieces of legislation that would have ended executions and transferred everyone from death row to LWOP, characterizing LWOP as a "lesser and more humane" sentence than death. While CCWP strongly opposes the death penalty, we believe that true abolition of the death penalty would include abolishing LWOP, or "walking death row," as it is called by people serving this sentence.[1] A Living Chance aims to educate people both inside and outside of prison on the realities of LWOP—specifically, the use of gendered violence and racism in sentencing that is inherent in the discrimination against LWOP within prisons and our movements.[2] Over the past four years, the storytelling project has catalyzed broadening movements against LWOP—facilitating advocacy for individual commutations to parole-eligible sentences and igniting the development of support groups inside prisons to build power among those surviving LWOP.

What follows are excerpts from individual interviews conducted at the Central California Women's Facility and the California Institution for Women between 2014 and 2017. Due to the limitations of legal visiting, we were able to interview only one person at a time; however, these excerpts are edited to read as one group interview. This format reflects our larger conversations with the LWOP community and demonstrates that LWOP is not an individual issue but a result of far-reaching systems of oppression that affect diverse communities and therefore need complex and broad strategies of resistance and resilience.

Adrienne: *How do you characterize life-without-parole sentencing?*

Ellen: [Being an LWOP] is like being an oarsman on a slave ship. When you first walk into prison, you see all these people that are already strong and used to their environment, and you're weak and scared. They find you this little seat and they attach you to this ore, and you're trying so hard to row like the rest of them. Everything we do is controlled by the beat of this drum on this slave ship. You know, you have to keep up with that rhythm.

The biggest role that LWOPs play is that we are that constant force that moves the prison because we're always here. So, as people leave, as people die, LWOPs are gonna always be there, ultimately working [our] way up to the middle of the ship that makes it go. Because without us, there's no constant slave labor.

Amber: Speaking about slave labor, we are not entitled to have any of the better-paying jobs. We can't work Joint Venture or Prison Industry Authority[3]—they came out with a discriminatory memo saying LWOPs can't work there. So we're very limited in terms of the positions that we hold. On average, I make twenty-five dollars a month, and that's high, you know, compared to some other people. I'm a literacy tutor. I help people in the honor dorm with any subject towards their high school diploma or GED. I do some college. I tutor women who speak no English, because I'm bilingual. And I've also tutored in Spanish, helping people who are taking Spanish for college. We [LWOPs] get up every day for no other incentive than to go out and do a good job.

Mary Elizabeth: We're kind of the dust in the crack. People sentenced to death receive a lot of legal attention, and then lifers go to the Board of Parole, but the LWOPs, we're just kinda like the dust in the crack that's not seen by the legal system. We just don't receive the same legal attention when we have the same needs [as people on death row]. We are [also] sentenced to death. It just happens naturally.

Adrienne: *Can you describe the kinds of relationships that are formed through this shared experience of LWOP?*

Stacey: All the people that have guided me to the right way of living in prison are LWOPs. People who I feel like if I'm really down and I need somebody to talk to, they're that person who I can go to. It just seems like because we do things sincerely and not for other motivations, like the parole board, we end up training and teaching other people how to do the same thing. When people parole or leave and come back, we're the ones that are still here and we're still carrying things on. I think that if they [the prison administration] was smart, they would invest in us, because we have a community in here that we can help. We are key players in the community. We can make a big difference in here, if they gave us the tools and the skills to do that.

Judith: Women in prison, it's a known fact, form families. I've got two hundred kids who call me Bubbie or Mom. I call Ellen my kid, and then my kid Deborah calls her Aunty. It's generational now. I've got some people who call me Grandma.

Amber: I've had the same bunkie [we share a bunk bed] for nearly sixteen years, and our other roommate has lived with us for a little more than fifteen years altogether. You do develop a familial bond with these people, because you live with them for so long. I lived with my family for eighteen years and ten days [before I was arrested], and now I have two other individuals who are coming up on that same time period. Of course, we get on each other's nerves now and then. It happens. But overall, knowing that you have somebody that you can trust and count on—no matter what else is going on—is huge.

Adrienne: *What kind of organizing is possible through the familial and critical connections among the LWOP community?*

Kelly: Organizing on the inside is difficult but needs to happen. There was no way for us to meet, because the [prison] administration feared that LWOPs meeting together would be difficult. So we decided together to meet at the chapel and get an opportunity to organize, educate, and support each other. This allowed us to see that most LWOPs were first-time offenders [and] survivors of some type of abuse; most were here under [sentences for] felony murder and therefore not the actual perpetrator of their crime.[4]

My most successful organizing would be our domestic violence education. I created a curriculum myself on boundaries and healing from incest and rape. We [went] into classrooms, substance abuse programs, and vocations to educate on what domestic violence is, the role it plays in our lives, and how to stop violence, [set] boundaries, and deal with the violence we see within the institution. I was able to teach approximately three thousand people. [Now] my full-time position is [teaching] a state-mandated class called "Beyond Violence." This class has four concurrent groups: one that is led in Spanish, one for youth under the age of twenty-one, and two for all other people. It runs for ten weeks. It is very rewarding to look at relationships, your community, society as a whole and see how our behaviors can affect ourselves or our children. This [education] is a big contributor to people changing their behaviors and stopping violence.

Rae: We started an organization called Networking to fill niches within the LWOP community and [provide] resources specifically for [our] community. I worked in the Parole Resource Center and had access to resources for employability, academics, and life skills [that I shared with other LWOPs]. In doing so, I found that there was other needs as far as appeals. So we created a habeas class, and I facilitated and actually taught people how to navigate through the law library and how to frame their [argument] when submitting [appeals] to the court. For myself, I lost time, I lost my appeal, so that's why I took an interest within the LWOP community to make sure that people understood the appeals process and that you don't have all day and night to submit an appeal or commutation.

Adrienne: *How do these forms of collective care and resistance give way to more freedom?*

Laverne: Without people who would sit down and be willing to teach me, and without community, I don't know. I would probably be dead. They've told us all our lives that our path is gangs or jails or death. And the only fortunate thing I see in jail is you can grow; you can learn things and skills that even the [outside] community doesn't have, such as classes on domestic violence and groups on healing childhood trauma. But is it useless if I can't apply it out there somewhere? The truth is, I'm a completely different individual now, one that [is] rehabilitated, yet this truth may never be examined by the state of California. As a LWOP, I may never get out of prison, so when shall I live, if not now? I cherish life, and whether it's here or there, I want to live. But now I [am not] content to die in prison. If I can have life out there with the knowledge I have now, the knowledge of how to live, how to appreciate people, how to treat people, I would be so incredibly different. So that just blows my mind. Before, I never even strived to get out; it's only in the last ten years that I threw myself into rehabilitation and into being a better person. It's only this year that I could even see a future out there, because it's always [been] a death sentence to me.

Barbara: In 2013 I filed for commutation. I had just met Sara Kruzan [a fellow LWOP whose sentence was commuted to a parole-eligible sentence by Governor Schwarzenegger]. Immediately when we looked at each other, she started crying and was like, "Wow, kindred spirits." I had my pen and my paper and was asking [her] a million questions. She asked me, "Did you kill anybody?" and I told her no. She said, "Do you have any vocations?[5] Have you done anything for yourself?" I said yes. She said, "Do you have an associate's degree?" I said yes. Sara said, "Girl, file for commutation of sentence! You have a good chance!"

So I got everything together—everything I've accomplished over the years. I prayed over it and even asked the Native Americans for sage and smudged it and sent [the commutation appeal] out. On July 21, 2016, I was interviewed by investigators from the Board of Parole Hearings. I was immediately crying and so grateful. I totally forgot that I had filed, because it's been three years. They told me that they had looked at my case and that they both agreed that I had too much time but that it is ultimately up to the governor. Now my commutation is sitting on the governor's desk as we speak, and I'm just hoping and believing that good things are to come.

Natalie: [Life without parole] has helped me change. I needed to see that sentence. When you don't have a date, when nothing is set in stone, you strive so hard to grasp it. If I knew I only had two years to do, I would plan my two years. But since I don't know, it makes me operate in faith, and it makes me push harder and develop my true character. In a sense, I was oppressed when I was out. I was in bondage. I wasn't me. So coming in here, it helped me find the true me. And I still have dreams just like I did back then. They say, "Have your dreams changed?" Sometimes people ask me that and I'm like, no. The same dreams I had when I was a kid are the same dreams that I have now. I'm still the same person. Because when I was being abused, all I did was dream. I still want a family, a husband. I still want the best. I still want to make a difference in people's lives. I want to travel the world with my dad when I get out. I see a big picture. Like Helen Keller said, "The greatest tragedy in life is to have sight and no vision." And I always have a vision.

It may sound so crazy, but I was like, "I'm gonna get this lawyer to take my case." And people were like, "They'll never pick you up." I kept striving and striving and knocking on every door, and I actually sent them Christmas cards every year and photos from recent visits. For three years I did this! And one day they just said, "We're taking your case." So it does happen. If you keep pushing, you'll get the right results. That's to encourage anyone [who thinks] it's impossible; if people tell you it's impossible, it is possible.

"Be a Panther When You Get to Angola"
A Conversation between Albert Woodfox and Beth E. Richie

Albert Woodfox spent forty-three years in solitary confinement in a Louisiana prison—more than any other person in the United States. Yet the cruelty and degradation of this form of carceral torture did not break his spirit. Woodfox, Herman Wallace, and Robert King became known as the "Angola Three" (A3) after they were charged with the murder of a prison guard in Angola Prison in 1972. Albert's conviction was overturned three separate times by judges before he was released from solitary confinement. At once a political coming-of-age story as a Black Panther and an inspirational memoir about collective resistance and individual survival, this interview is a call to action against the harsh conditions of confinement that have become routine in many penal institutions. At a September 2016 event hosted by the University of Illinois Chicago Social Justice Initiative, Woodfox shared his experience and the lessons he learned in moving detail, compelling readers to respond to the profound injustice of solitary confinement with demands for radical and urgent change. What follows are excerpts from the interview.

Beth E. Richie: *I want to say how moved and honored I am to be in this conversation with you, Mr. Woodfox, and to continue the conversation we already started. And if I may speak for the audience, I want to welcome you to Chicago. We really appreciate that you're here, for so many reasons. You've inspired many of us for a long time, and that's why this room is full. I think we've changed rooms three times already so that we could accommodate all of the people who are so anxious to welcome you. We're* *all welcoming you home. And when I say "welcome home," I hope you'll consider Chicago part of your home. Welcome to the Chicago family of activists who know and care so deeply about your struggle. It's reflected in our own struggle. Welcome home from where you were. We're glad you're here. We appreciate and admire you. I want to begin by simply asking you how you're doing.*

Albert Woodfox: I'm doing fine. Before we start, I would like to express my personal gratitude to the University of Illinois Social Justice Initiative as well as the Chicago Committee to Free Black Political Prisoners. I've been treated so wonderful since I've been here. I'm a little new at this, so bear with me.

Beth: *It's all good, it's all good. We're honored that you're here. How are you doing?*

Albert: I'm doing great. I'm enjoying reuniting with my family and my community. Right now I'm still adjusting to being able to walk beyond nine feet or turn beyond six feet. I've been reunited with my family; in spite of how young I look, I have a daughter, three grand-kids, and four great-grandkids.

Beth: *Imagine that family reunion. I know you've been busy since you've been here.*

Albert: I've been here since Saturday. And my gracious hosts have opened their homes and their hearts to me. I've been on several boat tours, to parks, and it's been a great experience. This morning I had an opportunity to meet with some young future leaders, and it's been a great experience all around.

Beth: *We want to hear about some of those meetings and lessons. Before we move forward too quickly, I hope the rest of audience is aware that as we honor and celebrate your freedom and feel the benefit of the wisdom of your work, we do need to pause for a minute and recognize the people who aren't here. The opportunity that we have with you needs to be understood as an opportunity that still millions of our brothers and* *sisters, comrades, don't have. So I'd like to take a minute and realize that there are a lot of people fighting for their freedom right now as they're behind those walls in those cages still. And our conversation has to be with them in our heads and hearts. Hopefully our conversation will dignify their struggle to survive.*

Albert: I'd just like to ask everyone to remember Herman Hooks Wallace. He is the deceased member of the A3. Forty-one years he made all the sacrifices, suffered all the pains, and he never complained; he never expressed regret of the path he had chosen. He's not here in body, but through me and through Robert King he lives on. And he is fighting as hard now with the ancestors as we are fighting here on this earth.

Beth: *Indeed, lift him up. I'd like us to continue by having you reflect on your experience, the big experience. I wonder if you would start by sharing a little bit of the background of your story, including your involvement in the Black Panther Party, and then walk us up to your time in prison and then specifically your activism around solitary confinement.*

Albert: Like most African American men of my generation, I started out as a petty criminal. It was more an act of survival, a choice between going hungry or having food to eat or having a roof over my head. I was raised in a single-parent home for a great part of my life, and eventually my criminal activity caught up with me. It's strange, though. I loaned my friend a car, [and] he was involved in an armed robbery. And as a result of that, I was charged with being a part of it, and I was sentenced to fifty years after being found guilty at trial: fifty years of hard labor in Louisiana State Penitentiary. Fortunately, I was able to escape that day, the same day I was sentenced to fifty years, and I eventually wound up in Harlem, New York, because I knew Harlem from my criminal days.

But there was a new force there, the Black Panther Party, and, you know, I was seeing the Panthers moving around the community, and for the first time in my life, I didn't see that fear in African American people. I saw pride, determination. I saw people controlling their own communities. And the sisters were so beautiful, you know? And so my initial contact with the party was personal. I was trying to get a date, and these sisters were talking about the revolutionary struggle—and the Ten-Point Program [the Black Panthers' party platform]—and the Black Panther Party, what it stood for. I'm like, "Huh?" I had never ever been exposed to this kind of thinking, this way of thinking, and this type of conduct by African American people. It was always fighting to survive just to live day to day.

I was arrested in New York for an armed robbery, which I was found not guilty of. And eventually I was returned, because of my political activism. I was in the Manhattan House of Detention, also known as "the Tombs." While there, three members of the Panther 21 were put on the tier, and it was my first chance to really face-to-face talk with someone in the Black Panther Party. Because of the political classes they were holding at the time, I would listen to what they were saying, but I wasn't hearing what they were saying. Eventually, another prisoner came down from upstate New York. He had filed a writ trying to get out, and he had a book called *A Different Drummer*. He suggested that I read it, and I read it. And all of a sudden, I started hearing what the Panthers were saying. I heard what African Americans and other progressive people in society were saying about the injustice. I began to realize that I, as a human being, had value. As a human being, I had a right to expect to be treated with dignity, pride, and self-respect. That basically was my journey.

I was involved in the riots in support of the Attica uprising and paid dearly for that: I had my head split, my arm fractured, and I was returned to New Orleans Parish Prison. The New Orleans chapter of the Black Panther Party had been involved in a shootout with the New Orleans Police Department, so I was placed on a tier with them. While there, I made a conscious decision to join the Black Panther Party. I was told that I could and what was expected of me, and so I joined the party, and that was the beginning of my rebirth. It was the beginning of going from a petty criminal and predator upon my own community and my own people to becoming a revolutionary individual who believed in social struggle, who believed in preserving the destiny of myself as an individual and of African Americans as an ethnic group. To preserving the destiny of other minorities as well as white citizens in this country.

Beth: *That's such a moving account and it's a shared account. Other people have kind of gone on the same journey with you and alongside you. I really appreciate you lifting up the sisters in the struggle, too. That's an important part of this.*

Albert: Those sisters taught me a lesson.

Beth: *We all need to remember that part of the history. So there you are, committed to the Black Panther Party. That's a transformative moment for you, and then you end up in solitary confinement. Can you walk us there and then talk about that experience?*

Albert: Prior to going to Louisiana State Penitentiary at Angola, there was some political activities in New Orleans Parish Prison because of the horrible conditions. You know, you think conditions are bad in prisons now, you should go back forty-four years. As a result of the agitation at New Orleans Parish Prison, I was shipped to Louisiana State Penitentiary. The comrade in leadership at that time, I asked him, "Well, what do I do now?" 'cause I felt somewhat lost. As they say, there is strength in unity, but I'm about to leave my comrades and fellow Panther members. So my comrade said, "Be a Panther when you get to Angola." Educate, agitate, organize. For me, that was the holy grail. I was transferred to the Louisiana State Penitentiary, and I went through the entry process that they have, and eventually I was placed in [the general prison] population. Because I started to try to raise the level of consciousness of people I had known all my life, who'd been involved in the criminal activities. Some thought I was running some kind of game, some thought I'd lost my mind, and who else knows what the others thought? But I continued to organize and try to raise the inmates' levels of consciousness.

At that time Angola had been designated the bloodiest prison in America. Someone was dying every week or being seriously injured, either from the security people or inmates themselves. I felt as though I had a responsibility to try to get these guys to understand they were in prison; prison wasn't in them. They had a right to see themselves as having self-worth, and they had a right to be treated a certain way.

They had human rights, first, and they also had a minimum amount of rights that the Constitution of the United States afforded them.

Eventually Herman Wallace was housed in another part of the prison at that time. Angola is a plantation, so it operates on a plantation system. Herman was in another area of the prison, but the building he was in had been condemned, so in order to repair the building, the inmates were moved into what's called a "new prison complex." Herman and I were aware of each other, and we were aware that we had joined the party, but we had never had an opportunity to live around each other. Herman was in a unit called Pine, and I was in a unit called Hickory. Together we began to organize. We used the football field as a disguise, because it was the only place where a large number of African Americans prisoners could get together and security not come down.

Beth: *Sounds familiar still. The football field as a very particular gathering space.*

Albert: We went out there and went through the motions like we were practicing football, but the conversations were always political. They were always about trying to raise the level of consciousness, and that evolved, too. I remember one day I was sitting on my bed in my dormitory, and a young kid about seventeen years old was sitting across from me, and he was totally crushed. He had been raped and forced into the sex slave market that existed in Angola. It was the most painful thing I'd ever seen in my life. There's nothing more sad than seeing a human spirit crushed from another human.

The next day, Herman and myself, we talked to some of the other guys who were trying to change things themselves, and we formed anti-rape squads. Every Thursday was called Fresh Fish Day, meaning young guys were coming in the system. Because of the violence in the prison at the time, we had to arm ourselves, and so we would go down, and when the guys would come in, we would talk to the young guys and tell them what to expect, what was going on, what to do, what not to do. And we made it known to the rest of the inmate population, especially the sexual predators, that these kids were under our protection and the path to them was through us. If you tried to travel that path, what would be left by the time you got to the end of the path wouldn't be in any shape to rape another kid. We organized and we fought against administrative corruption. Food and clothing that were meant for the inmate population were being confiscated by security staff and taken out of the prison. Basically that's what we were doing at the time. Herman and I established the only recognizable chapter of the Black Panther Party in a prison.

Beth: *Sometimes I think people who haven't listened carefully or heard about life inside don't understand how much prisoners are organizing all the time to take care of each other—to provide resources, to protect each other, to teach each other race consciousness, just like you were. You offer such moving accounts of that. Can you tell us about how something happened where you ended up in solitary confinement?*

Albert: April 17, 1972. A correctional officer was found dead in Pine dormitory. Because of my political activities in the prison, I automatically became a suspect and was automatically put in what was called "the dungeon." The dungeon was a prison within a prison within a prison. I was moved to solitary confinement, known as CCR. CCR stands for "closed cell restriction," where you were allowed a minimum amount of your personal clothing and virtually no other types of privileges. Herman, Robert, and myself—we were on different tiers of CCR.

Because of the things we had learned from the Black Panther Party, we instinctively knew that if we were going to survive solitary confinement, we had to turn toward society and not toward the prison. We had to not become institutionalized. Not embrace or contribute to the culture of prison, but to ensure that the values and the principles and the code of conduct created within ourselves be influenced by society and not the prison. As a result of that, we organized the tiers we were on, we taught men how to read and write, and we taught them how to do math. And it showed them that when you can read and write, the world opens up before you, and the possibilities of what can be achieved is unlimited. We turned our cells, which were meant to be death chambers—we turned them into high schools. We turned them into universities, we turned them into law clinics, we turned them into debate halls, and as a result of that, we were able to extract changes from the prison administration and the security people of CCR. And CCR began to slowly evolve, with the addition of TVs, and we were able to start getting newspapers and books out of the prison library.

Beth: *So you actually changed the institution regulations about what could happen in CCR?*

Albert: Yes, over a period of time. We fought on two fronts. The first front was physical confrontation against brutality and the racist acts against African Americans. We used hunger strikes, which is probably the most effective form of resistance in prison, but it is also the most brutal on the people. They used to feed us under a door. They used to put our food on a tray and slide it under a door. We tried to get it resolved administratively by petitions. When that didn't happen, we went on a forty-five-day hunger strike to get them to cut food slots in the bars so we could be handed our food rather than having it put on the floor and slid under the door. We became concerned with some of the men on the tier who were passing out from striking. We didn't want anybody to die. The prison, the camp administration, wanted the hunger strike to end, so we reached a compromise where we could stand at the bars and hold our tray in one hand and eat through the bars rather than have our food slid under the door. We had no idea that this was going to last eighteen months.

They say necessity is the mother of creation, and sometime at the beginning of the hunger strike, someone came up with the idea to make a shelf on the door of the cell with some string and a piece of cardboard. I think the idea came from Robert King. And everybody started doing that, so eventually it got to where we could sit the tray on the cardboard shelf and use both hands to eat with. We had no idea it would be eighteen months—that this is how we would eat. Eventually they came, and we knew they were cutting food slots in the other cell blocks in the prison. Those of us who organized resistance—we were in the camp RC [reception center]. If any of you have ever seen pictures of Angola, it's the big white building right at the front gate. Death row and CCR were housed in that building, so eventually they got to RC and they start cutting the bars. I was on D-tier and Herman was on A-tier, and those are the last two tiers they come to, to cut the food slots. And then when they got to the tier I was on—fifteen cells on that tier—they cut all of them except four. They claimed they ran out of material.

Beth: *And, let me guess: you were one of the four?*

Albert: No, but we all knew what it was. They were determined. They had been trying to force us for almost two years to eat under the door. And we were not going to give them that. So we made officers switch cells. At that time it was relatively easy to switch cells on the tier. The guys in there said, "Nah, man, we know what's going on here. We got this." So after about a month, a reclass [reclassification] board came, and we went out there and told them that there were four more cells on the tier that hadn't had food slots cut. And we told them if they didn't do it that day, we were going back on hunger strike. They claimed ignorance, that they thought all the food slots had been cut in all the cells, and so within an hour after the reclass board ended, they came and cut the other four cells. It was a victory for us.

Beth: *There's so many emotions I'm having hearing these stories. I'm sure you're having them telling them, living them for all those years. The constant march to live with your gaze turned outside instead turned inside. To try not to become institutionalized and at the same time seeing and feeling in the people you love and care about—and seeing and feeling in your own life—the brutality, the inhumane treatment, on and on every day. And still being able to organize and resist and teach and be creative. I'm sure people are wondering how you survived this. Where did you get the strength, and how did you stay focused or hopeful? How did you avoid feeling defeated or bitter or giving in, giving up?*

Albert: I always tell people that the power of the Black Panther Party was tremendous in my life. My mom struggled so hard to try to protect me and my brothers and sister from falling victim to criminal life of the street. But the voice of the street was louder than my mom, and the voice of the Black Panther Party was louder than the

voice of the street. It was the first time in my life where I understood that it wasn't who I was, but it was what I could be, what I
could become, what I could achieve. Then later on in life as I look
back—you know they always say hindsight is one hundred percent
perfect—I realize that other great men and women that I read about
in history books inspired me, and that I inherited from my mom the
quality of internal strength, determination, a strong sense of loyalty
and devotion.

I lost my mom in '94 to cancer, but before I lost my mom, I was
able to sit down and look her in the eye and apologize for the man I
was and let her know that she was my one true hero. She was the source
of whatever strength I had that allowed me to survive forty-four years
of solitary confinement. It was a difficult time. There's nothing more
difficult to live with than to watch another man go insane because
he's confined to a nine-by-six cell. And no matter how many toys or
trinkets they give you, like TV or radios or whatever, you're still confined to a nine-by-six area. And in some cases we were housed in areas
where the cells were smaller than that.

Beth: *And how often did you get out?*

Albert: You got one hour a day out of the cell. Originally we didn't
get any yard privilege or outdoor exercise. Eventually Robert and
myself and Herman, we taught ourselves how to litigate in courts,
and we filed suits in the court for us all to have outdoor exercise at
least three days a week. A lot of these prisons across the country,
they're in enclosed cells with steel doors and a food slot and a "peep-
hole," as they call it. CCR, solitary, in Louisiana State Penitentiary
was a bar system. The front of the cell was some configuration of
bars. But none of this matters when you confine a person to an area
no bigger than the average bathroom and when there's nothing he
can do or she can do that will allow her to be removed from solitary
confinement. The pressure of the whole thing—you know, I've seen
men go insane. We've fought so hard to try to give some of these
men reasons for wanting to live to be strong. We won some battles,
but, unfortunately, most of the battles we lost.

Beth: *I think about how solitary confinement is used all over this country, in almost every level of prison or jail or detention center. How unfortunately common it is. Yours is an unusual situation because of the remarkable duration of forty-four years, but it's not unusual that people who are incarcerated will spend some time in those conditions. And increasingly it's happening for longer periods of time for arbitrary kinds of reasons. In some ways when I hear you tell that amazing story, I deeply appreciate that to have survived would have been a victory. That would have been an accomplishment, a political act of resistance: to have survived. You not only survived, but you fought back; you organized from the inside both for your own well-being and also for the well-being of others on the issue of solitary confinement. And so I wonder if you can talk about how solitary confinement fits within the larger picture of racist carceral state processes. Where is solitary in that large map of criminalization and mass incarceration that this country is so committed to?*

Albert: As you've said, solitary confinement has become the means for the prison administration to kill off what they consider to be ills. The last information I read was that in any given year, over eighty thousand people are being held in solitary confinement, even juveniles. Either this year or last year, President Obama forbid the use of solitary confinement against kids held in juvenile facilities. You know, Herman was [in] for forty-one years, King for twenty-nine years, and me for forty-four years—well, actually forty-three years and ten months, but what's a few months? So we kind of round it off to forty-four years in solitary confinement. But I think one of the reasons that we were able to survive was because we knew that we could not remain the same men that were put in solitary confinement.

Our teachings as members of the Black Panther Party taught about materialism and dialectics and the contradictions that causes change. We knew that in order to survive we had to change. We turned our cells into something that they were not designed for, and given the qualities of humanity that I inherited from my mom and the inspiration I got from great men and women who have fought for change in society and in the world, somehow I managed not only to survive being held in solitary time but to prosper and progress as a human being.

Beth: *How do you see the larger activism now across the country around solitary confinement? As you said, there's now at least objection for juveniles to be placed in solitary confinement, and some move to have solitary confinement be used less often—for people with mental health conditions, for example. It's still a very common practice. What's the movement like on the outside, and how are you involved in that movement from the inside?*

Albert: Right now, Robert and myself are going around to speak. What we are trying to do is start an international dialogue about what constitutes a political prisoner. America is the only country that claims not to have political prisoners, but there are political prisoners: Leonard Peltier, Oscar Lopez, Sundiata Acoli, Herman Bell, Mutulu Shakur, and Russell "Maroon" Shoats. We're trying to start a national dialogue in this country, and we're trying to show people that these are not aliens from another planet. These people are grandfathers, fathers, husbands, brothers, sisters, mothers, and that what is being done to them is not only illegal; it violates the very core of humanity. It violates constitutional rights, but more than anything, it violates the moral standard that all human beings must ascribe to achieve in life. We think that the best way for us to start a national dialogue is by illuminating that the foundation of whatever we do stands on morality. Laws can change, people change, but morality pretty much remains the same.

Beth: *To what extent does that argument around morality and justice and the elimination of torture and all people are political prisoners, to what extent does that extend beyond issues like solitary and what I want to call more overt forms of torture? I'm asking this because I spent some time this morning at bond court over at 26th and California, Cook County Jail. And there were a lot of people in the room who work on the issue of mass criminalization, not in places like solitary confinement, but in the small places all around our city where people are suffering. And sometimes you organize around the worst case, like solitary confinement for forty-four years, and also want to be concerned about routine stops or in and out of the county jail—in other words, what's the link between the egregious torture that you experienced and the everyday more common*

experiences, especially of Black people, in the criminal legal system? Do
you see a connection there?

Albert: Yeah, because you know the criminal justice system in this
country is a pathway for a journey from society to prison. And I've
always said that institutions by themselves are concrete and steel and
computers. It is the human beings that function in these institutions
who give it dignity. We have a judicial system that no longer cares about
guilt or innocence or justice. The system mainly cares about due process. I always use the analogy, as long as you hanging right, that's the
concern. You use the right kind of rope, you'll have the right kind of
noose. And he or she is the right level in the air when you hang them.

I know justice, at least for me, is an abstract concept. But it is
a concept that works toward a more humane and organized society.
And so we live in a country now where a traffic ticket carries the
death penalty, where the police—whose responsibility is to protect
and serve—become judge, jury, and executioner on the spot. Because
prisons are virtually left without oversight, correctional officers and
administrators develop an attitude of invincibility. They don't have to
answer to anyone about how horribly they treat other human beings,
and it's okay. There's a syndrome we call the "Wyatt Earp syndrome,"
and it's when young guys come there to work and at first they are
pretty much humane. But as the days go on and the weeks go on,
they begin to realize, "Well, I could do anything I want; I don't
have to answer to anyone." So, you know, you see them, they come
down the tier, and I'm sure everyone has watched these old West-
erns where the gunslingers come down and they got their hands to
their side. And, I kid you not, that's actually how most of these guys
start walking—as though they're gunslingers. They psychologically
and mentally dehumanize you because it's the only way that they
can justify within themselves treating human beings in a subhuman
manner. And that's usually with beatings or gas.

It's pretty much like the police now: don't challenge them. No
matter whether you have the law, no matter whether you have the
Constitution. Even if you have human rights on your side, do not
challenge them. Their response is always violence; their response is
beatings or gassings. And when they gas one man, they really gas the
whole tier, because you can't gas one man. Gas spreads, you know?

Those are the things that constantly go on in the prison, and it goes on because there's no oversight. There's no oversight from the citizens. We have got to start being interested in what's going on in our prisons in our names. We have got to start remembering that the people who occupy the beds are no longer seen as being human, but they're being seen as profit margins. We have some of the wholesale companies that sign lucrative contracts with prisons, and you're good enough to work for them while you're in prison, but then once you get out of prison, you're not good enough. Those are the type of the things Robert and I try to speak on and to organize against. Our fight is for humanity. We believe that if the human race don't start evolving and start changing, that we're going to destroy ourselves.

Beth: *So let me ask you one last question. You brought up the police and people not having humanity, and I wonder if you could react to how frustrated people feel. I know you met with a group of young activists in Chicago this morning. And I'm sure that whenever you wake up in the morning, you've got to listen to some other story of what's happened to a Black person. And this room is full of people who have been on the streets organizing, trying to support each other, frustrated—you know, really tired, just tired, of the continued assault and the violence and the murder. What would you say to tired people who are admiring the perseverance and the courage and the dedication and the survival that you show through your story? What do you say to any of us today who are trying to survive the brutality that we have to witness and respond to it in some way that sort of dignifies it? We're worried about the struggle. What should we be doing?*

Albert: One of the things I asked the young ladies that I met with this morning was to see me as a witness to the strength and determination of the human spirit. You can survive almost anything if you're willing to struggle. You must take a stand and you must be willing to sacrifice. You can't allow yourself to be frustrated or to lose hope, and, most of all, you can't become predictable. These police departments, as well as the military, they have these squadrons of psychologists, and they sit down and they analyze and they pretty much know almost to the letter how we're going to respond to things that happen in society. And they use that as a mechanism to control or manipulate. We have to find new ways to become social activists. We have to realize that this is a lifestyle. Once you commit to becoming a revolutionary, an activist, a social struggle, or whatever you want to call yourself, you can't see this as *I'm working and I'm going to quit after ten years.* You have to say, *This is a lifetime commitment.*

Survival Kits

In 2017, artist and architect Andres L. Hernandez worked with a group of incarcerated artists—all serving long-term sentences—to develop a body of artwork about passing time, and the seemingly insignificant moments in between events. They looked at historical examples of artists who have creatively symbolized, documented, and measured time as inspiration for the creation of their own miniaturized survival kits. The items were designed to fit into the space of a plastic, state-issued soap box. Each kit represented what the artists needed to survive inside, for the long term.

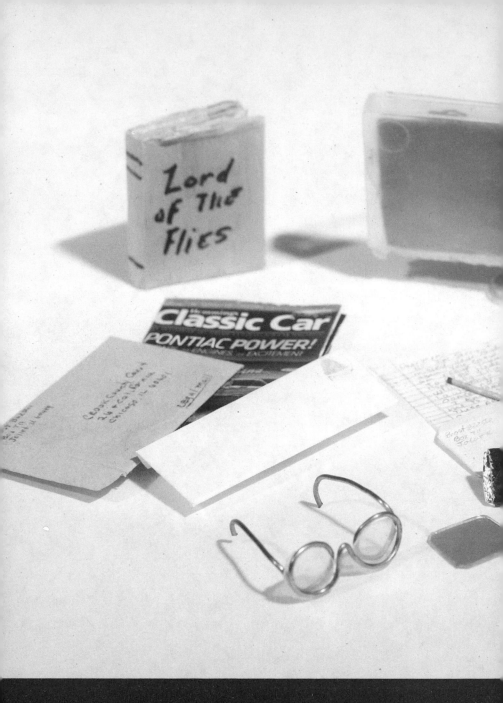

I have created items that I feel are necessary to help me pass time. Please understand that they may appear "rough" but the condition I exist in is not conducive to the creation of art. The pieces in this collection were created with items I have in my cell. For instance, I cut everything using fingernail clippers.

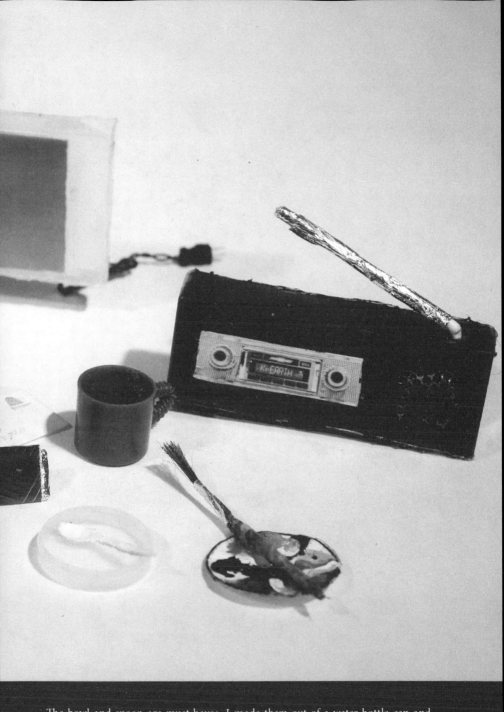

The bowl and spoon are must-haves. I made them out of a water bottle cap and paper. The chocolate bar allows me a small sense of normalcy, freedom. It is made with candy bar wrapper and foam. The letter and envelope represent the connection with my family, now fading after more than two decades inside. —Chuck Brost

I have included small boxes with jewelry as part of my survival kit to show the level of ingenuity of incarcerated people. The boxes are molded from cardboard and paper and are hand painted. Mattress foam is cut and inserted, providing a cushion. Making the jewelry is a separate and arduous process. I was first incarcerated at the

age of fifteen, released for two and a half months, and incarcerated again for the last twenty years. I'm condemned to a life sentence. I have never been engaged, married and I don't have children. The wedding band and heart pendant represents my hope and desire to one day come home and start a family. —Raul Dorado

"Two things have I required of thee; deny me them not before I die: Remove far from me vanity and lies; give me neither poverty nor riches; feed me with food convenient for me: Lest I be full, and deny thee, and say, Who is the Lord? or lest I be poor, and steal, and take the name of my God in vain." —Proverbs 30:7–9

This project is a representation of the truth found in Proverbs 30:7–9. The bread and water represent physical nourishment, while the bible represents spiritual nourishment. —Jason Muñoz

Section 2

Long-Term Sentencing, Illusions of Safety, and the Pursuit of Toughness

As early as the late 1800s people locked away in America's prisons described the experience as a "living tomb." The sentiment is not surprising: reformers who created these early institutions imagined the "ideal prisoner" as both dead and alive, a subject to be both corrected and severely punished, separated from the living. More than one hundred years later, the deathly experience of prison persists. In the twenty-first century, the prison conjures up images of a factory machine, fit with a moving belt determined to shape, stamp, and hold more and more people. Long-term sentencing—one critical cog in the machine—not only locks people up but does so for so long that the language of the eighteenth century is still echoed today. "Buried alive," "stretched out," and "earth slammed" are descriptions uttered to refer to people serving long term.

While the prison of today might be the same as it was at the beginning of the American penitentiary movement—still hinged on racist, sexist, and class-based frameworks of who is criminal— the scale of the project has drastically changed. This section details the incredible expansion of the prison system through the lens of long-term sentencing policies that are sometimes called the "other death penalty." Here we can see a literal reshaping of American communities. Specifically, low-income Black and Brown neighborhoods, targeted by policing, bear the marks of sentencing policies: high rates of vacancies, mental health impacts, and economic loss. Meanwhile, prisons are filled with people serving long-term sentences for crimes that would have resulted in shorter sentences had they been adjudicated in a different month or year.

Those sentenced in the late 1990s and early 2000s know the significance of these dates and policies all too well. One person, sentenced before 1999 (the year the state of Illinois enacted a truth-in-sentencing law), has done their time and prepares for life outside, while another, sentenced just days or weeks after 1999, will be 120 years of age before they see the free world. In this radical disparity, we can see how the vast policies of the "living grave" were not always this way. In the lives of our formerly incarcerated neighbors, friends, and leaders of movements—sometimes convicted for the very same crimes as those locked up today—we know that people can produce harm and not be harm itself. As many people inside prisons say, "I am not my crime." Further, studies show that long-term sentencing does not even produce safety or reduce harm. Long prison terms are, in fact, counterproductive for public safety, because they permanently remove parents, wage earners, and community members from the fabric of our society.

If the long-term prison sentence creates a living mortuary, what of the places from which the incarcerated were taken from, and who is left to carry on? And in what ways does the vital activity of life continue in a living grave?

Long Division

■ Tara Betts

How many decades of calendars reveal what is starkly plantation?
How wide the green fields are within the walls. Floors polished
spotless as walls sag with layers of paint older than me. It is endless
counting for the regimented lines to meals, walks within gated yards
for men on crutches, infinite uniforms to wash, dawns and nights,
but time hangs, looms for acts committed so quickly (or not). Time
lassoes anchors to their necks—most of those necks are dark
inheritors of knotted rope legacies. Moments in a classroom
with a broken window remind me of younger students, but they are
men, men who are fathers and uncles, in a place where books are
minted as rare capital. They think. I am sitting at a table full
of black and brown men in a classroom which never happens
outside these walls. The wrongness of prisons and schools collide.
The grand execution of an intentional mistake, and intentional means
a deliberate act, not an accident. An accident is not orderly rows
or an easy rhythm to follow. Recovering from accidents is easier.
The frittering away of lives behind concrete and bars punches
into registers, rings incessantly—calculated yet incalculable.

Lock 'Em Up and Throw Away the Key
The Historical Roots of Harsh Sentencing and Mass Incarceration

■ James Kilgore

I n 2016 more than 160,000 individuals were serving life sentences in the United States, more than four times the number in 1984. Of those, nearly a third were doing life without any chance of parole.[1] By contrast, the European Human Rights Court has ruled that life without parole is "degrading" and "inhuman"; German policy regards life imprisonment as "incompatible with the provision of human dignity."[2] Moreover, several European countries ban life sentences altogether. In the era of mass incarceration, the United States has become an outlier, virtually an outlaw in the international world of justice, the only country where "Lock 'em up and throw away the key" has become an operational slogan.

This country's propensity for extreme punishment extends beyond the increase in life sentences. Forty thousand people currently face "virtual life," terms of fifty years or more. Notions of mercy, second chance, rehabilitation, and redemption have been stripped away in the frenzied process of mass incarceration. Whereas in the 1960s and 1970s many prisons had extensive programs devoted to rehabilitation of people in prison, this approach rapidly fell out of favor during the era of mass incarceration as the country moved toward harsher sentencing. Tragically, the trend toward people spending more time in prison continues to accelerate. An Urban Institute study produced in 2014 showed that since 2000, the average time served by people in prison has risen in all forty-four states that responded to the survey.[3] In nearly half of those states, the average time served by the longest-serving 10 percent had risen by more than five years. These increases in length of time served are largely the product of sentencing policy, the cumulative effects of a hyperpunitive system.

To fully understand how the United States reached these extremes, we need to look at the punishment paradigm that swept the criminal legal system from the 1980s onward; in large part, this phenomenon represented a backlash against the massive social movements of the 1960s and 1970s, movements that questioned the nature of democracy in this country.[4] It is crucial to examine both the scale and ideological scope of these movements in order to comprehend the vehemence of the backlash that has taken place in the era of mass incarceration.[5]

Rebellions of the period went far beyond media representations of sit-ins, the counterculture, and the quest for legal equality.[6] Armed Native Americans occupied land on Alcatraz Island and at Wounded Knee demanding national sovereignty. Puerto Ricans fought for independence and campaigned for the freedom of imprisoned leaders like Lolita Lebrón, who had led an armed attack on the US Congress in 1954. Chican@ farmworkers and their allies mobilized international boycotts to secure the right to unionize and earn a living wage. In response to a US war machine that killed three million people in Southeast Asian wars, dissidents in nearly every community marched and protested, tens of thousands migrated to Canada and other countries to avoid conscription, and four thousand went to prison rather than be drafted.[7]

The period also saw the emergence of "new" social issue movements. Women's liberation and gay liberation challenged patriarchal power relations; ecology activists targeted environmental destruction. Jesuit activists like Daniel and Philip Berrigan destroyed records in selective service offices. Bomb attacks on buildings and offices related to the US war effort averaged nearly one a day from 1968 to 1970.[8] In 1972 the revolutionary Weather Underground organization bombed the Pentagon and US Capitol building in Washington, DC. The Black Panther Party organized armed patrols of local police and built ties to revolutionary freedom fighters around the globe. Predominantly Black neighborhoods in Newark, Detroit, and Los Angeles

were the focal points of urban rebellions—spontaneous sprees of setting fires to buildings and "liberating" merchandise from retail stores.
All told, these movements and uprisings amounted to open attacks
on a society that had left people of color and the global South out of
the American dream. These political movements and mobilizations
rocked a relatively comfortable, overwhelmingly white middle class
to its core with their rebellion.

Movements of incarcerated people and their supporters were
part of this trend. California prisons saw the formation of a United
Prisoners Union, acting on behalf of the "convicted class."[9] In addition, cases of racist abuse and institutional violence in high-profile
prisons like Angola in Louisiana and San Quentin in California
sparked efforts at reform. As historian Heather Thompson points
out, the demands of incarcerated people during that time "very
much mirrored those of activists on city streets—they spoke out
against racism, against the violence directed at them by officers of
the state, for better living and working conditions."[10]

No event of this period more clearly reflected the complexities
of prison struggles and their relationship to the movements of the
day than the Attica Prison uprising. And no event would have a
bigger impact on sentencing practice.

The Attica Uprising and Its Aftermath

On September 9, 1971, hundreds of men residing in the D-block of
Attica Prison in upstate New York seized control of one of the prison's buildings, taking thirty-nine guards hostage. Their demands focused on basic necessities: improved diet, better medical treatment,
and expanded recreation programs. But the men also pressed for
increased political freedom and an end to censorship of mail and
reading material. At the heart of their rebellion was a general issue of
human dignity. L. D. Barkley, one of the prisoner leaders, articulated
this demand in a famous speech to the men in D-yard during the
rebellion: "We are men! We are not beasts, and we do not intend to
be beaten or driven as such."[11]

Once the uprising began, the men in D-block organized. They
elected a team of negotiators from their ranks who ran daily affairs

in the prison and spoke on behalf of the population. The participants in the rebellion recognized the need to involve high-profile people from outside the prison to become part of the negotiations. *New York Times* reporter Tom Wicker and Black Panther leader Bobby Seale traveled to Attica and went into D-yard in an effort to broker a settlement. However, the highest-priority demand of the men of D-yard was not met: the call for then governor Nelson Rockefeller to speak to them in person. Despite pleas from many quarters, Rockefeller refused. Instead, on September 13 he sent in state troopers and other armed law enforcement personnel. The result was the killing of L. D. Barkley and twenty-eight other prisoners, along with ten guards. Those who survived were brutalized by law enforcement. Frank "Big Black" Smith, who became a well-known social justice activist upon his release, would later testify in court that when the troopers retook D-yard, guards had forced him to lie on a table naked for five hours holding a football between his chin and his chest. They threw lit cigarettes on Smith and told him if he dropped the football, they would shoot him. Somehow he managed to hold on. Other men reported similar abuse.

After the mass killing by Rockefeller's forces at Attica, hundreds of people rose to the defense of the men who survived the uprising. The Attica Brothers Defense Committee organized branches across the country and ultimately spent decades fighting in courts on behalf of those who took part in the rebellion while exposing the conditions at Attica and the violence of the prison staff after the uprising.[12] The slogan "Attica Is All of Us" became a popular mantra within movements of the day.

However, for many on the other side of the political fence, the uprising at Attica held a different meaning. Governor Rockefeller blamed the rebellion on a permissive criminal justice system, particularly what he saw as increasing illegal drug use. Over the ensuing two years the governor drove a set of measures through the New York State Legislature that in 1973 became known as the Rockefeller drug laws.[13] The laws broke new ground by instituting harsh, inflexible penalties, known as mandatory minimums, which prescribed fixed sentences for many crimes, especially in drug cases. For example, legislation set the sentence in New York for selling two ounces (57

grams) of heroin, morphine, opium, cocaine, or cannabis at a minimum of fifteen years to life. Possession of four ounces (113 grams) or
more of the same substances carried the same penalty. Mandatory
minimums meant that a judge had no choice but to impose these
sentences. The adoption of this legislation gave New York State the
toughest laws of its kind in the entire United States.

The Rockefeller laws provided a focus for backlash against
political and cultural rebellions of the day. The laws criminalized
not only drug usage but, by implication, actions and philosophies
deemed "anti-American" as well. In the criminal justice sphere, these
laws signaled a national swing toward the "lock 'em up and throw
away the key" approach.

The Rockefeller laws were not the only moves toward harsher
law enforcement and sentencing at that time. The increased prosecution of drug crimes went hand in hand with more repressive
policies directed at political activists. Leading this repression was
the FBI's Covert Intelligence Program, or COINTELPRO. Under
COINTELPRO the FBI infiltrated radical groups, gathering information and, in some cases, encouraging activists to engage in violent
political acts. The Black Panther Party, the Socialist Workers Party,
the American Indian Movement, the Puerto Rican Independence
Movement, the Communist Party USA, and Students for a Democratic Society all attracted COINTELPRO operatives. In 1969 these
federal agencies partnered with the Chicago police in the predawn
murder of Chicago Black Panther leaders Fred Hampton and Mark
Clark. COINTELPRO activities also contributed to processes that
led to lengthy prison terms for political prisoners, including Black
Liberation Army leaders such as Geronimo Ji-Jaga Pratt, Black
Panther Party member Mumia Abu-Jamal, and American Indian
Movement activist Leonard Peltier.[14]

The Further Spread of Harsh Sentencing Laws

As the radical political movements of the 1960s and early 1970s declined, law enforcement increasingly focused on drug laws. In 1973
Michigan enacted a "650-Lifer Law," which called for life imprisonment, without the possibility of parole, for the sale, manufacture,

or possession of 650 grams or more (1.43 lb) of cocaine or any other banned opiate. This spread of mandatory minimums accelerated after the launching of the "war on drugs" by President Ronald Reagan in 1982 and the increased use of crack cocaine in the mid-1980s.

Perhaps the most important of these measures were the federal sentencing guidelines passed by Congress in 1984, which were applied throughout the federal prison system. They spelled out required sentences for nearly every crime on the federal books and provided a clear indication that the tide in US criminal justice had turned from rehabilitation to punishment. Suddenly politicians, regardless of party affiliation, needed to appear "tough on crime" if they wanted to get elected. Ultimately this involved instilling racialized fear in the white population.

The 1988 presidential election actually turned on this fear. George Bush Sr. was trailing in the polls until he blamed his opponent, Michael Dukakis, for a program that granted a work release to Willie Horton, a Black man convicted of murder. During one of his work releases, Horton raped a white woman. The Bush campaign spread the media with photos of Horton, linking his offenses to Dukakis's being soft on crime. Ultimately, Bush overtook Dukakis, largely a result of his promoting fear of Black criminals like Horton.

Republicans were not alone in criminalizing Black men, however. As Michelle Alexander, author of *The New Jim Crow*, observes, "Soon Democrats began competing with Republicans to prove they could be even tougher on them [criminals] than their Republican counterparts, and so it was President Bill Clinton who actually escalated the drug war far beyond what his Republican predecessors even dreamed possible."[15] Clinton championed the 1994 Violent Crime Control and Law Enforcement Act, which fueled mass incarceration by setting aside $8.7 billion for prison building for states that enacted harsher sentencing laws. The law also rekindled capital punishment and financed one hundred thousand more cops on the streets.[16]

Spin-offs from Mandatory Minimums

The punitive philosophy behind mandatory minimums led to several other changes in sentencing laws across the country. The two most important of these were "truth in sentencing" and "three strikes laws," or "habitual criminal" legislation.

Truth in sentencing represents a rejection of the philosophy of indeterminate sentencing that dominated the criminal legal system throughout most of the twentieth century. First institutionalized by legislation in New York in 1877, under the indeterminate approach a person could serve far less time than stated in their sentence due to "time off for good behavior." This approach aimed to provide incentives for people to participate in rehabilitation and avoid disciplinary problems during their incarceration.

Truth in sentencing removed those incentives. Under a typical truth-in-sentencing law, a person would have to serve 85 percent of the time on their sentence before they could be released. So if a person received a ten-year sentence, they would have to serve at least eight years and six months. Their time could be extended to force them to serve the full ten years if they had disciplinary problems during their incarceration, but there was no option of time off for good behavior. In 1984 Washington became the first state to adopt truth in sentencing. By 1998 the federal system, plus some twenty-seven states and the District of Columbia, had truth-in-sentencing statutes in place.[17]

Three strikes laws applied the principles of mandatory minimums to people with extensive criminal histories. These laws often built on previous "habitual offender" legislation that allowed extra penalties for people with repeat offenses. As of 2016 twelve states imposed a mandatory sentence of life without parole for those convicted of three violent crimes.

The most stringent of these statutes was California's initiative, passed by a popular referendum named "Three Strikes and You're Out" in 1994. The ballot measure drew a 72 percent approval vote and made a sentence of twenty-five years to life mandatory for anyone convicted of a felony who had two prior convictions for violent offenses. An additional feature of the California law was a "second strike" provision, mandating double the normal sentence for someone convicted of a second crime of violence.[18]

According to a report by the Justice Policy Institute, in the first decade of implementation, California sentenced more than four thousand people to life under three strikes while thirty-five hundred received doubled sentences as a result of a second strike.[19] Some people received a third strike for relatively minor offenses. One of them was Jerry Dewayne Williams, known as the "pizza thief," sentenced to twenty-five years to life in 1995 for stealing a piece of pizza from some children at Redondo Beach. He served five years before a judge set him free.

While mandatory minimums and truth in sentencing were core policies in accelerating the growth of the prison population, three other developments in sentencing during the 1990s contributed further to the United States becoming a total outlier in the international world of justice: trying juveniles as adults; the increased use of solitary confinement; and the reemergence of executions. Under the slogan "adult crime, adult time," state and federal authorities accelerated the expansion of trying and sentencing juveniles as adults. Most states set a minimum age for a juvenile to be eligible to be tried as an adult. By 1997 two states, Kansas and Vermont, had reduced the age to ten. In 2014 Pennsylvania tried a ten-year-old for murder in an adult court.[20] Most other states fixed the age at fourteen. North Carolina, on the other hand, tries all sixteen- and seventeen-year-olds charged with felonies as adults.

The case of Kaliet Browder graphically illustrates the perils of sentencing youth as adults. Accused of stealing a backpack in New York at age sixteen, Browder was sent to the adult jail at Rikers Island and spent three years enduring extended periods of solitary confinement as well as numerous beatings at the hands of guards and incarcerated men. All the while Browder maintained his innocence, refusing to plead guilty and accept a plea bargain. Finally the prosecutor dropped his case for lack of evidence and released Browder. Once released, Browder suffered from depression and posttraumatic stress. He told an interviewer, "I'm paranoid. I feel like I was robbed of my happiness."[21] He spent most of his post-prison life in and out of psychiatric institutions. Finally, just after his twenty-second birthday, Browder committed suicide. The most extreme version of trying young people as adults has been the imposition of life without parole (LWOP) on youth, a practice prohibited by the International Convention on the Rights of the Child.[22] According to a Sentencing Project report, more than twenty-five hundred youth have been sentenced to life without parole.[23] Michigan and Louisiana account for more than a quarter of all juveniles doing life sentences.[24] After numerous appeals and public pressure, the Supreme Court banned life-without-parole sentences for youth in June 2012 in the landmark case *Miller v. Alabama*. Since that time at least twenty-seven states plus the District of Columbia have eliminated LWOP for juveniles convicted of murder. Some have made the ruling retroactive, making people sentenced to LWOP for crimes committed while a juvenile before the *Miller* ruling eligible for release.[25]

In the 1990s solitary confinement, or isolation, became both a permanent condition of incarceration and a form of temporary disciplinary action by prison authorities. This period also saw the advent of high-tech facilities totally dedicated to solitary confinement, the super-maximum prisons. The most well-known "supermax" is the federal Administrative Maximum Facility (ADX) in Florence, Colorado, which houses 490 men who are kept in their cells twenty-three hours a day, allowed out for only one hour a day of solitary recreation. For at least the first year of their sentence, they are not permitted to interact with anyone else in the prison. A former warden, interviewed on CBS's *60 Minutes*, described Florence ADX as "a cleaner version of hell."[26]

Many state prisons have also set up separate isolation blocks known by names such as "special housing units," "security housing units" (SHUs), "control units," and "behavior modification units." The watchdog group Solitary Watch estimated that between eighty thousand to one hundred thousand people were held in some type of "isolated confinement" in 2014.[27]

A final expression of the increased harshness of the US criminal justice system's sentencing regime has been the increased imposition of the death penalty. The US reinstated the death penalty in 1976 after a four-year suspension. Executions peaked at ninety-nine in 1999 and declined to nineteen in 2016. Over twenty people have been executed for crimes committed while a juvenile.[28]

The Impact of Harsh Sentencing Measures

Harsh sentencing has seriously impacted the prison and judicial system, with grave consequences for racial and gender justice. At the most fundamental level, harsh sentencing has torn individual lives apart by keeping people in prison for periods of time that are totally inappropriate for the offense for which they were convicted. Elvin Garcia, who spent twenty-seven years in New York state prisons, observed, "I've seen individuals do long sentences [and] by the time they're released, both parents died. They have no immediate family left. No one." Stanley Mitchell, who served a total of thirty-six years, reflected on long sentences, saying, "Does prison, long-term incarceration, change people? Sure it does. . . . It makes a person more bitter, more hateful, especially when . . . the rules are not applied fairly."[29]

But the impact of harsher sentences extends beyond what happens to the individual inside prison. At a systemic level, longer sentences have had an enormous effect on government expenditure. Longer sentences mean larger incarcerated populations, leading to heavily overcrowded prisons and jails and fueling constantly increasing demands to expand capacity. In 2015, Illinois prisons were filled to 145 percent capacity. The federal system hovered at around 130 percent capacity for the entire first decade of this century.[30]

In the short run, overcrowded prisons mean authorities convert gyms, dayrooms, libraries, and storerooms into living space, creating conditions that precipitate conflict and the spread of illness. In most cases the solution to overcrowding has been to build more prison and jail cells, perpetuating the cycle of draining resources from valuable social services such as education, health care, and public housing. Ultimately the pressure to expand carceral capacity has fundamentally reshaped the mission of the state to stress security and policing above all else.

In addition to contributing to expansion of the overall prison-industrial complex, harsh sentences have intensified the racial disparities in the criminal legal system. As early as 1991, a federal commission concluded, "The disparate application of mandatory minimum sentences (means that) whites are more likely than non-whites to be sentenced below the applicable mandatory minimum."[31] A 2014 report by the Urban Institute revealed that racial disparities among those serving the longest 10 percent of prison terms are even larger than the disparities in the overall prison population.[32] Pennsylvania is an example: Blacks make up 11 percent of the state's population, 49 percent of those in prison, but 60 percent of those serving the longest prison terms. The Urban Institute's report also noted that in at least eighteen states racial disparities for the longest sentences had grown in the previous decade.

The application of life sentences also reveals serious inequities, with people of color making up 66 percent of those serving life and 77 percent of those serving life for a crime committed as a juvenile.[33] Black people constitute 65.4 percent of those given life without parole for nonviolent crimes.[34] The application of the death penalty reflects similar patterns of racism. A report by Amnesty International on the first two decades of the resumption of capital punishment in the United States showed that roughly a third of those executed were Black.[35]

While many studies have focused on the racial impact of harsh sentences, the gender implications are equally significant. Though all sectors of the prison population have grown over the last three-plus decades, women's incarceration has grown the fastest—up 700 percent since 1980, outpacing the growth of men's institutions by 50 percent from 1980 to 2014.[36] This process was also racialized, with Black women incarcerated at a rate of 109 per 100,000 compared to 53 for white women and 64 for "Hispanic" women. But figures capture only a small part of the impact of harsh sentences on women. Likely even more important is the fact that when men go to prison, women typically are left to shoulder extra burdens.

While men make up nearly 90 percent of those in prison, according to a national study produced by the Ella Baker Center for Human Rights in 2015, 63 percent of those incarcerated relied primarily on family members for court-related costs associated with conviction, with 83 percent of those family members being women.[37] At the family level, a scenario in which men are serving long sentences implies the virtually permanent absence of a person in the role of parent, income earner, caregiver, or community builder. Typically, this means mothers, spouses, partners, grandmothers, and daughters take on these sets of responsibilities for most of their adult lives. As the Baker Center report stresses, taking on these responsibilities has a high cost. One-third of the families interviewed went into debt due to the costs of phone calls and visits to their incarcerated loved one. Two-thirds had difficulty "meeting basic needs." As one family member from Miami noted, "Whatever it is, you pay. When the call comes in, you take the call. It's time to visit, you visit. They want something, you buy it. The costs are astronomical." A mother from New Orleans reported going six months with no electricity in her house to fulfill her obligations to her incarcerated children.[38] With 80 percent of people in prison living below the poverty line, these burdens are an enormous challenge. Moreover, as the report points out, when a loved one is serving a long sentence, the loss of income can have implications for generations.

The costs are not only financial. Half of all people with a family member incarcerated have reported negative health impacts such as posttraumatic stress disorder, nightmares, depression, and anxiety. Shamika Wilson, whose husband has been locked up for three decades, described how stigmatization affected her: "My husband isn't the only person locked up; with an incarcerated loved one, I also feel like I've been doing time for the last thirty years. Society instills a sense of 'guilt by association' . . . which leads to additional pain, sadness and isolation."[39]

While the Baker Center report focused on individuals and families, loved ones of incarcerated people also come from communities. Studies have shown how those in prison tend to come from low-income neighborhoods where people of color are an overwhelming majority.[40] Given the scale of mass incarceration with so many people serving long sentences, the absence of a huge swath of community members leaves many gaps and imbalances, making the challenges of sustaining a healthy environment free of poverty and excessive police presence very difficult. Once again, these are challenges disproportionately borne by women.

The gender dimensions of harsh sentencing don't end there. Two additional realities are the excessive punishment of women who retaliate against abusive male partners and the hyperincarceration of transgender people. Cases like those of Marissa Alexander and Sara Kruzan illustrate the particulars of gender bias when violence is involved. Under a mandatory minimum, Alexander was sentenced to twenty years in prison for firing a shot at her abusive partner. The shot missed him and didn't harm anyone. At age seventeen, Kruzan killed a man she identified as her "pimp" after a long history of abuse and trafficking. She received a life sentence. Both women's cases were the subject of national campaigns by social justice activists. Alexander's decision was overturned after she had served three years. Kruzan eventually received clemency from the governor of California and was released after serving nineteen years. While these cases were overturned, few women are so fortunate. The Sentencing Project in 2013 reported that more than fifty-three hundred people were serving life and life-without-parole sentences in women's prisons.[41]

Though transgender people have almost been erased from discussions of sentencing and imprisonment, they are the most likely group to end up behind bars. According to Lambda Legal, nearly one in six adult transgender people in the United States have been to prison. For Black transgender people, the figure is almost one in two.[42] Additionally, the Sylvia Rivera Law Project reports that these arrest rates represent an intersection of "over-policing and profiling" of low-income as well as trans and gender-nonconforming people.[43] Long sentences add an extra burden. Transgender people are often placed in a facility according to the gender assigned them at birth rather than according to their gender identity. In addition, if they require hormone treatment or gender-affirming surgery, access is often difficult. Michelle Norsworthy, a transgender woman who has been in a men's prison since 1987, describes her life as "imprisonment within an imprisonment. . . . It's like suffocating."[44] Like a disproportionately large number of transgender people in prison, she has suffered rape and constant harassment from guards. Her confrontations with authority over her medication and other necessities have given her an unfavorable disciplinary record, reducing her chances of ever being released.

Changes in the Court System

In addition to the effects on individuals and communities on the receiving end of harsh sentences, mandatory minimums in particular have precipitated great changes in the actual functioning of the criminal legal system. To begin with, mandatory minimums have taken away much of judges' discretion in sentencing. Instead of examining the individual details of a person's history and considering possible mitigating factors such as employment history or family responsibilities, mandatory minimums reduce judgment to applying a formula from a fixed set of guidelines. Ultimately the charges a prosecutor files against an individual are more likely to determine the eventual sentence than anything a judge might do.

Furthermore, with the advent of mandatory minimums, more pressure lands on defendants to accept plea bargains. Risking a trial where a guilty verdict will almost certainly trigger the mandatory minimum influences defendants to accept a plea bargain, which means pleading to a lesser charge that does not include a mandatory minimum. In some cases, even people who are totally innocent of a charge may plead guilty because of the excessive risk of incurring a mandatory minimum if they are found guilty in a trial.

Most jurisdictions have complemented harsh sentences with fines often labeled as "restitution" or "victims' compensation" and court fees. These charges often go into thousands of dollars. Frequently the accumulation of fines and fees means a person released from prison faces a mountain of debt in addition to the other challenges of reentry. Researcher Alexes Harris, who investigated criminal justice debt for eight years in the state of Washington, argues that such fines have enormous impact on people who have otherwise served their time. As she puts it, "Because so many who are arrested and convicted are poor, unemployed, homeless, or suffering mental and physical illness, legal debt is a life sentence."[45]

Response, Resistance, and Transformation

Despite the widespread implementation of harsh sentencing policies, there is little evidence they have helped reduce crime. A National Institute of Justice publication summarizing the outcomes of this punitive approach concluded that "increasing the severity of punishment does little to deter crime."[46] Former attorney general Eric Holder, noting that in some cases mandatory minimums had resulted in "unduly harsh" sentences, issued a memorandum in 2013

that encouraged federal prosecutors to consider ways to avoid trig-
gering mandatory minimums in drug cases not involving violence
or extensive sales and distribution.[47] Opposition to mandatory minimums has been voiced by a number of active judges. In 2015 Iowa
judge Mark W. Bennett remarked, "Lengthy mandatory minimum
sentences . . . destroy families and mightily fuel the cycle of poverty
and addiction. . . . I am now sentencing the grown children of people
I long ago sent to prison."[48]

In recent years many organizations and individuals have campaigned against harsh sentences or for policy changes that narrow the
net for incarceration. The most obvious strategy is simply to pressure
lawmakers to change legislation. Efforts in this direction have had
some success, including the 2009 reversal of most of the Rockefeller
drug laws in New York. By 2016 twenty-six states had moderated or
eliminated mandatory minimums.[49] Oklahoma and California had
also taken steps to reduce some offenses from felonies to misdemeanors, and Delaware had modified three strikes laws.[50]

These efforts have been complemented by modifications in drug
law policy, from legalization of marijuana in several states to measures in New York and New Jersey that reduce low-level drug cases
to citations with just a fine or participation in a drug program as
punishment. In New York City alone, low-level marijuana arrests
fell from more than fifty thousand in 2011 to just over seven thousand in 2014.[51] These changes in sentencing for drug offenses, brought
about by years of grassroots campaigning by the Drug Policy Alliance and other organizations, have played a big part in reducing the
prison population in both states by about 25 percent. Both states
have also experienced a drop in crime rates as prison populations
fell, although those with long sentences for violent offenses largely
remain incarcerated.

However, with the arrival of a law-and-order voice in the White
House, strategies of the recent past seem less likely to bear fruit. The
present context demands a different political strategy, one based on
grassroots activism. For this we might need to hearken back to the
movements of the 1960s and 1970s. This is not a call to recreate the
past but rather to recognize that dismantling a system requires a systemic response, an agenda of transformational change, particularly

when efforts at gradual reform may be stymied. We can learn from movements of the past that fought for change at the systemic level. This involves connecting the struggles faced by those affected by harsh sentencing and mass incarceration with other vulnerable members of the community. Furthermore, a systemic response in this era requires theoretical frameworks and organizational forms that inspire activists of today—a new justice narrative born out of contemporary struggles. This narrative includes notions of intersectionality, decolonization, centering the struggles of transgender folk, fighting against anti-Black racism, promoting single-payer health care, imagining a world without borders, protecting our water, and, of course, prison abolition. Such notions may seem distant from the narrow, policy-wonk world of modifying mandatory minimums or freeing the elderly from prison, but any fights for specific reform must be linked to a broader agenda of mobilization and movement building. In the medium term, this will do far more to dismantle the maze of sentencing legislation that has captured millions of people in the era of mass incarceration than relying on experts and legislators to tweak draft after draft of legislation. Ultimately what is required is a counter-political power with an agenda of transformative justice that will get people out of prison; feed, clothe, house, and empower them once they hit the streets; and support families and communities impacted by mass incarceration.

Rethinking Truth-in-Sentencing in Illinois

■ Joseph Dole

Since the 1970s Illinois has been steadily increasing the length of sentences imposed for violent offenses.[1] In 1978 Illinois passed Public Act 80-1099, which made all life sentences in Illinois "natural-life sentences," meaning life without the possibility of parole.[2] Prior to the act's implementation a person sentenced to "life" might be eligible for parole in as little as eleven years. The act provided that anyone qualifying as a "habitual criminal" could receive a natural-life sentence. Habitual criminals were defined as those who commit a third or subsequent forcible offense.[3] Importantly, the 1978 law also abolished the parole system in Illinois, making all sentences determinate instead of indeterminate. The Illinois Department of Corrections found that determinate sentencing added approximately 3.5 years to the average sentence for murder and 1.4 years to the average sentence for a Class X crime.[4]

In the 1980s truth-in-sentencing (TIS) laws became increasingly popular in a number of states. In a study on TIS for the US Department of Justice's Bureau of Justice Statistics, authors Paula Ditton and Doris Wilson report that the state of Washington was the first to enact a TIS, and others soon followed.[5] Ditton and Wilson describe how these laws came about: "Sentencing reform policies have paralleled the mood of the country on crime and punishment, shifting between requiring a fixed prison time prior to release or allowing discretionary release of offenders by judges, parole boards, or corrections officials. Over the last two decades, sentencing requirements and release policies have become more restrictive, primarily in response to widespread 'get tough on crime' attitudes in the Nation."[6] "TIS . . . [were] designed to reduce the apparent disparity between court-imposed sentences and the time offenders actually serve in prison."[7]

While many states were enacting TIS in an attempt to address the public's desire for increased punishment for people who committed violent offenses, others chose a different route to achieve the same objective—they enacted mandatory minimum sentences and increased the sentencing ranges for violent crimes. Illinois initially resisted enacting TIS and instead chose the latter approach. For example, in 1987 Illinois extended the sentencing range for first-degree murder from 20–40 years to 20–60 years, and "the extended term was lengthened from 80 to 100 years."[8]

By 1994 Illinois had still not enacted a TIS when the US Congress passed the Violent Crime Control and Law Enforcement Act (the "Crime Act"). According to a US Department of Justice fact sheet, the Crime Act was "the largest crime bill in the history of the country and [provided] for 100,000 new police officers, $9.7 billion in funding for prisons and $6.1 billion in funding for prevention programs."[9] Some of the most significant provisions were the grant programs to encourage the states to enact TIS. These monetary incentives influenced Illinois, which was in the midst of building "nine new correctional facilities between 1990 and 2000."[10] By August 1995, Illinois's TIS was enacted under Public Act 89-404.[11] This law requires that people convicted of murder must now serve 100 percent of their sentence, and those convicted of other violent crimes must now serve at least 85 percent rather than the average of 44 percent of time that they would have served had Illinois not enacted TIS.[12]

In addition to abolishing discretionary release (i.e., parole) and extending the sentencing ranges for numerous violent crimes, Illinois nearly doubled, or more than doubled, the amount of time individuals would actually spend in prison. However, many speculated that the length of time spent in prison and the associated costs would not double, because judges would take TIS into account before sentencing.

While states such as Mississippi successfully adjusted after implementing TIS, the Illinois Department of Corrections (IDOC) was skeptical that this would be the case in Illinois. Department heads had concerns about "the fiscal impact if the law resulted in inmates actually serving longer sentences." Researcher David Olson and his colleagues sought to find out if "TIS changed the sentence lengths and lengths of time to serve in prison for murderers and sex offenders, and if so, to what degree." What they found was that the IDOC was right to worry, because unlike in Mississippi, in Illinois "the length of court-imposed sentences changed very little as a result" of TIS, and subsequently the time to be served "increased dramatically."[13]

Although TIS was enacted in Illinois over a decade and a half ago, not a single comprehensive cost/benefit analysis has been undertaken to determine what monetary effect enactment has had on the state. Other states that have enacted TIS legislation adjusted for the increase in time by reducing the sentence range; that way a prisoner ended up serving a similar amount of time in prison and didn't cost the state additional money. In Illinois, on the other hand, judges actually increased average sentences imposed or kept handing out similar sentences. With the sentencing ranges having already been increased, Illinois taxpayers are now being hit twice as hard.

In 2011 I compiled a preliminary report using rudimentary calculations and the limited statistics available on the internet or from the IDOC.[14] I found that even if one considers the meager funds received from the federal government from 1996 to 2004, which totaled less than $125 million, the additional costs incurred by the state for sentences imposed under TIS for 2002 to 2004 alone would be over $750 million. My estimates were extremely conservative. They were reached using a roughly $25,000 per year per person cost-of-incarceration figure, which is nearly $10,000 too low. Also, that number failed to account for the increased expense required to care for prisoners when they become elderly and require expensive medical care. Writing in an article for the *Chicago Reader* titled "Guarding Grandpa," Jessica Pupovac reported that the IDOC "spends roughly $428 million a year—about a third of its annual budget—keeping elderly inmates behind bars."[15] As Pupovac noted, "While keeping a younger inmate behind bars costs taxpayers about $17,000 a year, older inmates cost four times as much," or $68,000 per year. This is close to the $69,000 figure that the Centers for Disease Control arrived at as well.

According to the Vera Institute of Justice, the IDOC does

not calculate the full cost to taxpayers when reporting the average costs of incarceration.[16] They neglect to account for pension contributions, employee benefits, health-care contributions for both employees and retirees, capital costs, and statewide administrative costs. When one takes all of these costs into account as Vera did, it shows that Illinois spends an average of $38,268 annually per inmate to incarcerate one person.

Prior to TIS passage in Illinois, if a person received a fifty-year sentence for murder at age eighteen, he or she would have had to serve, on average, 44 percent of that sentence, or twenty-two years, due to the numerous types of "good time" awarded then. Thus, they would have been released at age forty, and it would have cost the state $841,896 to carry out that sentence.

After passage of TIS, that same sentence means the person must now serve the entire fifty years and won't be released until they are sixty-eight. Therefore, the first thirty-two years will cost the state $1,224,576, and the final eighteen years, when he or she is elderly,[17] will cost the state an additional $1,242,000. Before TIS a fifty-year murder sentence cost taxpayers $841,896, but after TIS it cost taxpayers $2,466,576—and this is in addition to the million dollars or so they may have already spent on a trial and appeals. Thus, TIS nearly tripled the cost to taxpayers, adding $1,624,680 to the tab for just one sentence. Each year, more than three hundred people in Illinois are sentenced for murder. Thousands more are sentenced for other violent crimes.

TIS sentences add up to the state's incurring well over a quarter of a billion dollars per year in added liabilities. How many more teachers, police officers, and firefighters can be employed for a quarter of a billion dollars per year? How many more of them will need to be laid off in order to continue paying for TIS? Every year that TIS remains law without action to adjust, reform, or repeal it we add another quarter billion dollars to the state's credit card that we'll all be paying for years to come.

Isn't it time we had a discussion about what constitutes a reasonable amount of money to spend to punish (i.e., incarcerate) someone? Isn't it also about time we consider more efficient ways to spend that money to reduce crime? Studies have shown that people who have served twenty-five years in prison and are fifty or older have less than a 1 percent recidivism rate. They also consistently show that "murderers," the so-called most violent criminals, have the lowest recidivism rate of any category of people. Keeping elderly people incarcerated well past the point where they cease to pose a threat to society may sate our appetite for revenge, but it does nothing to keep society safe. In 2005 the Pew Center on the States reported, "Statistics have long shown crime is an occupation of the young, so imprisoning offenders beyond the age at which they would have likely given up their criminal ways brings little benefit—but big expenses. . . . The graying of the nation's prisons suggests that policy makers have not paid much heed to this well-established criminological fact."[18] In fact, long-term sentencing policies like TIS actually produce an opposite effect: they take away funds that could have been used to employ police officers and teachers, fix dangerous bridges and roads, and rehabilitate the 90 percent of prisoners who will return to the streets. It's time to use some "common cents" in our criminal justice policies.

A Kinder, Gentler System?
A Look across the Border at Long-Term Sentences in Canada

■ Meenakshi Mannoe

While Canada is perhaps perceived by many outside and inside of our borders as a nation "soft on crime," with a penal system that upholds human rights and dignity, the history and current practices of indeterminate and long-term sentencing in Canada illustrate otherwise. Dangerously, this misconception of the "softness" of our prison system (particularly when juxtaposed with the United States) often justifies ongoing rallying for an expansion of the Canadian prison-industrial complex. Many antiviolence organizations, victims' rights groups, politicians, and hashtags demand punitive justice in the form of tougher laws and longer sentences and therefore obscure transformative measures that could take place in communities to reduce harm and build other forms of safety and security.

Two noteworthy sentencing provisions have produced long-term and indeterminate sentences in Canada. The first is the "dangerous offender" legislation, which dates back to 1947. The second is the "long-term supervision order" sentencing option, which dates back to 1997. To understand the impact of these provisions, it's worthwhile to name the various actors that shape and implement prison policy in Canada. First, judges (in either a provincial court or the Supreme Court of Canada) determine the sentence meted out once someone is found guilty. Typically, less serious crimes are dealt with in provincial court, and more serious crimes are dealt with in Supreme Court. Following sentencing, provincial and territorial governments oversee people serving any sentence of two years or less, while the federal government oversees people serving any sentence of over two years.

Correctional Service of Canada, also known as "CSC" or "Corrections Canada," which oversees all longer sentences, operates federal prisons across the country, including maximum-, medium-, and minimum-security penitentiaries. CSC also funds halfway houses operated by nonprofits. Importantly, CSC does not determine whether or not prisoners get parole—this is done by an "independent administrative tribunal" known as the Parole Board of Canada.[1] Finally, the Office of the Correctional Investigator operates as an ombudsman for anyone held in a federal institution and is responsible for investigating and resolving individual complaints as well as bringing attention to more systemic policy issues.[2]

During the recent era when the Conservative Party of Canada headed by Prime Minister Stephen Harper was in power (2006–2015), the party worked to lead the country (some say astray) with the familiar "tough on crime" refrain. The sentencing landscape in Canada was significantly altered. Among the most consequential legislation was the 2012 Safe Streets and Communities Act, which created mandatory minimum sentences for nonviolent drug offenses, and the 2009 Truth in Sentencing Act, which denied prisoners "enhanced credit" for time spent on remand if they were denied bail.[3] The Truth in Sentencing Act was intended to minimize and even deny prisoners any credit for time served if they were denied bail, despite a long-standing practice of "2 for 1 time," which meant that every day spent on remand was worth two days if someone was found guilty.[4] Eliminating pretrial credit would have disproportionately impacted prisoners and exacerbated systemic inequality, and in *R v. Summers*, Justice Andromache Karakatsanis noted that remand centers are often rife with problems, and "conditions in remand centres tend to be particularly harsh; they are often overcrowded and dangerous, and do not provide rehabilitative programs."[5] Consider that Indigenous people in Canada are more likely to be denied bail and are overrepresented in prisons, including remand facilities, where they constitute more than 20 percent of the institutional population.[6] Ultimately, the Supreme Court of Canada struck down the mandatory minimums and reinstated enhanced credit for time on remand in 2016.[7]

Dangerous offenders and long-term offenders are referenced in the Criminal Code of Canada (CCC) in part 24. Sentencing options available to judges following a guilty finding typically involve a forensic psychiatric evaluation. A long-term supervision order (LTSO) may result in up to ten years of community supervision following the completion of a sentence (CCC, sec. 753.1[3][b]), and breaching the LTSO can result in imprisonment. Individuals serving an LTSO have essentially served their prison sentence but remain under the supervision of CSC, because there is "substantial risk the offender will reoffend" (CCC, sec. 753.1[2]). Similarly, the dangerous offender (DO) designation is applied when a judge is satisfied that an individual convicted of a serious personal offense (1) constitutes a broad threat to the life, safety, or well-being of people, following an assessment that outlines a basis of persistent aggressive behavior, and the level of brutality demonstrates that the offender is unlikely to be inhibited by "normal standards of behavioural restraint" (CCC, sec. 753[1][a][i–iii]), or, (2) "has shown a failure to control his or her sexual impulses and a likelihood of causing injury, pain or other evil to other persons through failure in the future to control his or her sexual impulses" (CCC, sec. 753[1][b]). The DO designation leads to an indeterminate sentence, meaning there is no statutory parole date, although the parole board does review parole applications of individuals held indeterminately (CCC, sec. 761[1]). The imposition of an indeterminate sentence represents the most extreme type of sentence in Canadian criminal law, meant for "the worst of the worst."

The Supreme Court has grappled with the DO designation in the context of the Charter of Rights and Freedoms, which is part of the Canadian Constitution. The decision in *R v. Lyons* (1987) recognized that indeterminate sentences primarily function to segregate a residual class of habitual criminals from mainstream society and that this preventive detention may unfairly deprive individuals of their liberty. Yet, ultimately, the DO legislation was upheld but was only meant to apply to a limited group.[8]

This interplay of judicial sentencing, prison administration, government operations, and ombudsman oversight might lead one to assume that Canada has a well-organized correctional system, where punishment is fair and met with administrative safeguards. But the conditions of individuals serving indeterminate, life, or long-term sentences illustrates that this is not the case. During their sentenced lives, this population is subject to the whim of politicians who promote policies and regulations that cater to fearmongering and harsh punishment, with little evidence that these broad policies deliver the results promised. The most recent data show that there were 681 people serving sentences and labeled dangerous offenders in 2016 and 705 active long-term supervision cases in 2012.[9] Again, Indigenous people continue to be overrepresented in these sentencing categories—23 percent of dangerous offenders and 17 percent of people serving LTSOs are Aboriginal—reflecting how persistent systemic racism is in the Canadian carceral state (approximately 4.3 percent of the total Canadian population identifies as Aboriginal).[10]

In 2008 the Tackling Violent Crime Act amended the CCC to mandate that judges make a dangerous offender finding when the legislative criteria were satisfied, whereas they previously had retained judicial discretion. The Conservative government again advertised this legislation as "providing for more effective sentencing and monitoring of dangerous and high-risk offenders."[11] In reality, however, "more effective sentencing" leads to indiscriminate application of indeterminate sentences, capturing people who have a history of violent offenses but are more marked by living on the margins of society, surviving untreated mental health issues, negotiating significant substance use, and being involved in street-based economies. The original dangerous offender provisions date back to the early 1900s, referencing "hardened criminals for whom 'iron bars' and 'prison walls' have no terrors, and in whom no hope or desire for reformation, if it ever existed, remains."[12] Victorian-era sentencing cannot capture the complexities of life in a settler-colonial society such as Canada, which rests on violence at its core. Consider people like Renée Acoby, an Ojibwa woman from Manitoba, currently the only female DO in the county. Acoby has been held in prison since 2000, and she has never taken a life or committed a crime of a sexual nature but was involved in several hostage-taking incidents while incarcerated.[13] Or consider the recent DO designation of Donald Joseph Boutilier, a man described as a "drug addict who was abused as a child [. . . and who] had a long criminal record for offenses including assault and kidnapping."[14] Boutilier, whose most recent convictions stem from an armed robbery of a drugstore and subsequent car chase in 2010, was designated a DO in 2016, and the designation was upheld by the Supreme Court of Canada in 2017.[15] The indeterminately criminalized lives of Acoby and Boutilier reflect the reach of long-term sentencing in Canada. People who may be better categorized as "violent recidivists" (likely receiving inadequate supports along the social services continuum) have now been caught in a scheme that was sold to Canadians as protection from the "worst of the worst"—serial predators or sadistic killers. The current application of the dangerous offender designation is becoming analogous to the "three strikes" laws that contribute to mass incarceration in the United States.

Lengthy sentences and the net they cast continue to morph in alignment with political, social, and economic machinations. As a prison abolitionist living on unceded Indigenous territory in the nation called Canada, I believe it is crucial to closely examine how our carceral state uses long-term sentences to cage increasing numbers of people. Those living on the fringes of this state—whether due to their indigeneity, in the case of First Nations, Metis, or Inuit peoples; or their lack of immigration status, in the case of immigration detainees; or their health needs, in the case of people living with addictions or mental health issues—are swept up by broad legislation. Politicians tell us it is for our protection, our safety, the safety of our children and communities, but in actuality these designations and laws are meant to disappear undesirables from our daily lives. In the specific case of dangerous offenders, what was originally conceived to protect people from significant violence and harm has been turned on many people whose survival relies on struggle.

Thank you to my colleague Anthony Robinson for his guidance and mentorship in writing this article.

Football Numbers

■ Phil Hartsfield

Shootings in Chicago have risen to numbers not seen since the 1990s, with more than three thousand shootings and seven hundred murders last year. Police Commissioner Eddie Johnson has stated over and over in the media that we need tougher gun laws to "solve" the problem.

Aaahh, yes, stiffer penalties for guns—this will solve everything! Sentence everyone who is caught with a gun or commits a crime with one to extraordinarily long prison terms like the higher numbers on the backs of football jerseys. Stiffer sentences will supposedly deter crime, because "criminals" will fear the consequences. So, let's see, the gangbangers won't shoot at each other, because they're afraid of the consequences. And those who do commit crimes will go to jail forever, so they won't be able to ever do it again. The logic of this argument is that stiffer penalties will make us safer. But nothing could be more wrong.

Let's ponder here: What is the correlation between longer prison sentences and lowering crime rates? In the 1980s there was a prison population boom and yet crime rates went up. Then in the early 1990s crime rates dropped while the prison population grew again. The Sentencing Project points out that "the number of people sentenced to prison for property and violent crimes has also increased even during periods when crime rates have declined."[1] So how have stiffer penalties made a difference? Should we be asking if longer prison sentences actually contribute to the rising crime rate?

In Illinois, judges have been handing out football numbers by way of statutes that enhance prison sentences for gun possession. The term "football numbers" was coined by the incarcerated community to signify how extraordinarily long their sentences were: 35, 48, 59, or 75 years.

Someone might ask, "How much time did he get for that case?" "Man, they gave him football numbers."

These sentences are sometimes for crimes in which no one was injured, such as robbery with a gun or attempted murder. Mind you, I am in no way condoning these crimes.

Illinois gun laws state that if you commit a crime while armed with a gun, an extra fifteen to twenty-five years will be added to your sentence. That's not suggestive; that's a mandatory minimum sentence added on to whatever sentence you get for the crime. It's for simply having a gun—and it doesn't have to be used; it could be in your back pocket. These laws have been in effect for almost twenty years without having any major impact on the crime rate. If anything, the rate's gone up.

If you commit a robbery with a gun, the sentence is a minimum of twenty-one years—fifteen years for possessing a firearm and six for the actual crime of robbery. If convicted, you would get more time for having the gun than committing the crime itself. However, in my experience, individuals rarely receive the minimum and are more likely to receive a sentence of over thirty years.

In such cases as crimes like murder, there is a mandatory minimum of forty-five years—twenty-five for the gun enhancement and a minimum of twenty for the actual crime of murder (a class-M felony carries a sentence of twenty to sixty years). Once again, there is potential for more time for the gun than for the actual crime itself. The logic of gun enhancements means that if a person used another method to take someone's life, they would receive less time for the same crime.

There are instances in which an individual can receive two enhanced sentences for the same gun. An aggravated battery and robbery with a gun could result in fifteen years added for the battery and another fifteen for the robbery with a gun. That's thirty years before you get sentenced for the actual crime. Two enhancements for the same gun, and more time for the gun than for the actual crime. Football numbers!

Two Terms
The Effects of Long-Term Sentencing

■ Benny "Don Juan" Rios

On April 29, 2002, I was found guilty of first-degree murder and aggravated discharge of a firearm. I caught my case in May 1999, just a few years after the Illinois Truth in Sentencing law came into effect, which meant I fell under the new and revised law that would send me to prison for the rest of my life.[1] I was sentenced to forty-five years at 100 percent. That means no possibility of parole, no time cuts for good behavior, and no incentives whatsoever. My punishment and the punishment of so many others is to be warehoused for the rest of our lives until our out date, if we don't die first. Who can serve forty or fifty years in prison and still make it home alive and well? The answer is hardly anyone. By the time those of us serving long-term sentences are ready to come home, we will be old and in bad health, leaving society to deal with ailing senior citizens who have no family to care for them.

I was born and raised in the Pilsen community of Chicago, where it was very rough and dangerous growing up. I did not have a father in my life. Instead my male role models were my older brothers, my older cousins, and, of course, the gang members. I was raised by my mother and grandmother, as well as my aunt. By the time I was nine years old, I had already lost two of my brothers, one to prison and the other, at age seventeen, to a gang murder.

As a small child, I was already labeled a target because of who my family was and where I lived. I soaked up everything about my environment: the gang culture, who our enemies were, how to spot an enemy coming to attack, how to dodge bullets when shot at, and how to defend myself. At the ages of four and five, I learned the importance of family and brotherhood, love, honor, loyalty, respect, and protecting our neighborhood with our lives. By the time I was twelve, I had already been shot and was a hard-core gang member. Instilled in my heart and my brain was the belief that the gang and my family were my everything. I felt destined to end up either dead or locked up by the time I was eighteen. I can honestly say I had no choice in transforming into what I became.

Several months after I got shot, I became a ward of the state and lived in several boys' homes until my cousins took me in. They were ex–gang members and pastors of their local church. I lived with them for two years in Cicero, Illinois, with their five sons, who were a good and positive influence on me. They treated me like their own son, but in my mind I was already an adult and I was still so connected to gang life. When I was fourteen years old, I met a girl who was six years older than me and I eventually ran away with her. The relationship lasted a year and a half before we broke up and I went to look for my mom, who suffered from schizophrenia, manic depression, and bipolar disorder. I was sixteen years old when I found that she was living in a park, so I rented an apartment in Pilsen and moved her in with me. We lived together until I got locked up.

I remember when I turned twenty-one, being so happy and proud because I had made it without going to prison or getting killed—having run-ins with other gangs made me a constant target. A few months after my twenty-first birthday, I was charged with first-degree murder.

My brother got locked up when I was only six years old; he got out when I was twenty-one. We were able to spend about a year and a half together as adult, free men until I was convicted. I took care of my mom until my brother finally got of prison. He was sentenced before the passage of Truth in Sentencing and served half of a thirty-four-year sentence. I was sentenced after the passage of the law, meaning I had to serve all of my forty-five-year sentence. While I was home with my brother, I was able to show him how to take care of our mother. She had become diabetic, and I had to teach my him how to keep my mom on a healthy diet, how to keep

up with her medications and doctor's appointments, where to find
her prescriptions for the lowest price, and how to keep her away
from alcohol, as she'd also battled with alcoholism in the past. I also
taught my brother to manage my mother's finances. She functions
well, but not when she's alone or off her medications. I also helped
my brother adjust to all the changes that had taken place while he
was gone. He left in 1984, and by 2000 there were a lot of techno-
logical advances, one of them being cell phones. One day he took
the cordless phone with him to run errands. He told me he'd taken
the phone with him in case I called. I laughed and had to explain
the differences between a cordless and a cell phone. My brother has
been out of prison for sixteen years and he has never returned. He is
still taking care of my mom and living in Texas.

I've been locked up for fifteen years and I'm thirty-eight years
old now. I'm no longer the little kid who believes that gang life is everything. Instead, I am an adult who has come to the realization that
the gang life destroyed the lives of numerous families. The things I
participated in as a child and adolescent are behind me. Through the
support of family, friends, volunteers in prison, faith, and my fellow
prisoners here, I've been encouraged to stay on a path that's good.
Even my enemies have played a role in reconditioning my mind and
heart. In prison I've developed close relationships with people who
were once considered enemies when I was out of prison instead of
having hate for them. Things look bleak for me because, as of yet,
there's no guarantee that I'll ever make it home. But I still have hope.
One thing I do know for sure is that I'm not a threat to society, and
if given a second chance, I know that I'll be a positive influence in
the community.

Long-term imprisonment takes a toll on one's mind, body, and
spirit, and one's familial relationships. We are held in an inhumane
environment, locked in a small cell with another human being most
of the day, and fed unhealthy food and contaminated drinking water,[2] with little hope for ever coming home. The justice system does
not offer any possibility of reconciliation with our families or with
victims and their families, which could lead to forgiveness, closure,
or healing. Our families are discouraged from visiting, writing letters, and accepting phone calls because of difficulties imposed by the

institution. Letters get held up in the prison mail system and delay communication. Phone calls have to be approved by the institution. And when families visit, they have to deal with unruly guards, being turned away from reconnection because of a small tear on their jeans or some other made-up rule.[3] Once in the visiting room, the costs of the snacks from the vending machines are ridiculous. A sandwich from the Stateville vending machine costs more than double that of the same item at the nearby gas station.[4] These things heavily burden our loved ones, making it hard to continue relationships. Incarceration takes a toll on their lives, too. Fortunately, I still have a small circle of family and friends who still love and support me, but that's not the case for many people who are incarcerated. However, it's one's mental state that is most vulnerable and dangerous. The idleness of being warehoused can lead to depression, mental illness, hopelessness, misery, and so many other negative things. When a person is in this state, it can cause them not to care anymore, which can lead them to hurt themselves or someone else or to get hurt by someone else. This place is designed to drain you of all hope.

In recent years there have been new programs in this particular prison that are positive, and we desperately need more. They offer hope and give us a sense of humanity once again. But programs alone won't suffice. We also need the possibility of coming home. Currently there is absolutely no option for early release for people categorized as long-term offenders. Reforms only focus on people with nonviolent offenses and disregard those of us with violent offenses and longer sentences. Studies show that people who are older and have served longer terms have a low chance of returning to prison; my brother is a perfect example. Truth-in-sentencing laws need to be repealed, and restorative justice practices should be widely implemented to heal families and communities.

In October 2016, when Illinois governor Bruce Rauner closed down F House, a unit here at Stateville prison, he said, "The people of Illinois believe in redemption; we believe in second chances. All of us at one point or another need a second chance to turn a wrong into a right. We should not be needlessly tearing families apart."[5] I believe he is sincere in these sentiments, and I hope and pray that other lawmakers feel the same way. It's time for change. The "lock 'em up and throw away the key" approach does not work. It causes prison overcrowding, broken families, ailing elderly people in prisons, and billions of dollars wasted on something that doesn't work. It is time to invest in redemption, rehabilitation, reconciliation, transformation, forgiveness, and second chances.

Coming Out of the Digital Closet

■ David Booth

C oming out as registered for a sex crime is a lifelong process, usually grounded in concerns for safety and survival.

Early morning light illuminated the rise and fall of his chest as I lay next to him, gathering the courage to be vulnerable. We'd only been dating a few months, but my family already welcomed him and I'd adopted his friends. It only got more serious after I word-vomited an *I love you*. Keeping my secret threatened not only my relationship but also the terms of my probation. How could I disclose my registered status for a sex crime without risking my relationship?

An inescapable feeling of panic crept over me as seconds ticked by. All of my imagined scenarios abruptly concluded as they did in reality—a slammed door and footsteps retreating, with me left a little more broken. The panic settled as he awoke and scooped me into a hug.

I'd already been rejected from innumerable employment opportunities, evicted from home after home, and watched my support network crumble because of my registered status. Worry crouched deeper. Would disclosing cause me to lose the one good thing to have happened since my release from incarceration?

His lips brushed mine as he drowsily clambered out of bed. I lay there long after he left, wondering if this was goodbye, and prepared for the worst when he returned home. *Captain America, my love*, I began, *you're stirring up things that have long lain dormant, and it's terrifying. Experience has taught me that all good things will end. I've been plagued with lies, broken promises, and heartache from the start of good things. The scars left behind etch indelible marks on my heart. Yet, for all their disfigurement, you find each more beautiful than the last. I'm*

119

terrified this next revelation will be my thickest scar tissue yet.

My fingernails drew pinpricks of blood from my palm as he read my letter. I studied him, searching for clues. His hazel eyes darted across the pages, but they didn't widen in surprise nor did his brows furrow in perplexity. His jaw didn't clench in anger, nor did his shoulders signal resignation. Whatever he was thinking or feeling in those moments was hidden from me—and making me anxious. I leaned back on the bed and closed my eyes, and struggled to control the panic.

One. Two. Three. Trace the embroidered stitching on the comforter.

One. Two. Three. Feel the plushness of the carpet under my feet.

One. Two. Three. Listen to the creak of stairs as roommates move about.

One. Two. Three. Over and over I counted, until I heard him sigh and set down the letter. I couldn't bring myself to open my eyes. I felt his lips brush mine and I leaned away, shocked. His arms embraced me and pulled me close.

"I love you. This," he said, gesturing to the letter, "isn't who I've grown to love. There is so much more to you than being registered."

My panic evaporated.

Disclosure is always challenging, because registrants are often imagined as Frankenstein's monster, a miscellany of advertised fears. It's not even revealing oneself as registered that's challenging—it's the potential for the ensuing judgment, questions, invasiveness, and lost relationships. Your identity, your narrative, no longer belongs just to you. You're an entry in a table of contents, erased by the broader narrative of the registry.

The registry isn't a nuanced portrayal of what it means to be registered, but merely a list of people at a specific point in time. The focus is on a registrable act with no space for repairing harm and restoring lives. While challenging sexual violence is critical, research suggests that registration doesn't reduce sexual violence. Instead, it's an indefatigable mechanism for state-sponsored violence. For revealing our convictions, we are harassed and even killed. We're also systematically denied access to housing, jobs, and social support. Our families feel shame, discrimination, and stigma, and our children are bullied, alienated, and experience higher suicide rates.

Our past actions are used to justify extreme forms of lifetime punishment in the name of *community safety*. What's at stake isn't whether to protect against sexual abuse but how to do so effectively and meaningfully. We must support and, if possible, heal people harmed by violence and create avenues for accountability and change for those who have harmed others. Research indicates that current practices are failing at prevention, but perhaps my former love has a solution: to humanize registrants. After all, we're more than the worst act we've ever committed.

Concentrating Punishment
Long-Term Consequences for Disadvantaged Places

■ Daniel Cooper and Ryan Lugalia-Hollon

The incarceration rate for parts of Chicago's predominantly Black West Side is dozens of times higher than Chicago's highest-incarceration white community. In West Garfield Park, for example, the incarceration rate is "forty-two times higher than the highest-ranked white community on incarceration (4,226 vs. 103 per 100,000)." Robert Sampson, the sociologist behind these findings, declares, "This is a staggering differential even for community-level comparisons," one suggesting that entirely different social realities exist within the same city, created by policies and systems that are poles apart.[1]

In the West Side's 60644 zip code, the Austin community, between 2005 and 2009 there were 6,700 residents who were convicted and sentenced to prison. In neighboring Oak Park, a predominantly white suburb just across Chicago's city line, just 311 residents were sentenced to prison during the same time.[2] These differentials point to profound gaps in how residents of many low-income African American areas experience relationships, family, and a general life trajectory. All prison sentences handed out to West Side residents, regardless of the actual length of time served, have long-term effects. They have lasting consequences for neighborhoods that unfold across generations. Every prison sentence marks a forced migration trail, spanning living rooms, courtrooms, and prison cells, where punitive policies actively remake city blocks, disrupting households and shifting the ways many neighborhood residents experience time.

As these numbers show, mass incarceration feeds on the punishment of people in places like the West Side. In fact, Sampson and his colleague Charles Loeffler have said the very term "mass incarceration" is a misnomer.[3] According to them, the United States' unparalleled rates of imprisonment are really the result of "concentrated incarceration," meaning that a relatively small pool of neighborhoods accounts for the great majority of those imprisoned. In these predominantly Black areas, poverty is high, few can afford private lawyers in the courts, and risky strategies for making ends meet are abundant. Residents of these areas are more likely to be arrested, tried, and convicted of felony charges. Given legislative shifts that started in the 1980s, once convicted these residents are more likely to be sent to prison and to stay there for years on end. Furthermore, once a prisoner is released, no matter where they might have lived before, they are more likely to return to a neighborhood like those on the West Side, thereby fueling a "revolving door" effect that further strains limited community resources.[4]

We use the term "concentrated punishment" to describe how the effects of mass incarceration are experienced in places like Austin, where prison sentences are felt not only by the person behind bars but also by their neighbors, loved ones, and communities at large. However, the term "mass incarceration" is still helpful in describing a national criminal justice infrastructure that locks up nearly 25 percent of the world's prisoners.[5] We use "mass incarceration" when referring to the laws, prison buildings, criminal justice professionals, and varied private interests that compose this infrastructure. They are what gives incarceration its mass. And when describing how some places bear the brunt of this mass, we use the term "concentrated punishment."

Not only is incarceration itself geographically concentrated, but so are its ripple effects. For example, concentrated incarceration is associated with depression and anxiety among *all* neighborhood residents, regardless of their individual history with the criminal justice system.[6] One of the key drivers of these effects is widespread parental absence due to incarceration, which has profound consequences for youth and families. In Austin, during 2005–2009, 5,983 men and 1,123 women were sentenced to prison.[7] Their absence disrupted family dynamics. The proliferation of Black households led by single mothers follows the growth of the prison rate very closely. During the initial phase of the prison boom, from 1980 to 1990, the number of single female–headed Black households grew by 19 percent.[8] As a result, children often missed out on having the stable influence of more than one active parent.

Moreover, parents who experience incarceration are less likely to obtain a college degree, will accumulate less in lifetime earnings, and are less likely to ever own a home. This is important because home-ownership stabilizes neighborhoods, lowers crime rates, and is a source of wealth that can be passed on to the next generation.[9] Such benefits are less likely to be transferred to children of the incarcerated. Instead, vulnerable children are made even more vulnerable. At the same time, those returning to the community after completing a prison sentence face employment and other barriers that result in roughly half ending up back in prison for a parole violation or a new sentence.[10] Because of this, all prison sentences should be thought of as long term in that the effects last much longer than the actual time spent behind bars. They often result in extended contact with the justice system, and the lasting consequences of each and every one of them continue unfolding across generations.

Globally, there is little precedent for the United States' incredible reliance on prisons. At any given time, Chicago's 60644 area has more people behind bars than several small countries combined. Incarceration rates on Chicago's West Side are ten times that of Russia (442 per 100,000), which is among the other top jailers on earth. Meanwhile, the incarceration rates of even the most impacted white areas are nothing extraordinary. The rate of Chicago's most affected white neighborhood is roughly the same as all of South Korea's (104 per 100,000), which is very close to the global average (100 per 100,000). These numbers make clear that some areas endure concentrated punishment while many others are largely immune.[11]

If you live in one of the most affected areas, it would be commonplace to know many people with felony convictions or to have a record yourself. One of the residents we interviewed for a research project about the impact of incarceration on West Side Chicago neighborhoods told us, "Out of the people that I know from [the]

Austin [community], about 60 to 70 percent of people have felony convictions. I know hundreds of people. Out of 300 people, probably about 180 would have felony convictions." Tragically, this resident's estimate is well aligned with West Side averages for African American males in his age group.[12] Males make up 86 percent of all convictions in Austin, although in recent years women have become one of the fastest-growing jail and prison populations.[13] These convictions have profound implications in the larger world, often determining who can get job interviews, access educational loans, or secure subsidized housing.

Thus, the effects of concentrated punishment take many forms, with many interwoven consequences. While Black men are more likely to be removed from the home and incarcerated, Black women are more likely to bear the brunt of the added responsibilities, challenges, and vulnerabilities. Matthew Desmond, in his book *Evicted*, writes, "If incarceration had come to define the lives of men from impoverished black neighborhoods, eviction was shaping the lives of women. Poor black men were locked up. Poor black women were locked out."[14] He reports that in Milwaukee, similarly divided and segregated like Chicago, one in five Black women renters are evicted, triple the rate of white women. In segregated Black neighborhoods, women are twice as likely as men to face eviction. One of the consequences of single female–headed households is a heightened vulnerability to housing instability, just one of the additional strains that incarceration places upon families.

Though mass incarceration affects cities across the country, it is especially bad in Midwestern states like Illinois and Wisconsin, where more than one-third of Black men will serve time in state prisons, and where Black men have a higher cumulative risk of imprisonment than in any other region.[15]

In theory, high incarceration rates in areas like 60644 can simply be explained away by levels of crime. But no such simple correlation exists. Crime is not a pure predictor for levels of imprisonment. "Punishment's Place: The Local Concentration of Mass Incarceration," Sampson and Loeffler's pioneering 2010 study of how incarceration concentrates in certain urban areas, details how neighborhoods with high levels of both crime and other markers of disadvantage—such

as low education levels and sparse capital investments—have much
higher incarceration rates than high-crime areas with few markers
of disadvantage.[16] In the words of these scholars, "communities that
experienced high disadvantage experienced incarceration rates more
than three times higher than communities with a similar crime rate."
As their work implies, you cannot understand incarceration without
also looking at social forces beyond crime.[17] During Lyndon Johnson's "war on poverty," the prevailing policy assumption was that
poverty and disadvantage caused crime. Poverty was seen as the root
cause to address in order to produce better public safety outcomes.
In the 1970s this idea was turned on its head with the "war on crime"
and later the "war on drugs," both of which assumed the opposite—
that poverty was caused by crime and disorder. This shift ushered
in concentrated punishment in urban areas of color, along with the
steady rollback of services and welfare aimed at addressing poverty.[18]

How Concentrated Punishment
Shapes Neighborhoods

The parents missing from places like Austin are also absent from
participating in the civic life of their community. While involvement in neighborhood life may seem to be a leisure activity at first
blush, the bonds that form between neighbors who know and look
out for one another have been shown to actually regulate crime and
disorder. Across Chicago, neighborhoods that have strong norms of
trust and cohesion between residents have less violent crime.[19] These
norms might not be as strong in Austin as in other neighborhoods,
because parents are constantly being removed or cycling back into
the community after being released from prison. This has major de-
stabilizing effects. Criminologist Todd R. Clear has demonstrated
these effects through decades of research that points to incarceration
as a primary driver of disorder and crime.[20]

Neighbors only get to know one another when there are opportunities for interaction and expectations of permanence. But concentrated incarceration disrupts social networks and bonds among
neighbors. A resident may not feel any motivation to form a strong
connection with others if they believe either of them will be there

only temporarily. These connections, between people and also be-tween individuals and institutions in a neighborhood, build social capital. This kind of capital affords residents access to resources that might otherwise be out of reach, giving them a psychological and social bond that allows for greater opportunity and stability.[21]

Meanwhile, concentrated punishment keeps urban Black neighborhoods segregated and disadvantaged, thereby making the uphill battle for success even steeper. Racist institutional practices such as redlining—where the federal government drew red lines around whole, largely black neighborhoods and refused to issue home loans—gave way to private sector predatory lending, which during the Great Recession resulted in Black neighborhoods dis-proportionately experiencing high rates of foreclosure.[22] Many market forces have already created disorder and instability in urban Black neighborhoods. As mentioned previously, women are even more vulnerable to negative housing trends. Concentrated incar-ceration is only adding more neighborhood disorder, creating a cumulative punishment effect that extends well beyond the justice system. This amounts to a one-two punch of neighborhood insta-bility, with multiple forms of forced community removal that are ultimately responsible for more crime and disorder.[23]

Many Black neighborhoods are trapped in a downward spiral of absent parents, stressed and traumatized youth, and highly mobile, unstable households that decrease opportunities for strong bonds be-tween residents. More crime and disorder results, which further alien-ates residents from their neighborhood—violent crime leads residents to pull back from participating in civic neighborhood life out of fear.[24] These are the ripple effects of concentrated punishment. Youth, fam-ilies, households, and whole neighborhoods are trapped in this spiral of disadvantage, which is passed on to the next generations. Trauma, broken households, a lack of social capital, and violence only widen the inequalities in educational attainment, employment, wealth accumu-lation, and other outcomes. This is precisely why our cities are divided into two different places: one of thriving white or ethnically mixed neighborhoods and one of disadvantaged neighborhoods of color.

But instead of investing in solutions to these complex prob-lems, we continue to employ a one-dimensional approach—trying in vain to police and incarcerate our way to public safety. In doing so we've only made neighborhoods worse. This has been demonstrated through careful research across numerous cities. In neighborhoods where prison cycling is high—including a steady rotation of parental absence and return—the crime rate is actually often higher as a result.[25] Conversely, if fewer people had been forcibly removed from places like Chicago's West Side, we might see more families who live in one place for a longer period of time and who spend more time in the workforce, allowing them to save money for things like homeownership and enabling the expanded sense of investment that comes with it.[26] In turn, greater trust and interaction among residents who aren't forcibly removed may lead to greater opportunities for young people. This is what a virtuous cycle looks like, as opposed to the current vicious cycle in place.

Seeing Prison Sentences as a War on Black Neighborhoods

Between the years of 2005 and 2009, there were roughly 322,000 people sentenced to the Illinois Department of Corrections from Cook County. It is an astonishing number but only a fraction of the total number of forced removals that have occurred since the late 1970s. The boom in mass incarceration began more than twenty-five years earlier, meaning hundreds of thousands more were sent to prison before and after that time period. And that is just in one county.[27] Meanwhile, other forms of community investment have struggled to see the light of day. Though community leaders of all stripes have never stopped doing the vital labor of neighborhood building—from creating opportunities for youth to providing healing resources for those who need them—even their most successful efforts have struggled to receive the funds needed to be brought to scale. Instead, one conviction at a time, massive amounts of money have been poured into the punishment of African American residents from low-income neighborhoods.

This concentrated punishment is one of the most sophisticated operations of structural racism the world has ever seen. Policy makers have all but abandoned the effort to uproot poverty and disadvantage in urban areas. Instead, concentrated incarceration has been a perverse attempt to manage such conditions, which, in turn, has led to an extreme overreliance on the criminal justice system.[28] In so doing, concentrated punishment extends a long legacy of anti-Black policies and practices, one of the few true constants in US history.[29] And its true legacy is the long-term destruction of neighborhoods and the perpetuation of disadvantage.

But despite the evidence, the idea that punishment is concentrated and therefore inequitable is not a widely accepted truth. There is a pervasive and persistent myth that says people are equally likely to be arrested, prosecuted, and convicted for their actions no matter where they live, how they look, or what conditions they may be striving to overcome. Within this myth, incarceration is empowered by one of four basic rationales: retribution, incapacitation, deterrence, and rehabilitation, each of which is based on a different set of assumptions about how change will happen given a particular series of rules and enforcement mechanisms.[30]

Retribution is based on the idea that people who break society's laws inherently deserve to receive some measure of harm in return. *Incapacitation* says that those who break laws can and often should be removed from their social contexts for a designated period of time. *Deterrence* asserts that by damaging those who damage others and their property, we send an important social message that wrongdoing is not acceptable and triggers substantive consequences. Finally, the *rehabilitative approach* says that isolation from society can help people to improve themselves, creating space to change whatever characteristics led them to their acts of wrongdoing.[31]

Under each of these justifications, prisons are a way to govern disorderly people who cause significant harm to others. Separation from the rest of society is presented as a form of individual-level population management, where the law is enforced, interpreted, and applied on an individual basis as a way of assessing the degree of past harm and future risk. Based on due process and the weighing of evidence, the idea of individual-level application of the law is foundational to the American legal system. In the minds of many Americans, the behavior of police officers and judges is consistent across geography, punishing only people who are guilty beyond reasonable doubt. In reality, the definition of both guilt and doubt is

directly influenced by the geography in question and the poverty
and skin color of the people living in that geography.[32] What police
officers see as suspicious behavior depends largely on the areas they
are patrolling, just as the ways judges conceive of threat hinge greatly
on the lawyers presenting the case to them. For these reasons, actual
crime is only one predictor of the incarceration rates of an area, with
levels of poverty and structural disadvantage being a close second.[33]

Consequently, in high-incarceration neighborhoods, the law is
not just applied individually. It has become a vehicle for collective
punishment, used as a basic public policy response to the struggles of
marginalized African American communities, not only in Chicago
but also in Milwaukee, New York City, New Orleans, Baltimore,
Detroit, Los Angeles, Dallas, Houston, Louisville, Memphis, and
dozens of other US cities suffering from deindustrialization and selective community divestment.[34] In New York City, for example, just
five neighborhoods, the South Bronx, Brownsville, East New York,
Harlem, and Bedford-Stuyvesant, were targeted for over a third of
the entire state's prison population.[35] Within these areas there is now
a major gap between the logic of the law and the actual, on-the-
ground reality of the law. Only by interrogating that gap is it possible
to see how the law is experienced by residents of these communities,
where police officers have lost much of their public respect, deterrence has lost its power, children and families frequently become
incapacitated, and rehabilitation often doesn't stand a chance.

Despite these failings, the law, not social safety nets, remains the
primary force for social intervention among the most disadvantaged
communities in the United States. Policy makers have leaned heavily on the criminal justice system to hide, rather than solve, many
of society's most entrenched challenges. But penal institutions have
limited power to heal the traumas that drive so many to offend. Nor
can they uproot the pain that often torments survivors and the loved
ones of victims. Incarceration does nothing to change the dilemmas
and difficulties faced by residents of high-incarceration neighborhoods. It makes them no less dependent upon survival strategies
such as selling drugs or their own bodies. It neither removes the
abundant stressors they face nor expands the limited opportunities
they can claim in the face of those stressors. Rather, arrests, felony

trials, and prison time all become the basis for society to further condemn these residents, pile on the stressors, dismantle supportive family structures, and further narrow any redemptive opportunities.[36]

When prison sentences go unquestioned, they complete a tidy but dangerously false story line for how society creates safety on the streets. But when we take a critical look at imprisonment patterns in areas like Chicago's 60644, a more difficult story emerges. What has so often been called a "war on drugs" was part of a larger war on neighborhoods, a prolonged and costly period of conflict that has destabilized low-income African Americans and the communities they call home. Fueled by concentrated punishment, this war is waged every time society attempts to make the world safer simply by forcibly removing African Americans from the general population. The war is carried out through both the broken logic and the broken tools of the law, propelled by policies that respond to economic isolation with disinvestment, to trauma with confinement, and to missing parents with the further fragmentation of families. It amounts to a legally codified attack on pain and dysfunction, through which high rates of conviction and imprisonment have become both a self-fulfilling prophecy and a long-term addiction across the United States, and urban neighborhoods of color bear the long-term scars of this addiction.

Suspension[1]

■ Kristiana Rae Colón

players

yansa turner—17-year-old Black girl, hs junior
mika hampton—18-year-old Black girl, hs senior
voltaire pride—16-year-old Black girl, hs junior
ms max—26-year-old Becky, success development specialist

voices

demarcus—15-year-old Black boy, hs sophomore
main office—56-year-old Janice
mr. turner—yansa's guardian
captured main office—the voice of liberation

location

urban charter high school

time

a future we hope is more distant than it is

> (a sterile classroom with a white board, perhaps a repurposed science
> lab. from the ceiling grid, **yansa**, a young Black woman, is suspended
> by her ankles, bound in a thick straitjacket cocoon, with a belted latex
> intubated gag fastened to her mouth. two thin black bungee cables
> stretch from two hooks above each breast of the jacket and disappear
> into the ceiling grid. **yansa's** long locks sweep the floor as she hangs. the
> heavy sigh of respirator machinery whirs from above, where the gag
> tubes disappear into the ceiling. a large computer monitoring system
> tracks her vitals.)

*(**yansa** becomes suddenly alert and struggles against her restraints. the machine responds with a series of beeps and a rush of pharmaceutical gas forced through her tubes and gag. she falls slack again.)*

(a school bell rings. the roar of teen voices fills the hallway. shadows of passing students clamor beyond the door's frosted glass.)

(the door opens)

ms max

no   no   you're fine demarcus you have two minutes   come on let's move   we're not doing this today

demarcus (off)

maaaaaaaaaan who the fuck is you!

ms max

there you go   you're done
(into a vest radio)
240 on 2 over

radio

copy that 240 go

(the shadows of two heavily vested armed security marshals rush the hallway)

demarcus (off)

get the fuck off me nigga! youooonno who the fuck i am get the fuck—

*(a high-voltage zap crackles in the hallway. student laughter. the shadows of the marshals drag **demarcus** away. **ms max** shouts down the hallway.)*

ms max

tardy tickets in 5 4 3 2

> *(school bell rings. **ms max** tucks herself back into the classroom and closes the door behind her. she retrieves the long pole of an animal release stick and aims it toward **yansa**)*

ms max

ha or not

> *(she tucks the pole away again)*

ms max

your interval's up but you seem so peaceful there

> *(**ms max** flops into the mesh swivel chair behind the desk)*

ms max

hang tight for a few

> *(she props her stilettoed feet up on the desk)*

ms max

you guys are wearing me out today and it's not even 3rd block

> *(she pulls her iPhone out of her purse and begins swiping)*

ms max

you won't snitch, right? breathe for 5 minutes

(mock thug voice)

NO SNITCHIN

> *(**ms max** lets her head fall back and does a few luxurious neck rolls then*

resumes swiping. and swiping. and swiping. and swiping. a tinder notification—it's a match! **ms max** *tap tap taps. spreads her heels to the edges of the desk and clicks a pic between her legs. giggles. tap tap tap send.* **yansa** *jolts alert again and begins struggling.)*

ms max

alrightalright   you're cooked   come on down

*(**ms max** slips the cable loop of the animal release stick around **yansa**'s ankles and flicks a lever on the computer monitor. the two black cables attached to the chest of her jacket raise into the ceiling grid as another cable lowers, releasing her ankles from above. the pulley whirs until she's upright.)*

ms max

here we go   gravity and bathroom

*(**ms max** flicks another lever then unfastens the latex belt of the gag. it flops away from **yansa**, but remains dangling in front of her face by the respirator tubes hanging from the ceiling grid.)*

yansa

gravity and bathroom? i'm done

ms max

you've got one more interval

yansa

nuh uhh i'm done! i had twelve points i did twelve points

ms max

you had fifteen points

yansa

i ain't have no fifteen points i had twelve and i did my twelve

ms max

is that another contradictory disruption i hear? eighteen?

> (*ms max* *flicks another lever and* *yansa* *steps out of the suspension* *boots.*)

ms max

cuz you max out at twenty-four you know that

> (*ms max* *works the cable loop of the animal release stick up over the* *boots and tucks the pole away*)

ms max

like you want to go to 4th block anyway   you can't seem to get through one day of american history without racking up a ticket

yansa

cuz mr. focelli is a nazi and he stank

> (*ms max* *flicks open the straitjacket buckle and the sleeves fall slack*)

ms max

gravity and bathroom   let's go   you've got two minutes

> (*yansa* *seethes as she retreats to a narrow closet of the classroom,* *squeezes inside, and closes the door.* *ms max* *flops back into her swivel* *chair and continues swiping on her phone. another match. she unfastens* *the top button of her blouse, tussles her hair, bites her finger, and clicks a* *high-angled pic with her iPhone. she lifts one stiletto up to the edge of* *the desk again and begins to set up a shot, when the classroom intercom* *beeps. she's startled upright.*)

main office

max come in

ms max

copy max

main office

those were the days

ms max

just can't help yourself can you janice

main office

it's just funny every time listen is turner with you?

ms max

yansa turner   *(as much for yansa's benefit)*   gravity & bathroom 60 seconds

yansa

   (from inside the closet)
copy 60

main office

listen max   we've got a situation in accounts with her guardian
and i just want to confirmturner was up for four intervals or five?

ms max

fifteen points   going up for her last interval at the end of this 60
and then i'll escort to fifth block

main office

okay because the guardian is here to pay the reinstatement and he
insists it was only a twelve-point suspension

ms max

she was booked for twelve and we had an incident after the second interval   contradictory disruption ticket tacked on another
three points

main office

mr. turner that total is correct that's $25 dollars per suspension
interval

(mr. turner's muffled voice through the intercom)

mr. turner

disrupt what? what she do? what she do now? act like you don't
know how to talk to kids! sheeeeeeeit needa be disrupted   you
ever just talk to kids

i gotta pay another twenty five dollars cuz yo gray's lake headass
don't know how to talk to kids!

main office

mr. turner you're going to have to calm down

mr. turner

and it's twenty a interval! think you slick

main office

in-school suspension now features success inversion therapy with
our new success development specialist we sent home a notice of the

updated discipline & honor rates last week

ms max

you got this under control janice?

main office

we're all good   stand by for two

ms max

which two?

main office

hampton and pride

ms max

which hampton?

main office

shamika

ms max

shamika hampton never fails   what's the ticket?

main office

assault with a lunch tray four points

ms max

i thought three hundreds were an automatic O.S.S.?

main office

lunch tray was dropped to a 200-level ticket   that article's got
downtown shook

ms max

downtown's always shook

main office

i'll resend the new point schedule several tickets were dropped to
200s to keep more of them in the building more of the time

ms max

right

main office

so you'll have your hands full 'til the install on the other inversion
grids is finished

ms max

so what are the three hundreds?

main office

fighting and above

ms max

lunch tray to the face isn't considered fighting?

main office

it was lunch tray to the buttocks max
4th block bell   standby for hampton and pride

ms max

hampton and pride copy

main office

tango mike   over

ms max

time's up turner! you growing a new rib in there?

yansa (from inside the closet)

you ever hung upside down on your heavy day before!

ms max

that sounds like a three-point excuse to me!

yansa (from inside)

i'm coming!

> *(school bell rings)*

> *(the classroom door opens. two heavily vested armed security marshals deliver **mika hampton** and **voltaire pride**, each guard guiding his prisoner by an animal release stick with the cable looped tight around the girls' wrists. they release the girls into the classroom.)*

ms max

thanks guys! stay safe out there alright ladies   boots

voltaire

put my boot up yo narrow ass

mika

i didn't even do nothing! she hit me!

voltaire

you liked it

ms max

alright! two verbal assault tickets coming right up

*(**ms max** starts tapping on the touch screen of the vitals monitor)*

mika

see what you did bitch! cuz you can't shut yo fuckin mouth for three seconds

voltaire

look who fuckin talkin?! only time you shut up is when you deep-throat the defense

ms max

let's go ahead and make that FOUR tickets   you guys wanna keep going? you know you max out at twenty-four and then it's an O.S.S.   zip it!
and step into your boots

*(pods of red, mechanized boots form a grid around the classroom floor. **mika** and **voltaire** each step into the pair of boots on either side of **yansa**'s pod. **ms max** flicks another lever on the vitals monitor, and with a mechanized whir, the suspension boots fasten themselves around the girls' ankles.)*

mika

i can't take this shit right now   ms max please can i just do a regular in-school?

ms max

sorry hampton your guardians signed the waiver for enhanced
jackets

> (*ms max flicks another lever and the black bungee cables holding the
> straitjacket cocoons lower from the ceiling grid and dangle in front of
> each girl.*)

mika

i can't take this shit right now   it make my eyes hurt ms max
my eyeballs feel like they gonna explode when i go upside down

ms max

arms out

> (*voltaire defiantly extends her arms*)

mika

no! no! no! i can't

> (*mika struggles from her locked-in booted position and loses her
> balance. she falls forward but is held in place by her mechanized boots
> locked into the floor grid.*)

voltaire

cho goofy ass

mika

i can't ms max   PLEASE! PLEASE! PLEASE!

> (*mika lets out a chilling animal scream. voltaire laughs.*)

ms max

arms out

mika

PLEEEEEEASE!

*(**ms max** sighs and flicks another lever on the wall that sends a jolt through **mika**'s body, subduing her. she flicks another lever and respirator tubes lower a belted latex gag from the ceiling grid. she walks over to force **mika**'s limp arms into the jacket. she pinches **mika**'s cheeks together 'til her jaws fall open and she forces the gag into her mouth and belts it around her head.)*

voltaire

i like it   it make me feel high

*(**ms max** walks back behind the desk and flicks another lever. with another mechanized whir, the straitjacket cocoons tighten around the ankles of the suspension boots, then belt themselves around the calves, the hips, the chest.)*

voltaire

feel like a hug   mika's just a big baby

ms max

if you're lucky it'll make those grades feel high

voltaire

yall dumb for thinkin this make my brain better   you can't make my brain better

*(**ms max** flicks another lever and **voltaire**'s gag lowers from the grid.)*

voltaire

hangin upside down don't do nothin but make me feel high can't
nothin make my brain better but god

> *(**ms max** walks over and fits the gag into **voltaire**'s mouth.)*

ms max

i am god

> *(**ms max** returns to the desk and flicks a lever to tighten the gag belt
> around **voltaire**'s head. she flicks another lever and the suspension boots
> are unlocked from the floor grid. another lever and the pulley begins to
> roll up the black bungee cables attached to the girls' chests and ankles.
> they raise about six inches above the ground, then the chest cables release
> as the ankle cables lift into the grid so that they are slowly brought
> horizontal. **ms max** lets them linger there in a horizontal swing for a
> moment. she smirks. **mika** regains consciousness and begins to grunt
> and struggle behind her gag. **ms max** flicks another lever and the pulley
> continues to draw their ankles up toward the grid and release their
> chests toward the floor, gradually completing the inversion.)*

ms max

alright turner that's an aggravated defiant tardy four points
let's go! right now!

yansa

it was a fuckin butcher shop in my panties you fascist cunt   i'll   be
out in a second!

ms max

oh you are gunning for an out of school turner
i don't know what the new point schedule says about aggravated
verbal assault but by my count you just maxed out

> *(a disaster alarm begins to wail)*

main office

code black   code black   all marshals go
good afternoon learning specialists of climb & succeed charter academy! we are currently at a code black please stay in your rooms while
marshals secure each floor and exit your classroom doors will automatically lock in ten seconds

marshals will come around to escort you and your scholars outside
when we get an all clear i repeat   your doors will lock automatically in ten seconds please stay in your—

> *(the sound of a high-voltage zap crackles through the intercom. a grunt
> from **janice**. the thump of a body hitting the floor. the lights in the hallway
> flicker then go black. the lights in the classroom flicker then go black.)*

ms max

what the fuck

> *(**ms max** paws around in the dark for her phone and taps it alive for
> light.)*

ms max

what the fuck is a code black?

> *(the blue emergency lights flicker on, revealing **yansa** standing behind
> **ms max**'s swivel chair with a success saber to her neck.)*

yansa

i am

> *(**yansa** delivers a high-voltage zap to **ms max**'s neck and she slumps
> over the desk. the shadows of security marshals bloom behind the frosted
> glass of the classroom door. they are met with a barrage of high-voltage
> zaps. the percussion of several big men hitting the floor drums in the
> hallway. **yansa** smiles. a new voice crackles through the intercom.)*

captured main office

good afternoon! survivors of climb & succeed charter academy

*(yansa flicks a lever and **voltaire** and **mika** are lowered and brought upright.)*

captured main office

make some noise if you ready to stand up straight

(the roar of Black children from classrooms all over the building)

captured main office

that's what we believed
and who are we?
your brothers & sisters

*(yansa flicks three levers and **voltaire** and **mika**'s boots, jackets, and gags are released)*

captured main office

or so you'll see

(with a mechanized whir, the classroom door floats open. from a distance and growing closer, the song of doors opening.)

(blackout)

"Mass Incarceration" as Misnomer

■ Dylan Rodríguez

"Mass incarceration" has become a misleading, largely useless, and potentially dangerous term—a newly designated keyword, if you will, in the steadily expanding political vocabulary of post-racialism. We must ask ourselves what "mass incarceration" has actually come to mean, to what uses this phrase is being deployed, and whether, in our incessant and perhaps under-examined use of this phrase, some of us are becoming unwitting accomplices to the very regime of US state violence to which we profess to be radically opposed. Who, exactly, is the "mass" in mass incarceration? If it is not the case (really, not even remotely the case) that Euro-descended people and those racially marked as "white" are being criminalized, policed, and incarcerated en masse—that is, if the commonsense usage of "mass incarceration" already presumes casual and official white innocence and decriminalization—then isn't this phrase closer to being a clumsy liberal racist euphemism for mass Black incarceration, and in many geographies, mass Brown incarceration? There is an emerging liberal-to-progressive common sense about US policing, criminalization, and human capture that uses the language of mass incarceration within a sometimes sterilized rhetoric of national shame, shared suffering, and racial disparity. Notions of fundamental unfairness, systemic racial bias, and institutional dysfunction form the basis for numerous platforms advocating vigorous reforms of the criminal justice apparatus, largely by way of internal auditing, aggressive legal and policy shifts, and rearrangements of governmental infrastructure (e.g., "schools, not prisons").

What is largely beyond contestation is that this reform agenda rests on two widely shared premises: (1) that the current structure of US incarceration is bloated beyond reasonable, justifiable, or sustainable measure; and (2) that equal and rational treatment under the (criminal) law is both a feasible and desirable outcome of mass incarceration's imminent reform. What is less clear, however, is whether those who subscribe to this commonsense formulation of liberal-progressive solutions are willing to concede that they may have radically misconceived the problem. While we cannot reproduce them here, every conceivable statistical measure clearly demonstrates that the impact of the last four decades of state-planned criminological apocalypse is historically, fundamentally asymmetrical. (For lucid and concise summations of this evidence, see sentencingproject.org or criticalresistance.org, among many other sources.) In other words, the post-racial euphemism of "mass incarceration" miserably fails to communicate how the racist and anti-Black form of the US state is also its paradigmatic form, particularly in matters related to criminal justice policy and punishment. Put another way, there is no "mass incarceration."

The persistent use of this term is more than a semantic error; it is a political and conceptual sleight-of-hand with grave consequences: if language guides thought, action, and social vision, then there is an urgent need to dispose of this useless and potentially dangerous phrase and speak truth through a more descriptive, thoughtful activist vocabulary. The twenty-year history of "mass incarceration's" entrance into the popular vocabulary illuminates the lurking dilemma at hand: while its etymological origins can be traced further back in time, the contemporary use of the phrase emerged in the mid-1990s, owing in significant part to the work of the National Criminal Justice Commission between 1994 and 1996. The commission generated a comprehensive analysis of what it then deemed "the largest and most frenetic correctional buildup of any country in the history of the world" and summarized its findings in the widely cited text *The Real War on Crime*, published by the mega–trade press HarperCollins.[1]

The terms "mass incarceration," "mass imprisonment," and similar ones persisted through the latter 1990s and early 2000s, surfacing in academic, activist, and public policy rhetoric as well as influential texts like Marc Mauer and Meda Chesney-Lind's 2002 anthology

Invisible Punishment: The Collateral Consequences of Mass Imprisonment and, of course, Michelle Alexander's widely read, deeply flawed 2010 book, *The New Jim Crow: Mass Incarceration in the Age of Colorblindness.*[2] Since the publication of Alexander's text, "mass incarceration" has not only entered the post-racial lexicon as a euphemism for racist criminalization and targeted, asymmetrical incarceration, but it has also been absorbed into the operative language of the US government and its highest-profile representatives.

Let us briefly consider three prominent examples of this creeping co-optation, spanning ten months in 2014–2015. US attorney general Eric Holder's keynote address on "over-incarceration" at NYU Law School in September 2014 was one of the early indications of a reformist shift in the US state's internal deliberations on national criminal justice policy. Crucially, Holder's speech occurred just one month after the police killing of Michael Brown in Ferguson, Missouri, amid an unfolding national revolt against anti-Black, racist police violence. Against this burgeoning climate of antiracist protest, Holder pandered to law enforcement in the same breath in which he decried the "rise in incarceration and the escalating costs it has imposed on our country": we can all be proud of the progress that's been made at reducing the crime rate over the past two decades, thanks to the tireless work of prosecutors and the bravery of law enforcement officials across America.[3]

Soon after Holder's resignation from the attorney general post, newly declared presidential candidate Hillary Clinton called for a new era of criminal justice reform in an April 2015 speech at Columbia University. Echoing Holder's verbal genuflection to police power, candidate Clinton lamented the "era of mass incarceration" while lambasting the contemporaneous uprisings in Black Baltimore over the police torture and killing of Freddie Gray. Scolding the Baltimore protesters for "instigating further violence," "disrespecting the Gray family," and thus "compounding the tragedy of Freddie Gray's death," Clinton declared, "We must urgently begin to rebuild bonds of trust and respect among Americans, between police and citizens."[4]

Not to be outdone, President Barack Obama resoundingly hailed the onset of carceral reform in a somewhat remarkable July 2015 address at the NAACP's national convention in Philadelphia.

To a series of standing ovations, Obama declared, "Our criminal justice system isn't . . . keeping us as safe as it should be. It is not as fair as it should be. Mass incarceration makes our country worse off, and we need to do something about it."[5] Amplifying the Holder-Clinton script, Obama proclaimed the need for more policing of African American communities, to the audible praise of the NAACP crowd.

Obama's subsequent historical mischaracterization of policing under US apartheid is peculiar at best; historically, in fact, the African American community oftentimes was under-policed rather than over-policed. Folks were very interested in containing the African American community so that it couldn't leave segregated areas, but within those areas there wasn't enough police presence. Herein lies the punch line of the multiculturalist racial state's co-optation of the mass incarceration rhetoric and its conjoined reform agenda: as Obama et al. sang alongside the liberal-progressive chorus of demand for an end to mass incarceration, they simultaneously advocated for a redistribution of state resources away from prisons and toward the police. For Obama, the salve for rampant racist police violence and mounting popular revolt against the default prestige of the badge and gun was "hiring more police and giving them the resources that would allow them to do a more effective job [of] community policing."[6]

There is something lurking beneath this still emerging liberal-progressive, and now official state reformist, discourse of mass incarceration that is worth some critical, radical scrutiny. We are witnessing the early stages of a subtle though potentially significant shift in the statecraft of policing: the reform of mass incarceration is becoming insidiously linked to calls for a kinder, gentler, and expanded form of law-and-order policing. This growing, technologically enhanced, and body-camera-strapped police power, in turn, implicitly promises to kill and maim fewer unarmed (Black and Brown) people while also subjecting them to more effective forms of surveillance, control, and discipline (community policing or "peacekeeping"). Riding the wave of a mass incarceration reform renaissance, the multicultural racist state—in loose coalition with an ensemble of liberal-progressive consensus makers (professional activists, academics, nonprofit and foundation executives, policy think tanks, religious leaders)—is building a refurbished pro-police national consensus by naturalizing the utterly bogus connection between decarceration, "community safety," and expanded police capacity/power. This is a statecraft that intends to win hearts and minds even as it focuses its punitive, disciplinary crosshairs on those fitting the profile of "real criminals" (whatever that might mean in a given time and place).

If the current political discourse on mass incarceration is allowed to remain intact, it is almost certain that the technologies and institutional reach of policing will increase, expand, and intensify even as the thing being called "mass incarceration" is subjected to reformist scrutiny from within and beyond the racial state. Perhaps, then, it is the moment when the public intellectuals and figureheads of the US state begin to deploy the allegedly critical language of mass incarceration that we must admit to ourselves that this term may have reached its point of explanatory and analytical obsolescence—that is, if it ever adequately explained and analyzed anything to begin with. It is becoming increasingly clear that the US racist state is both willing and capable of re-narrating the story of mass incarceration as a call for better—in other words, more tolerable and consensus-building— technologies of criminalization, policing, and incarceration. The historical rhythm of US nation building plays on the percussive terrors of domestic warfare and gendered racial criminalization (literally, the creation of crime and criminals through the raw material of racial- and gender-marked bodies). A spectrum of selective, targeted forms of incarceration—from Middle Passage slave ships and California missions to Mexican labor camps and federal supermax prisons—has produced multigenerational terror, suffering, and freedom struggle for populations at the underside of white American (and now multiculturalist, post-racial) civil society across its various phases of historical development. In addition to challenging and ultimately dismantling the idiom of mass incarceration, we must come to terms with the need for a more comprehensive, flexible critical/activist language that does not fixate on prisons and jails—or even on "criminal justice"—as the exclusive sites of institutionalized racist state violence.

Contemporary systems of human incarceration, from Pelican Bay to Guantanamo Bay, are inseparable from both the growing ideological, institutional, and militarized regime of US policing and the larger cultural-legal technologies of criminalization, including popular entertainment, corporate and social media, and the law it-self. Thus, the problem is not merely one of "incarceration"; it is also a matter of an overlapping, symbiotic ensemble of institutions and systems that implicates the entire apparatus of the law-and-order United States as a form of asymmetrical, domestic war against crim-inalized people and places. Certainly, the rebellions against police violence across the US over the last two years are forcing a partial disruption of classical white supremacist and anti-Black policing strategies such as those seen in places like Ferguson and Baltimore. Yet at the very same time, in response to this climate of protest and uprising, the statecraft of criminal justice reform is premised on a strengthening and re-legitimation of police authority and prestige. As the phrase "mass incarceration" is absorbed into the operative language of the state, does it not become necessary to consider how this rhetoric is becoming more of an accomplice to the racist state than an effective language of opposition to it?

On Being Human

■ Kathy Boudin

We crowd into each other, pushing ourselves up against a window in the prison school. Through the wire and bars, we can see two of our friends surrounded by guards as they walk toward a small building; they disappear through one door, entering a space we may never see. A few minutes later they reappear, coming out of a different door. They are no longer in captivity. They are free women. We wave. They can't see our heads or bodies; only our fingers stick out, waving our love and support, waving our dreams.

This is the "waving goodbye ritual." We stick our fingers through the bars to say goodbye to friends with whom we have shared a life. I crane my neck to catch a last glimpse. The sun's rays bounce off the razor wire, row on row, circle on circle, silver gleaming. I wonder what happens to birds and butterflies. Do they get caught? Do our dreams? I can barely see my friend. Now I can't see her at all. My gaze is caught in the wire.

Back then, when I was still in, we were waving goodbye to women with nonviolent convictions; they were the only ones the parole board released. Would it, could it, ever be our turn? Would society ever see those of us who had committed a violent crime as human beings with potential; someone who had served her many years; suffered, served, and learned a lot and was more valuable to society outside than inside?

◆

In our green pants and green denim shirts, we sat around the long table in the parenting center. Allie taught foster care and child custody law, Beth oversaw the nursery and taught the caregivers about

154

newborns, Miranda spent weekends as a caregiver with the visiting children. All of us were teachers, caregivers, or advocates in the children's center. We were also prisoners at the maximum-security women's prison in New York State, Bedford Hills Correctional Facility, where I shared twenty-two years with other long-termers. Professionals in education and child development and staff from other prisons often came to meet with us because they had heard about the Bedford Hills Children's Center and wanted to learn about our work.

"Most women are in prison for nonviolent crimes," the civilian staff member who was introducing the program, and us, assured the visitors. We stared at each other, swallowing what we knew, our histories. Almost all of us had been convicted of a violent crime in which someone died, but we did not dare to break the narrative that erased us.

We are women who committed violent crimes. We are also worthy human beings. We knew that the civilian staff person was afraid to acknowledge that. And we each knew that even though she genuinely cared about us and respected our work as caregivers and teachers, she was stymied by the question of how a person she knows to be kind and empathetic, hardworking and disciplined, could also be someone who took a life, or agreed to risk that someone would be killed, or seriously hurt others? How should society respond to a person who has killed someone? She would find it hard to answer the question: When a life is taken, how much punishment is enough?

We were both grateful to have the opportunity to do meaningful work while in prison and afraid to jeopardize it. And we ourselves were in a process of trying to answer those same questions, from within our own experience. We tried to imagine how to ever make up for the harm we had caused; we worked at connecting the pieces of our lives so that it made sense. We saw in each other the growth, the good that was possible in helping others; "Each one, teach one" was our mantra. It takes courage to speak about the reality of our lives, the bad, the good, to wipe away the pretense, the simplifying. One of us who often sat at that table with the visiting professionals displayed that courage when she wrote:

> I am the voice you locked away and do not want to hear. But I echo through your conscience. I am your average woman prisoner: black, poor, with a history of family abuse. I came before

your ice chamber, a 17-year-old girl, naïve to the system, accused of two counts of murder. No, I'm not innocent in the legal sense, because I was *there*: I permitted an entry that caused
two human lives to be halted suddenly in an unplanned violent
act. I take full responsibility for everything I did. You gave me
50 years in a state penitentiary. Yet the story of my life is not so
alien from yours. The abuse I survived might be abuse in your
home. Like you, I've overcome obstacles. The love I feel for my
child is as intense as yours for your child. Just like you, I want
to make the world a better place. I am a statistic. But I am also
a woman—a friend, a teacher, a creator of life. I am powerless
and powerful. I am a human being.

—Roslyn Smith, in her thirty-eighth year of a fifty-to-life sentence, arrested when she was seventeen

◆

John MacKenzie's friends found him hanging by a bed sheet in his cell
in Fishkill prison, in the state of New York. It was August 23, 2016. He
had been sentenced to twenty-five years to life. He had served forty
when he hanged himself. He was first eligible for parole when he turned
fifty-five. He was seventy when he decided he could bear no more.

John MacKenzie was in prison for a failed robbery in which he
killed a police officer. During the early years of his twenty-five-to-
life sentence, he faced the terrible harm that he was responsible for.
He went on to create a victim awareness group for other men. He
became educated; he became a Buddhist. Over time, he became part
of the growing elder population and a mentor for the young people.

After twenty-five years he expected to get out. He had done
everything right. And more. Much more. He had a perfect score
on the risk and needs assessment used to measure the risk to public
safety if he were released. He was a model of growth and transformation under the most difficult conditions. But the parole board
repeatedly denied him freedom on the basis of the one thing he
could never change: the crime.

In reality, the parole board simply ignored the judge's sentence
that made him eligible for parole after twenty-five years. The board

decided that more punishment was needed. This denial of parole for violent crimes is a common practice in New York and many other states. The "nature of the crime" supersedes good behavior, remorse, rehabilitation, and lack of risk to public safety. The seriousness of the crime is exactly what prompted the sentencing judge's decision to impose a twenty-five-year punishment; the parole board, in fact, overrode the judge and changed the sentence to more than forty years. Ultimately, it condemned John MacKenzie to despair and death.

After being denied parole *eight times*, a judge repudiated this sickening routine and ordered the board to conduct a "de novo" (new) hearing so that MacKenzie could be released. It held the hearing—and turned him down for the *ninth* time. The judge held the parole board in contempt and ordered another hearing. MacKenzie, with forty years of his sentence completed and now part of the growing population of aging prisoners—he was seventy years old—left that hearing denied *a tenth time.* In response, he hanged himself.

Shortly before he died, John MacKenzie wrote to his friends, saying, "If society wishes to rehabilitate as well as punish wrong-doers through imprisonment, society—through its lawmakers—must bear the responsibility of tempering justice with mercy. Giving a man legitimate hope is a laudable goal. Giving him false hope is utterly inhuman."[1]

I went to a memorial for John MacKenzie at the National Black Theatre of Harlem. We sat in a circle and introduced ourselves. Some of us were long-termers, including men who had known him inside and had made it home to freedom. Also in the circle were advocates and activists; a woman whose son had been murdered and had met John when she spoke inside the prison at a victims' awareness group; one of John's daughters. Each spoke about him, about what brought us to the memorial. A long-termer who had served eighteen years of extra punishment imposed by the parole board's denials said, "Prison is like being among rocks. But John MacKenzie was a rose in my life."

Postscript

"Please do not let my father's death be in vain," said Danielle, John MacKenzie's daughter, at the end of the memorial. In the years since

John MacKenzie died, we[2] have tried to carry the torch forward: Demonstrations in Albany have demanded the governor appoint new parole board commissioners and not reappoint old ones. Advocates and lawyers, long-termers inside prison, and family members outside have campaigned for new parole regulations. And some victims/survivors/representatives have told the parole board that not all survivors want interminable sentences.

MacKenzie's death shone a light on what was a hidden inhumanity. The struggle continues. Today the issue of parole denials extending sentences is no longer a secret. Some progress is being made. But parole denials are just a part of the problem. They are part of a punishment paradigm that grips the soul of our country. So often driven by race, it is a paradigm that not only dehumanizes people in prison, guards, and survivors/victims but also permeates the entire culture.

Listen to former president Obama as he began to push for criminal justice reform. It was a historic, hopeful moment. But even as he opened the door for some, he double locked it on over half the people in prison when he argued to let those with nonviolent crimes out but not "the murderers, thugs, drug kingpins."[3]

As a society, we have yet to understand the dynamics of social responsibility and individual acts. We tend to reduce the problem of violent crime to the comforting notion that it is produced by a bad person. We put him or her away, out of sight, as if that is the end of the story. Individuals sometimes make bad choices, but they are capable of much more than they were at their worst or weakest moment. We fail to acknowledge the role of poverty and discrimination in denying education, jobs, and hope to whole communities. Racism demonizes whole communities.

The life and death of John MacKenzie and the courage of Roslyn Smith and thousands of others who have emerged from decades behind bars to become educators, beacons, wise men and women in many walks of life and in many communities is an important lesson in human complexity and creativity. They demonstrate our capacity to learn and grow, to accept responsibility for awful harm while striving to heal and live as complete human beings. We need more roses like Roslyn and John MacKenzie in the free community. They have a lot to teach us about being human.

Section 3

For Feminist Freedoms
Confronting Misogyny and White Supremacy through Abolition Politics and Anticapitalist Practices

This section of the book carries a particularly heavy burden because of the demands that it makes on how we understand long-term work for freedom. The seven pieces that follow are written by feminist organizers who are or have been incarcerated and by activists who are working on the outside for freedom and justice for our communities. Although the starting points for making claims about how to approach work against the devastating impacts of the long term differ by author, when taken together the contributors make a very convincing argument that *the only way to fully realize a true revolution against carceral injustice is to put radical feminist analyses and praxis at the center of the work.* That is to say, each individual struggle for justice, every community organizing campaign, every legal or legislative reform, and all resistance movements must be based on a commitment to radical feminist principles and actions. Radical feminist freedoms are at the root of all liberation from carceral control of human bodies.

What exactly are radical feminist freedoms? And how are they linked to carceral injustice? Feminist freedoms against carceral injustice are, first and foremost, broad, radical demands against systemic oppression as opposed to those that focus on narrower issues or concerns associated with policing, imprisonment, violence prevention, surveillance, or conditions of confinement. While these are real concerns for people harmed by carceral control and must certainly be addressed, the authors whose writing appears in this section take a wider view of what freedom looks like. They focus on issues like economic security; recognition of native sovereignty and the rights of First Nations people; demanding visibility and supporting leadership of women, queer, and trans people of color, as well as survivors of state violence. The collective argument is that these broader issues are critically linked to carceral injustice and that addressing them increases the likelihood of radical social transformation of the carceral state into safe and secure communities.

This approach to freedom work requires a centering of feminist concerns about gender violence, the oppression that women face in political formations, the lack of visibility of queer and gender-nonconforming leadership work, and the degradation of mothering and other issues related to gender and sexuality. The authors implicitly challenge the exclusive focus on men's incapacitation and imprisonment (particularly those identified as Black cisgender) that tends to characterize most discussions of the carceral state and its long-term damage to individuals and communities. Instead they bring attention to how violence by intimate partners; stigma and shame associated with family members' long-term incarceration; challenges to those "left behind"; and the ongoing pain of multiple forms of simultaneous abuse and degradation of women, queer, and trans people operate alongside what is often foregrounded as the most important concerns in the struggle for justice. The writing reminds us that carceral injustice is not just about cages and bars but also about poverty, attacks on immigrants, failing schools, rape, denial of health care, lack of jobs, food instability, and, in particular, how misogyny and capitalism conspire with white supremacy to leave Black and other women of color and trans people captive in a prison nation.

Importantly, several pieces in this section decry the specific damage that carceral feminism has done to liberatory work for freedom and justice. Citing the work by INCITE!, Critical Resistance, and other groups that challenged the ways that mainstream antiviolence organizations advocated for state intervention by police, judges, probation officers, and others in situations where harm had occurred, the authors in this section are absolute in their demand that we find alternative ways to respond to harm that comes from reliance on the violence of the carceral state. The broader context of this critique, articulated by Mariame Kaba as "Prison Is Not Feminist," helps frame a broader politics of abolition, one that centers radical feminist concerns in the work against the long term. Several authors remind us of this and, in so doing, set out an agenda for radical, inclusive, feminist struggles for freedom—not just from the bars and cages but from the capitalist, misogynistic, white supremacist, settler-colonialist systems that hold them in place.

There is tremendous benefit from this analysis. First and foremost, it makes a more inclusive political process possible, where we will see more people (women) engaged in the work at the local, national, and global level. We benefit from more leadership, and we have more human resources to put into our projects for transformation. Moreover, it means that our work will be better. When we work for radical feminist abolition of the entrenched apparatus of the carceral state, the future will hold the possibility of justice for all people for the long term. Feminist freedom, and nothing short of this, is required.

Prison is Not Feminist, laser print, 2017, Sarah Ross, print; Mariame Kaba, quote

"Do We Want Justice, or Do We Want Punishment?"

A Conversation about Carceral Feminism between Rachel Caïdor, Shira Hassan, Deana Lewis, and Beth E. Richie

Rachel Caïdor: The way that I define "carceral feminism" is to explain it as the way that, in the spirit of protecting women, people have used the state to set up really big penalties that ultimately mean that entire communities, including women, are targeted—particularly women of color, or people of color, and people who have complicated legal identities, like people who are undocumented, people in the sex trade. I also usually say that people who tend to be carceral are kind of in two camps: either people who haven't really been given the space and opportunity to think through other solutions, or people who have benefited from the state. And those people tend to be white.

Beth E. Richie: The second group, or both groups?

Rachel: The second group tends to be white. I see a lot of carceral feminism among young people of color—and people of color in general—because we haven't actually been given a space to think through other solutions, and we get so obsessed with making the system do right by us that we haven't actually had the space to think about what we really mean by that. And then the minute you do give people in the first group that space, they're like, "Oh, yeah, fuck that."

But in the second group, that conversation doesn't matter, because they've benefited from the state, and the state has protected them. In a certain second-wave white feminism, people actually weren't seeking liberation. People who invested in these carceral systems were not marginalized from humanity, but marginalized from power. These people aren't angry at a social inequality or political inequality but

163

that they're on the wrong side of that inequality; rather, they are "this type of violence shouldn't happen to me." There is no actual critique of the inherent violence of the capitalist or imperialist carceral state.

Deana Lewis: I'll offer some examples of what carceral feminism looks like every day in practice. Taking a sexual assault survivor, locking her up so that she is able to testify against her abusers to make sure that the people who assaulted her are locked up and get jail time. Carceral feminism is taking a law like Title IX—which is supposed to protect women on college campuses—and then demanding that all campus employees are mandated reporters. And so if a survivor discloses to us, the duty for protection is to tell the authorities—tell the Title IX office—about the assault, and then don't provide any type of confidentiality or anonymity to the survivor. Carceral feminism is also advocating that a homeless woman's children be taken away because she left them in a car while interviewing for a job.

Shira Hassan: I would add to those examples that many domestic violence shelters do not let anyone in who has a criminal record, under the auspices that this will keep the "women" in the shelter safe.

I want to share this one other thing that was a real-life story that happened with Lynne Johnson when she was the political director of Chicago Alliance Against Sexual Exploitation [CAASE]. When CAASE was rolling out all their anti-trafficking legislation at an event at Hull House, they tried to present all the "different sides" of the sex trade. It was so sad and bad.

Beth: I remember that.

Shira: This anti-trafficking legislation made the penalties around the sex trade stricter. Basically, it changed the definition and made it so that you could be arrested for trafficking yourself, but the law was dumb. A comrade Lara was there and raised the point that the way that the law is written allows for police officers to arrest young people as trafficking themselves. Lynne first denied that the law was written that way. Yet someone else in the audience who was a lawyer stated, "Nope, that's the way the law is written. That's true. That can happen."

Then Lynne stated, "But that will never happen. That's not who we're going after." Yet within six months, a huge story broke one morning about how this new legislation was used to arrest, literally, probably

fifty or sixty different young people on the South Side who were pre-
sumed to be either gang-involved or related to trafficking rings.

There's two points from this story. One, there's a dismissiveness
around the harm of the state—either because the state has always
benefited you, it won't harm others, or the people who it's harming
deserve this harm. Second, they add in things to laws—like wiretap-
ping to anti-trafficking legislation—to make the legislation tricky
and complex so that more people get caught who don't have anything to do with the original intention of the law.

Beth: From that story there's also an assumption in carceral feminism that the law will err toward doing the right thing versus doing
the wrong thing.

Shira: Yes. What's so strange about carceral feminism as I see it,
especially playing out in institutionalized antiviolence work, is that
the same people, in the same breath, will explain up and down how
the law doesn't work and the system doesn't provide any justice for
survivors. They're very articulate about how the system inherently
doesn't work, but then they woxrk so hard to get people to use the
system, knowing the possibility of a conviction is minimal in cases
of sexual and intimate violence. When you're having conversations
with these advocates and suggest solutions that do not use carceral
systems—solutions where people who cause harm will actually be
held accountable through a long process of transformation, and that
can be done immediately, for free, and doesn't need permission from
the state to happen—they get mad at you and label you a "rape apol-
ogist." Even though it's the system that is actually protecting mass
rape in prisons. That ability to live with a cognitive dissonance only
makes sense for people because, for them, there is something at their
core that feels really invested in protecting the system, because when
they do benefit from it they feel deep validation and recognition.
So that dismissal of "Oh, Lara, you don't know what you're talking
about," they would never be used in that way. The "you-gotta-break-
a-few-eggs-to-make-an-omelet" kind of mentality—that is a real
red flag of when someone's not on the right team.

Beth: What does race and class have to do with this? Each of you
have talked a little bit about that, but what about carceral feminism,

really explicitly, is about white supremacy? Or is carceral feminism about white supremacy?

Deana: To me, carceral logic and feminism should be antithetical to each other, because a carceral logic is relying on systems of oppression—and systems of oppression punish people for what is seen as going against the state's rules and sometimes harming an individual or sometimes harming an institution or a company. And feminism is about breaking down these systems—at least my feminism is—and saying these systems don't work. These systems are oppressive to us, and we can't rely on these tools and institutions to liberate or even support us. For me, it's not just about the white feminists as individuals, but it's about that mentality, a white feminist mentality, that believes that feminism is about equality, that all people were born equal.

It's not just about the bodies of white women; it's about the way that white supremacy has snuck into, or has always been in, our social justice movement, in our collective conscious and our public imagination.

Rachel: White supremacy and carceral feminism feed each other— only when you occupy whiteness in a certain way or you aspire to whiteness in a certain way do you have the luxury of deluding yourself that the laws of this country will work *for* you, not against you. To walk around and feel like the state is somehow out to protect you is the white supremacist weird programming that we've all been raised with. That programming comes from white supremacy, because white supremacy really needs us to believe that the state and the way that its laws work are going to protect all of the people. But that's actually just not true.

That very basic fiction of the law being devised to support people of color—Black people, formerly enslaved people, trans people, sex workers, all of those people—the idea the laws of this country have ever protected these people is a fiction that white supremacy really has tried to program in a lot of us. Carceral feminism has relied on taking that programming and running really far with it, because in so many ways, we—and I'm going to say "we" because I'm at a conference; we're crisis line directors—we really were able to go far with it. We have the Violence Against Women Act, Victims of Crime Act—all of these things where the state has allowed us to believe this to be true and allowed us to indulge in this fiction that the law actually works for us.

Beth: Rachel, how does that work, then, with the two groups that we've talked about at the beginning of this discussion: the white women who are trying to get the benefit, and then the people of color who haven't had a chance to think of other solutions yet?

Shira: The young people who haven't had a chance to think of other solutions yet are most of us who have gone through any sort of system. No matter how radical we are, and no matter how subversive we are, we still are exposed to those ideas at some point. Like Officer Friendly, or on *Law and Order* where we are organized to sympathize with Olivia Benson, this is what it means to be a person who lives in this country. Part of living on the margin is dealing with and trying to make sense of the way that the world tells you the world works, and reconciling your experience of the way the world works. This idea of a world that's so orderly and works for you and is actually out to protect you is the world we all want to live in. But our country is structured in a way that relies on that world being impossible for a significant number of some people, for other people to feel safe in their privilege or whatever. There's a set of people who never had to think of a different way. Carceral feminists or white feminists, they say, "Oh, the system is broken." But the system is brilliant.

For those of us who grew up with these messages, no matter how many people in your family are caught up in the criminal legal system, or no matter how many times you see them caught up for survival or because of racism, there is the constant drumbeat of "you are in these systems because you did something wrong."

Deana: But it's also not just because you did something wrong. It's also because you're a bad person. And so we can maintain this dichotomy or binary of bad versus good, which helps to fuel the idea of a "perfect victim" advanced by mainstream sexual assault and domestic violence organizations.

Rachel: And this is what makes it okay to throw people in the jails for the rest of their lives. They didn't *do* something wrong; they are just *bad* people.

Shira: I also think there's this thing that's very specific to race and class connected to extreme patronization. Brown people are always the villain and always the victim. Rescue is very alive in carceral feminism. You're not supposed to know what's right for you. You're a victim who needs to be saved, and therefore there's the "white savior" piece.

We were always to be rescued, and the law always made us the villain, to the point where they created a law where we could traffic ourselves: literally the victim and the villain simultaneously in our own bodies.

Deana: Shira, what you're also making me think of is just how carceral feminism, white supremacy, and white feminist logic or ideology also fueled imperialism and wars. In *Do Muslim Women Need Saving?* Lila Abu-Lughod writes about the idea that the Middle East is savage.[1] The men are savage barbarians; the women need saving because they're in a *hijab*, or *niqab*, or burqa. The women are fragile and they need white people to go over there, wage wars in the name of saving Muslim women. And if they do speak out against these wars or imperialism, then they are villainized. Carceral feminism is not just rotated in the US, or doesn't just stay in the US, but travels internationally, fueled by white supremacy and imperialism.

Rachel: What is blowing my mind, Shira, about what you said is if you're thinking about it as a circle or cycle—I can't think of how to picture it—but you can be either a villain or a victim, and they're actually not that far apart from each other. You're never just a person, and you're never a full person, and you're never actually competent, or you don't make a life or a world for yourself. Inherent in all of that is that you are not full, and you're not human. And you need white people to just fix you, in some way, shape, or form. Or their laws.

Beth: Sometimes carceral feminism is reduced to the current moment of the Violence Against Women Act, and not with deep roots in all of these other ways that the state creates dangerousness in people (in their body and their behavior) and oversimplifies what our antiviolence work really is.

Let's talk about the people who advocate for long sentences for people who cause a lot of harm. If you assume that the system works, then you assume that you either get in a situation that you're in—in opposition to the criminal legal system—either because you belong there or because you're a bad person. And there's so much language or work around how people who use intimate partner violence—or any kind of violence, really—are bad people. The assumption, therefore, is that carceral feminism works for them. As a system it works because it does take away the bad people, if you follow that assumption. What do we say to people who have been harmed by a person who they think is "bad," because they were harmed badly, and they don't have any other recourse—or they think they don't have any other recourse—but to use the system?

Deana: I want to have faith to push back against the idea that they are actually safer. Trans kids are not safer in schools. They're not protected by the school police. They're not protected by the police on the street. They're not protected by the system; they're targeted by the system. That one person might be put behind bars, but that doesn't make the world any safer, because we haven't done anything to restore the community—however you define the "community"—and we haven't done anything to heal the harm that the survivor is carrying. We haven't done anything to heal the harm that the harm-doer is feeling and has done. And that one person locked up does not equal a safer world.

Beth: Does it mean a safer world for one person?

Deana: It doesn't even mean a safer world for that one person.

Rachel: Conversations often set up people who are survivors to be the ones who are the punishers, because they want to feel safer. The system is what's offered. Of course, survivors deserve that people who harm them are held accountable and face consequences that feel real. Yet the system we have very rarely is effective, because it either targets people falsely or when you try to use it because you have been told it will work, it doesn't. It's not actually delivering consequences and any kind of, as Deana was saying, big-picture transformations to end harm.

Shira: These systems have really taught us how to bind our own idea of safety with someone else being unsafe. But sometimes violence is the only thing that's going to separate this person from the person that they're harming. I'm not pretending that is not a thing that happens. But, then, I'm also not going to contribute to a conversation around prisons, especially long-term sentencing, as a mechanism to keep people away from other people that they can do harm to, because that's not what happens in prisons.

If your uncle Charlie is sexually assaulting all of the children in the family, Uncle Charlie might actually not need to be in that house or even that neighborhood for a long time until he gets his shit together. Does Uncle Charlie need to go into this prison, where he is going to be further dehumanized, further isolated, not address whatever is his fucking problem, and, furthermore, the young children are not going learn that they have a right to be whole again?

We have learned in this culture to want to see people hurt. When people talk about getting a sense of justice, what they actually want is for people to suffer. It's a super "eye-for-an-eye" situation. At the root of it is that violence upon me is wrong but upon someone else it is okay.

There are some real fundamental questions that we have to ask ourselves. Do we want justice, or do we want punishment? Do we want punishment, and do we want that punishment to be violent? The answer is often yes, we want to see people hurt. We often create a whole other generation of harm-doers with that very logic.

I think it's okay to want to kill your rapist. Building a system on that is not okay, and making decisions about what happens from that place is not okay. And not everyone actually just gets to go kill their rapist. It's just not that simple. And who gets away with killing their rapist is also what's important, too.

Rachel: Exactly. Who even gets named as a rapist?

Shira: Where I also struggle with is, we go so philosophical when survivors are asking us, "Are you saying that the person who hurt me doesn't have to deal with what they did to me, and that what they did to me is okay?" And I really don't like how we as a TJ [transformative justice] community have gotten into this cycle of responding to those sort of deeply emotional—and also very concrete—questions with philosophy. I think the answer is equally concrete. The person who hurt you deserves consequences, and you have a right to want them to be punished. The problem is how those two things have become mechanized. And what we want to do is figure out how both of those things can . . . how we can transform it so that punishment isn't what's even needed, and that the consequences are actually real for what you experienced. Because using the system isn't going to get us there. And you have a right to use the system. I'm starting to get anxious about—not in this conversation but in life—about how often we tell survivors of violence not to use the system, because it's starting to feel like another victim-blaming thing where we don't have a better resource built up yet. If every single survivor started running a community accountability process instead of using the system, we would be failing them just as badly as the system would be.

Beth: That's part of what arises for me when I think about the long term. It is going to take a long time to build up capacity and change—it's not just to change ideology; it's changing values and ways of being—in order to really hold an alternative. It took a long time to build this system as it's built, so it's going to take a long time to build the alternative.

Deana: Not only values and ideology but materially. We're using our money—material resources—for the state to do a job to help support us, and so if we're paying these taxes, then they need to show up and do the job that we're paying them to do. And the alternative is, we need to take that money and put it towards material resources that are alternatives to these oppressive systems.

Shira: I do think that there is this pendulum swinging towards victim-blaming if people access the system, but what becomes really hard is that when a lot of survivors access the system, it really becomes hard then to access anything else.

And I think there is a side of "don't call the cops under any circumstances" that is naïve, and also it's similarly disempowering, but unprivileged. And the thing about carceral feminism, if I'm feeling really generous, is that people thought that it was going to have X effect, but it's like the tentacle of an octopus. The collateral damage of one phone call to the cops can mean so many unforeseen things.

For me, it's not about telling people not to call the cops, but it's just as impossible to explain to people all of the possible outcomes of either or both choices, because right now it feels like there's only two. It can't be like, "Call the cops for this person beating your ass but not for the drugs." I wish that, as a community, we were talking more about, "What is your bottom line for calling the police?" Because I have called them and will call them again. There is this one particular situation where, after fifteen years of not calling the cops, calling them was the thing that actually did make the biggest difference. And it did result in someone going to jail. It wasn't a long sentence, but it was long enough, and it did dramatically change the pattern of violence in that family. It's like we're not good salespeople because we're not acknowledging that there's this very real truth also about the system. And so transforming the system itself instead of abolishing it becomes more appealing, because everyone knows that there's been a time in their life when it's worked. Or a time in someone's work life where it's worked, you know what I mean?

Beth: Or it worked for a minute.

Shira: Or it worked for a minute, which was long enough. For me, that then sort of snowballs into what's your line for . . . I feel like there are still three or four things in between someone calling the police for an immediate stopgap and then how people end up incarcerated for life. It is like when you thought you were going to Target for toilet paper, and five hundred dollars later you have a dehumidifier and you don't even know what it does.

Beth: Exactly. The other piece that I am thinking about around this part of our conversation is, in my classes at Stateville prison, I think every man at one point—every single one—has disclosed their use of violence toward a woman. Some of it's been really casual. Others have been these really scary, horrific stories of what they've done. They feel—especially on the issue of violence toward the women—"you don't want these brothers out on the street." Many of them think that the system works, the carceral feminism—which is what led to harsher sanctions for them—works . . . for everybody else, but not for them. It's just a tricky thing.

Rachel: It actually makes perfect sense to me, 'cause it's like they're the perfect people for community accountability processes because they are aware of how much harm they've caused, and they don't want to do that harm again. If we just for a half second left this planet, and we were on a planet without jails and cops, and we were on a planet where we could not use violence—like our arms didn't

work or there were no guns—how would we hold people accountable? What would we do?

Deana: If we could not use violence, that's huge. If we could not
use any type of violence, how do we right wrongs? How do we move
forward? What kind of world do we create?

The Longest Long Term: Colonization and Criminalization of First Nations' Land and Bodies

■ Boneta-Marie Mabo

My name is Boneta-Marie Mabo. I am a proud Piadram woman of the Meriam Lag language group of the Torres Straits and a Munbarra woman. Munbarra Country was colonized and given the name Palm Islands. I live on Yugara Country ("Country" refers to a particular area rather than Australia as a country), which is situated south of the Brisbane River in Queensland's capital, Brisbane, in a suburb called Moorooka, which means "iron bark."

It is important to state who I am, where I come from, and where I live.

It is traditional practice for First Nations people of Australia to acknowledge the traditional custodians and seek permission to enter or use resources from other countries' land and sea. It is cultural practice to acknowledge traditional custodianship of the land to pay respect to the traditional custodians, ancestors, and continuing cultural and spiritual practices of First Nations people.

Australia is the only commonwealth country colonized without a treaty or the consent of the First Nations people, so to acknowledge is also to pay respect to the fact that one is on unceded First Nations land.

First Nations people of Australia continue to resist prison, policing, and punishment in a "long-term" fight that began with colonization in 1788. Since colonization, First Nations people have experienced many different forms of punishment and criminalization—prisons, missions, child removal, and indentured servitude/labor (the whitewashed terms for slavery). The prison officers were the governors, nuns and priests, matrons, everyday white men and women, and the "protector of Aborigines" (an official state job modeled after the "protector of slaves"). Historically there's little difference between missions and prisons. We had to have permission from the protector of Aborigines to move, to travel, to work, to marry. This position controlled every aspect of First Nations people's lives.

Colonization, racism, and capitalism are ongoing processes of white control over First Nations bodies and land, and the latter is the most highly valued. Today many laws primarily affect First Nations people, including mandatory sentencing; paperless arrest laws (laws that make it possible to arrest and hold people because the police suspect they might commit a crime); imprisonment for unpaid fines, public nuisance, or "poverty" offenses (e.g., begging, drinking in public, not paying for public transport); and heavy penalties for "violence" against police. All of these charges are disproportionately used against First Nations communities, leading to the overrepresentation of First Nations people in the criminal justice and child protection systems. These laws perpetuate the "stolen generations," the forced removal of Aboriginal children from their families, and the attempted genocide of First Nations people.

First Nations women have always resisted and will always resist settler-colonialism, racism, and state violence perpetrated against our people by prisons, police, and bureaucracies. Our resistance and activism is often made invisible—white supremacy and misogyny operate to exclude our voices, priorities, and ideas from public discussion.

One of Australia's founding and still persistent myths is that First Nations people are a "dying race." We resist settler-colonial Australia by living—reminding white Australia of the ongoing sovereignty of First Nations people and practicing our culture proudly. Women have always played a strong role resisting the old and new stolen generations and fighting for the survival of our families. Teaching my daughter to grow up proud in her culture is an important way that I resist the erasure of First Nations people and identity.

I also practice activism and resistance through art to create a better world for my people. I use art to show representations of strong First Nations women and men and to critique and replace the false and harmful representations of First Nations women in popular culture and

mainstream media. I'm currently working on a project—*Submerged*—
that will involve painting and writing about strong Black women
activists. I also run the Aboriginal and Torres Strait Islander Young
Artist Group at Sisters Inside, an independent community-based organization in Queensland, as part of a decarceration strategy.

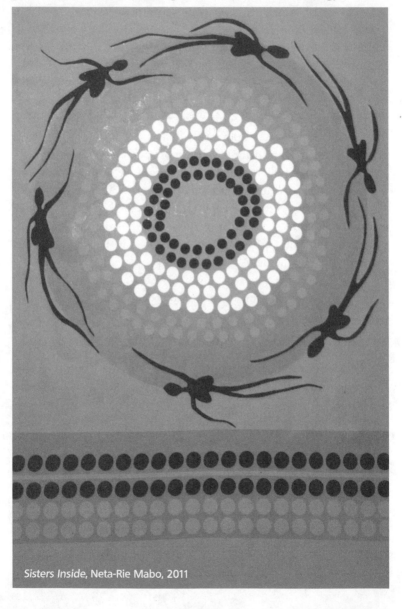

Sisters Inside, Neta-Rie Mabo, 2011

Sisters Inside advocates for the collective human rights and interests of women and children affected by the criminal injustice system. Our work is always directed by the needs and priorities of women and girls with lived experience of criminalization and imprisonment.

The image on the previous page was designed and inspired by Sisters Inside values (www.sistersinside.com.au). We exist to challenge and change racist and unjust social structures by empowering women to have control and make decisions about their own lives.

The circles in the center represent society—the unjust social structures, the privileged, capitalism, patriarchy, and racism. The women around the circles represent Sisters Inside and the women we walk with. They are positioned on the edge of the circles to represent how society marginalizes criminalized women and their children. They are going in one direction because we as an organization will always work toward decarceration and abolition.

Against Carceral Feminism

■ Victoria Law

Cherie Williams, a thirty-five-year-old African American woman in the Bronx, just wanted to protect herself from her abusive boyfriend. So she called the cops. But although New York requires police to make an arrest when responding to domestic violence calls, the officers did not leave their car. When Williams demanded their badge numbers, the police handcuffed her, drove her to a deserted parking lot, and beat her, breaking her nose and jaw and rupturing her spleen. They then left her on the ground.

"They told me if they saw me on the street, that they would kill me," Williams later testified.[1]

The year was 1999. It was a half decade after the passage of the Violence Against Women Act (VAWA), which deployed more police and introduced more punitive sentencing in an attempt to reduce domestic violence. Many of the feminists who had lobbied for the passage of VAWA—most of them white, well-heeled feminists—remained silent about Williams and countless other women whose 911 calls resulted in more violence. Their legislative accomplishment did little to stem violence against less affluent, more marginalized women like Williams.

This carceral variant of feminism continues to be the predominant form. While its adherents would likely reject the descriptor, "carceral feminism" describes an approach that sees increased policing, prosecution, and imprisonment as the primary solution to violence against women.

This stance does not acknowledge that police are often purveyors of violence and that prisons are always sites of violence. Carceral feminism ignores the ways in which race, class, gender identity, and immigration status leave certain women more vulnerable to violence and that greater criminalization often places these same women at risk of state violence.

Casting policing and prisons as the solution to domestic violence both justifies increases to police and prison budgets and diverts attention from the cuts to programs that enable survivors to escape, such as shelters, public housing, and welfare. And finally, positioning police and prisons as the principal antidote discourages seeking other responses, including community interventions and long-term organizing.

How did we get to this point? In previous decades, police frequently responded to domestic violence calls by telling the abuser to cool off, then leaving. In the 1970s and 1980s, feminist activists filed lawsuits against police departments for their lack of response. In New York, Oakland, and Connecticut at that time, lawsuits resulted in substantial changes in how the police handled domestic violence calls, including reducing their ability to not arrest.

Included in the Violent Crime Control and Law Enforcement Act, the largest crime bill in US history, VAWA was an extension of these previous efforts. The $30 billion legislation provided funding for one hundred thousand new police officers and $9.7 billion for prisons.[2] When second-wave feminists proclaimed "the personal is the political," they redefined private spheres, such as the household, as legitimate objects of political debate. But VAWA signaled that this potentially radical proposition had taken on a carceral hue.

At the same time, politicians and many others who pushed for VAWA ignored the economic limitations that prevented scores of women from leaving violent relationships. Two years later, President Bill Clinton signed "welfare reform" legislation. The Personal Responsibility and Work Opportunity and Reconciliation Act set a five-year limit on welfare, required recipients to work after two years, regardless of other circumstances, and instated a lifetime ban on welfare for those convicted of drug felonies or who had violated probation or parole. By the end of the 1990s, the number of people receiving welfare (the majority of whom were women) had fallen by 53 percent, or 6.5 million.[3] Gutting welfare stripped away an economic safety net that allowed survivors to flee abusive relationships.

Mainstream feminists have also successfully pressed for laws that require police to arrest someone after they receive a domestic violence call. By 2008 nearly half of all states had a mandatory arrest law. The statutes have also led to dual arrests, in which police hand-cuff both parties because they perceive each as assailants or they can't identify the "primary aggressor."

Women marginalized by their identities, such as those who are LGBTQ, immigrants, women of color, or even women who are perceived as loud or aggressive, often do not fit preconceived notions of abuse victims and are thus arrested.

And the threat of state violence isn't limited to physical assault. In 2012 Marissa Alexander, a Black mother in Florida, was arrested after she fired a warning shot to prevent her husband from continu-ing to attack her. Her husband left the house and called the police. She was arrested and, although he had not been injured, prosecuted for aggravated assault.

Alexander argued that her actions were justified under Flor-ida's "Stand Your Ground" law. Unlike George Zimmerman, the man who shot and killed seventeen-year-old Trayvon Martin three months earlier, Alexander was unsuccessful in using that defense. Despite her husband's sixty-six-page deposition, in which he admit-ted abusing Alexander as well as the other women with whom he had children, a jury still found her guilty.

The prosecutor then added the state's 10-20-Life sentencing en-hancement, which mandates a twenty-year sentence when a firearm is discharged. In 2013 an appellate court overturned her conviction. In response, the prosecutor has vowed to seek a sixty-year sentence during her trial this December.[4]

Alexander is not the only domestic violence survivor who's been forced to endure additional assault by the legal system. In New York State, 67 percent of women sent to prison for killing someone close to them had been abused by that person. Across the country, in Cal-ifornia, a prison study found that 93 percent of the women who had killed their significant others had been abused by them. Sixty-seven percent of those women reported that they had been attempting to protect themselves or their children.[5]

No agency is tasked with collecting data on the number of survivors imprisoned for defending themselves; thus, there are no national statistics on the frequency of this intersection between domestic violence and criminalization. What national figures do show is that the number of women in prison has increased exponentially over the past few decades.

In 1970, 5,600 women were incarcerated across the nation. In 2013, 111,300 women were in state and federal prisons and another 102,400 in local jails. (These numbers do not include trans women incarcerated in men's jails and prisons.) The majority have experienced physical and/or sexual abuse prior to arrest, often at the hands of loved ones.[6]

Carceral feminists have said little about law enforcement violence and the overwhelming number of survivors behind bars. Similarly, groups organizing against mass incarceration often fail to address violence against women, many times focusing exclusively on men in prison. But others, especially women-of-color activists, scholars, and organizers, have been speaking out.

In 2001, Critical Resistance, a prison-abolition organization, and INCITE! Women, Gneder Non-Conforming and Trans people of Color Against Violence, an antiviolence network, issued a statement assessing the effects of increased criminalization and the silence around the nexus of gender and police violence. Noting that relying on policing and prisons has discouraged the organizing of formal and informal community responses and interventions, the statement challenged communities to make connections, create strategies to combat both forms of violence, and document their efforts as examples for others seeking alternatives.[7]

Individuals and grassroots groups have taken up that challenge. In 2004 antiviolence advocate Mimi Kim founded Creative Interventions. Recognizing that alternative approaches to violence need to be demonstrated, the group developed a website to collect and publicly offer tools and resources on addressing violence in everyday life. It also developed the StoryTelling and Organizing Project, where people can share their experiences of intervening in domestic violence, family violence, and sexual abuse.

In 2008 social justice organizers and abuse survivors Ching-In Chen, Jai Dulani, and Leah Lakshmi Piepzna-Samarasinha compiled "The Revolution Starts at Home," a 111-page zine documenting various efforts in activist circles to hold abusers accountable.[8]

Piepzna-Samarasinha described how trusted friends helped devise strategies to keep her safe from a violent and abusive ex who shared many of the same political and social circles:

> When he showed up at the prison justice film screening I was attending, held in a small classroom where we would have been sitting very close to each other, friends told him he was not welcome and asked him to leave. When he called in to a local South Asian radio show doing a special program on violence against women, one of the DJs told him that she knew he had been abusive and she was not going to let him on air if he was not willing to own his own violence.
>
> My safety plan included never going to a club without a group of my girls to have my back. They would go in first and scan the club for him and stay near me. If he showed up, we checked in about what to do.[9]

In their article "Domestic Violence: Examining the Intersections of Race, Class, and Gender," feminist academics Natalie Sokoloff and Ida Dupont mention another approach taken by immigrant and refugee women in Halifax, Nova Scotia, one that tackled the economic underpinnings that prevent many from escaping abusive relationships.[10] The women, many of whom had survived not just abuse but torture, political persecution, and poverty as well, created an informal support group at a drop-in center. From there, they formed a cooperative catering business, which enabled them to offer housing assistance for those who needed it. In addition, women shared child care and emotional support.

As these examples demonstrate, strategies to stop domestic violence frequently require more than a single action. They often require a long-term commitment from friends and community to keep a person safe, as in Piepzna-Samarasinha's case. For those involved in devising alternatives, like the women in Halifax, it may require creating not only immediate safety tactics but also long-term organizing that addresses the underlying inequalities that exacerbate domestic violence.

By relying solely on a criminalized response, carceral feminism fails to address these social and economic inequities, let alone advocate for policies that ensure women are not economically dependent on abusive partners. Carceral feminism fails to address the myriad forms of violence faced by women, including police violence and mass incarceration. It fails to address factors that exacerbate abuse, such as male entitlement, economic inequality, the lack of safe and affordable housing, and the absence of other resources. Carceral feminism abets the growth of the state's worst functions while obscuring the shrinking of its best. At the same time, it conveniently ignores the antiviolence efforts and organizing by those who have always known that criminalized responses pose further threats rather than promises of safety.

The work of INCITE!, Creative Interventions, the StoryTelling and Organizing Project, and "The Revolution Starts at Home" (which sparked so much interest that it was expanded into a book) is part of a longer history of women of color resisting both domestic and state violence. These efforts show that there is an alternative to carceral solutions, that we don't have to deploy state violence in a disastrous attempt to curb domestic violence.

Circles of Grief, Circles of Healing

■ Mariame Kaba

M rs. Brown could be thirty-five or fifty-five. As she walks through the door and takes a seat at the conference room table, I see an ageless and world-weary Black woman.

Right now her face is impassive. She eyes me skeptically. After a quick round of introductions, I begin my workshop: "What comes to mind when you hear the words 'trauma' and 'separation'?" I ask the women (they are all women) in the group to write down any thoughts. "Don't analyze your responses," I tell them. Some of the women scribble on pieces of paper that I've distributed. Mrs. Brown does not. She's slouched in her chair looking down at the blank paper in front of her.

I'm nervous even though I've facilitated many workshops for different kinds of people over the years. I wonder if there will be a disruption or confrontation as the workshop progresses. After ten minutes I ask the women to share what they've jotted down about trauma and separation. A couple of women mercifully offer their ideas: trauma is pain, it's suffering; separation is lonely and is a loss. Mrs. Brown abruptly gets up and leaves the room. I think to myself, *This is definitely not going well.*

I invite the women to share the names of their incarcerated children. Oh, that's right—I forgot to say that this group is made up of mothers who have a child currently jailed at the juvenile detention center. All of the mothers are women of color, which is unsurprising since 97 percent of the children and youth in the detention center are Black or Brown. I struggle to stay focused, but I'm distracted by Mrs. Brown's absence.

"What's your child's name? And tell us the story of how/why you chose that name," I say. The moms become animated as they share their children's name stories. I'm only half listening, though, as I steal glances at the door watching for Mrs. Brown's return. Ms. Diaz catches my attention when she says, "I was in prison when Angel was born. He's my miracle, so I named him Angel." Poignant words that perfectly illuminate both a mother's love and the inter-generational cycle of incarceration.

About twenty-five minutes later, Mrs. Brown returns. Her eyes are red. There's no mistaking that she's been crying. Some of the mothers look away as if meeting her eyes will lead them to crumble too. Another mom, Ms. Gardner, I think, puts her hand on Mrs. Brown's shoulder and whispers, "We're here for you." Four decep-tively simple words that contain so much love. Mrs. Brown drops her head and takes some deep breaths. We all wait. Someone passes her a Kleenex and she furiously dabs her eyes. Ms. Jenkins breaks the interminable silence. "Is it Manny? Is he okay?"

We hold our collective breath. After what seems like an hour, Mrs. Brown finally speaks. "He tried to kill himself again last night." More silence. What is there to say? Then various voices combine—"Sorry." The words are painfully inadequate compared to the scale of hurt and harm.

Ms. Diaz interjects, "What you need right now, sis?" After what feels like another eternity, Mrs. Brown says, "I need Manny home. I need him out of here, but that's not gonna happen."

I feel helpless. I ask if they want to end the session early. A woman who hasn't spoken yet responds emphatically, "No, this is our time. It's the only time I have with people who understand what I'm going through."

I'm a guest here. I don't know these women, but they know one another. I look around and other heads nod as she speaks. I watch Mrs. Brown, who is staring at me through glassy eyes. She nods im-perceptibly. "Okay," I say. "Does anyone know what affirmations are? We're going to work on writing our own for the next few minutes."

◆

In the last decade, greater attention has been paid to incarcerated parents and to the children they leave behind. According to the Pew Charitable Trusts, more than half of the people who are incarcerated have children under the age of eighteen, including more than 120,000 mothers and 1.1 million fathers.[1]

But there are also tens of millions of invisible victims and survivors of the mass incarceration epidemic, people like Mrs. Brown, Ms. Diaz, Ms. Jenkins, and their peers. They are parents, wives, husbands, partners, siblings, cousins, and best friends of those who are locked up. Most never have the opportunity to gather together regularly to address and discuss the challenges and traumas of having incarcerated loved ones. In that respect, this group of women is privileged.

Mrs. Brown's sixteen-year-old son was in juvenile detention. For his seventeenth birthday, he'll be transferred to the adult county jail. He had been tried as an adult the previous year and found guilty. As an automatic transfer, he will be moved to county jail and then, when he turns eighteen, to prison, where he will serve the remainder of his twenty-five-year sentence. Mrs. Brown may not have her son home until he is forty-one.

Manny's trauma was top of mind for his mother. But there was no doubt that she was suffering too. Manny at least had a counselor to hear him out at the juvenile detention center, but his mother and siblings were left to fend for themselves; their grief remained unaddressed.

That evening all of us in the room watched as Mrs. Brown struggled to keep her emotions contained. She took deep breaths as she tried to keep calm. Incarceration carries an emotional cost for her and her family as well.

Collateral Damage

Years ago a friend asked me to facilitate a healing circle for the family of a young man who had been sentenced to seven years in prison. After speaking to everyone involved, it became clear that the family primarily wanted to process their grief and anger.

Many tears were shed over three and a half hours. The young man's family members and friends shared the anger that they felt toward him. They were furious that he would do something "to get himself locked up." Sobbing, his best friend raged, "He knew that they were out to get us. *He knew.* They want to put all Black men in the pen. Why help them do it?"

However, their anger was rooted in a deep sense of hurt, loss, and, most acutely, grief. The incarcerated young man was locked up far from home. It wouldn't be easy for his family members to visit, a reality that saddened everyone in the room. Being incarcerated far from family and friends increases the likelihood of disconnection. Expensive phone calls make it difficult to communicate and keep up with news about everyone's life. Letters, while very much appreciated by prisoners, can feel dated and are time-consuming to write. Everyone in the circle feared that this lack of connection would irrevocably alter the family. "How would he reintegrate once he was released? Would he come back home a 'hardened criminal'?" his mother wondered aloud. His younger sister, wringing a Kleenex in her hands, worried that prison would "take his heart."

Toward the end of the circle, we discussed how family members might constructively support both one another and the incarcerated young man through this ordeal. They decided that two people from the circle would arrange to visit him at least once a month during the first year. We made a plan for this together. We also strategized about how his younger siblings who were part of the circle could talk about their brother's incarceration. They were nine, twelve, and sixteen years old and felt ashamed that their brother was in prison. Everyone offered their ideas for how they might address their brother's plight with their friends and others. We practiced talking about what happened and encouraged them to use their own words to describe this circumstance. Brainstorming how to talk about the incarceration of their brother helped to break through their feelings of shame.

That day I learned that people who are experiencing the trauma of incarceration of their loved ones need space to vocalize their fears, hurt, anger, shame, and grief. Perhaps even more importantly, they also need opportunities to start making concrete plans to help lessen those feelings. Stories like this are frequently obscured in debates about policy, systemic change, and social justice. But these "small" stories—of individual people who are struggling daily to repair families ravaged by the plague of mass incarceration—are central to the experiences of criminalization in our communities.

Too often, though, when we do think of these people, we think of them as "collateral damage." But they are, in fact, human beings:

our neighbors, coworkers, family members. They are us. Individual relationships provide solace and support. Healing and support circles offer meaningful contact with an empathetic, understanding person. We cannot resolve our hurts alone. Within a landscape that can appear bleak and hopeless, it is important to point out that we can all still be "keepers" for one another.

Family members often say that they do the time along with their incarcerated loved ones. Families suffer both visible and hidden costs when a loved one is criminalized. A 2015 report by the Ella Baker Center and others found that criminalization and incarceration harms families emotionally, physically and financially:

> The findings show that the long-term costs extend beyond the significant sums already paid by individuals and their families for immediate and myriad legal expenses, including cost of attorney, court fees and fines, and phone and visitation charges. In fact, these costs often amount to one year's total household income for a family and can force a family into debt. Latent costs include, but are not limited to, mental health support, care for untreated physical ailments, the loss of children sent to foster care or extended family, permanent declines in income, and loss of opportunities like education and employment for both the individuals incarcerated and their family members, opportunities that could lead to a brighter future.[2]

Incarceration causes trauma and injury. Healing demands acknowledgment that incarceration leaves a wound. That societal acknowledgment is usually not forthcoming, leaving families on their own to navigate the impacts of trauma.

Mothering an Incarcerated Child

In *Twelve Years a Slave*, Solomon Northrup describes the closing moments of a New Orleans auction in 1841:

> The bargain was agreed upon, and Randall [a Negro child] must go alone. Then Eliza [his mother] ran to him; embraced him passionately; kissed him again and again; told him to remember her—all the while her tears falling in the boy's face like rain.

Freeman [the dealer] damned her, calling her a blabber-
ing, bawling wench, and ordered her to go to her place and
behave herself, and be somebody. . . . He would soon give her
something to cry about, if she was not mighty careful, and *that*
she might depend upon.

The planter from Baton Rouge, with his new purchase,
was ready to depart.

"Don't cry, mama. I will be a good boy. Don't cry," said
Randall, looking back, as they passed out of the door.

What has become of the lad, God knows. It was a mourn-
ful scene, indeed. I would have cried if I had dared.[3]

There are no photographs of Eliza. But her face is familiar. It's a
face I recognize in Mrs. Brown's. Eliza cried as her child was ripped
from her embrace and was admonished to stop "bawling" by Freeman, the slave master. Over 150 years later I watch as Mrs. Brown
tries desperately to hold back her tears. One wonders if Freeman's
threat to Eliza not to cry has carried over to the present. We ad-
monish Black women who are seen publicly grieving their dead or
disappeared children. Think of the images of Sybrina Fulton or Lu-
cia McBath, Trayvon Martin's and Jordan Davis's mothers, standing
before the cameras, stoic, pained, and tearless. Having to be "strong."

Forced separation from one's child damages mothers. Incarceration shapes people's ability to mother. Mrs. Brown was helpless to
console her son after his suicide attempt. She had only limited access
to him through restricted, supervised, non-private visits. Their interactions were monitored, and sustained contact was prohibited. In this
context, motherhood is corrupted. Outside of the workshop, many
would judge Mrs. Brown to be a "failed" mother. Having birthed a
"criminal," she is denied our empathy and instead demonized and
blamed. This is particularly true when mothers are poor and Black.

In the United States Black mothers have been and continue to
be punished and controlled in various ways. Sociologist and legal
scholar Dorothy Roberts writes brilliantly about this phenomenon
in two books and several articles. For example, "Prison, Foster Care,
and the Systemic Punishment of Black Mothers" provides a good
analysis of how the criminal legal and child welfare systems collaborate to police and control Black women's bodies and families.

Roberts writes that the systems "function together to discipline and control poor and low-income black women by keeping them under intense state supervision and blaming them for the hardships their families face as a result of societal inequities." She also points out that stereotypes about Black women as "Welfare Queens" and "Matriarchs" subject them to and reinforce punitive policies.[4]

Anecdotal and empirical evidence support Dr. Roberts's claims. Over the past few years, however, I've been considering the idea of "un-mothering" as it relates specifically to Black American women. Scholar Connie Chung has used the term "(un)mothering" in her discussion of "the politics of representation in documenting the homeless female 'other.'"[5] The concept of un-mothering that I advance focuses on the ways the state and society actively and violently threaten, remove, disappear, and kill Black women's children. Through this process, Black women become un-mothers, having (sometimes) given birth and then had their children disappeared through death, removal, or the prison-industrial complex. For women whose children are still in their care, the threat of un-mothering always looms. It's unclear what impact this might have, since the concept of un-mothering isn't explicitly articulated within our culture. Failed mothers are punished while un-mothers are often made invisible. Both are forms of violence.

Prison Is Not Feminist

The silence of contemporary feminism on matters such as these is an indictment of feminist thinkers and organizers. Mrs. Brown, a single mother working two jobs while struggling to meet the financial and emotional needs of her incarcerated son and other family members, is a member of a group that is currently unrepresented in most organizing efforts. Organizing with mothers like Mrs. Brown would illuminate the ravages of late-stage capitalism and offer opportunities for truly transformative justice. But often their voices and presence remain left out.

The imperative to build radically inclusive communities and to actually live in solidarity rather than merely to demonstrate it is urgent. We live, as scholar Beth E. Richie has termed it, in a prison ·

nation.[6] The needs of families with incarcerated loved ones must be prioritized—and not only by those struggling with prison issues. This should be a concern of a feminism focused on fighting oppression and on pursuing freedom. It should be a concern of a politics focused on the sources of people's suffering and pain. It should be a concern of a movement that posits, as Saidiya Hartman teaches us, "care as the antidote to violence."[7]

◆

That evening years ago, we wrote affirmations in a conference room inside the juvenile detention center. Mrs. Brown's face crumbled as she read hers out loud: "My son will not die in prison. He'll eventually be free."

Fund Black Futures as an Abolitionist Demand

■ Janaé E. Bonsu

B orn after the prison boom, I grew up seeing mass incarceration as a norm. The concept of abolition was once a pipe dream in my mind, but today's freedom movements taught me that it doesn't have to be.

I joined an organization of young Black freedom fighters called Black Youth Project 100 (BYP100), which emerged out of George Zimmerman's acquittal for killing Trayvon Martin. One of BYP100's first organizational efforts in Chicago was opposing legislation that would enhance penalties for weapon-related felonies, along with a campaign to fully decriminalize marijuana by eliminating police discretion to make arrests. We knew that long sentences don't work as a deterrent, they don't make people safer, and they wholly discount the humanity of people accused of these crimes. We also knew that Chicago police made more arrests for low-level marijuana possession than for any other offense—and almost 80 percent of those arrests were Black people. These arrests cost taxpayers at least $78 million and 84,000 police hours per year but weren't making the city any safer. Taken together, we recognized that systems of punishment are maintained with resources that we desperately need. The real solution lies in divesting from these systems and reallocating funds to build community infrastructure, services, and other investments that can truly make communities safer.

Through direct action and grassroots organizing, we've been calling for both *divestment* from systems that punish our people and *investment* in the things we need to survive and thrive. In October 2015 we concretized this analysis in our first major civil disobedience action at the annual International Association of Chiefs of Police (IACP) conference in Chicago. We put our bodies on the line with coconspirators to shut down all entry points to the IACP conference, proclaiming that we need to #StopTheCops to #FundBlackFutures. The #FundBlackFutures framework is grounded in the idea that if we took all the money the state spends on systems of punishment and invested it in building strong communities through a social wage (e.g., housing, jobs, health, education), we wouldn't need those institutions to be safe.

#StopTheCops to #FundBlackFutures: International Association of Chiefs of Police conference shutdown, October 24, 2015, Sarah-Ji

We're trying to do this work from several entry points, including educating ourselves about governmental budgeting processes and participatory budgeting, moving public policy to prioritize resources such as those spent on decriminalization and ending cash bail, direct action organizing, and base building. BYP100's "Agenda to Build Black Futures" captures much of what we're working toward: a living wage regardless of education or experience, worker rights for incarcerated laborers, reparations, comprehensive health care, universal child care, and ultimately the elimination of the prison-industrial complex. Abolition is the grand strategy.[1]

We must believe that we can keep one another safe in more

effective ways than police and prisons ever can. That means not only a fundamental shift in resources but also a shift in the ways we relate to each other daily. Through both divestment and seeking safety and accountability without relying on the state systems that harm us, a world without prisons and police is possible.

Meditations on Abolitionist Practices, Reformist Moments

with Rachel Herzing and Erica R. Meiners

Despite campaign promises to restore "law and order," the Trump administration might not be able to halt the momentum of prison and policing reform movements, which intensified under the Obama administration with Black communities at the forefront of these struggles. Yet over the past year, across the United States many reforms proposed by the state are far from innovative. They are instead deeply familiar—calls for more research data, police review boards, more "scientific" risk assessment tools. Other reforms reflect changing technologies and times: cops must now wear body cameras. Importantly, these proposed reforms are fully compatible with a "law and order" agenda and do not challenge the prison-industrial complex (PIC), an important target of abolitionist movements.

As people committed to building freedom through reducing harm and building responses to harm that do not rely on imprisonment, surveillance, or policing, this political moment offers an opening and a caution for abolitionist organizing. Galvanized by the changing landscape of abolition and reform, the two of us participated in a roundtable event to discuss our collective investment in creating changes that lead to increased self-determination and in movements that build community power rather than increase the size, scope, and power of the carceral state.

Our work and thinking originate from our shared investments in abolition. The Oakland-based organization Critical Resistance offers on its website a working definition of "abolition," which can be understood as encompassing global movements working to eliminate "imprisonment, policing, and surveillance and creating lasting alternatives to punishment and imprisonment."[1] As both an organizing tool as well as a goal, an abolitionist perspective challenges the "belief that caging and controlling people makes us safe" and that "basic necessities such as food, shelter, and freedom are what really make our communities secure."[2]

Our shared commitment to abolitionist liberation requires us to think beyond reform and toward the abolition of the PIC in all its forms. As such, in the dialogue that follows we are interested in a common question: *How can we move beyond reformist limitations and build strong communities that do not rely on the state violence that is inherent in systems of imprisonment and policing?* This dialogue reflects our individual work in overlapping movements in the United States: abolitionist initiatives to decrease people's reliance on imprisonment and policing, creating dialogues and practices capable of reducing sexual and gendered violence, dismantling sex offender registries and community notification laws, and building quality and accessible public education for those both inside and released from prison. This dialogue offers a discussion about how abolitionists are organizing in the US, some of the current limitations we are seeing, and some ideas about how to move forward.[3]

What are the openings for abolition in the areas in which you work, study, and resist?

Rachel Herzing: Across the US, policing reform is a hot topic right now. Everyone seems to be getting in the game: law enforcement agencies from the Department of Justice to municipal police departments, academics and think tanks, politicians, NGOs [nongovernmental organizations], and grassroots organizations. This high level of activity has opened both interesting opportunities as well as challenges for those committed to the abolition of the PIC. One challenge has been that conversations about policing are increasingly reduced to conversations about Black people being killed by the police. The United States' genocidal policies and practices against Black people are real and date back to the foundation of the nation-building project. It is also true that Black people are disproportionately policed and killed as a result of that genocidal drive.

That being said, the tendency to narrow the conversation and analysis about the violence of policing to its role in killing Black people obscures the breadth and range of the violence of policing. Additionally, it limits our abilities to bring a wide range of constituencies into the fight against the violence of policing and runs the risk of exceptionalizing instances in which people are killed by law enforcement rather than highlighting how central physical harm is to everyday policing practices. Similarly, the fanfare around reform efforts that have emerged since 2014, such as those mentioned above, have attributed all recommendations for change to a single group or handful of people, thereby reducing a long-standing, varied, and dynamic movement against the violence of policing into a single tendency. That inclination is dangerous, and those of us working on these issues need to resist that.

Don't get me wrong. There are also opportunities presented by the increased interest and agitation about policing in the US. American culture increasingly reflects this shift, from professional basketball players wearing "I Can't Breathe" shirts on the court, to fashion designers running clips of policing violence before their shows during New York Fashion Week, to prime-time television show plots revolving around resistance to policing. New laws and policy proposals have flooded state legislatures and city council chambers. Resources have flowed into the nonprofit sector ostensibly to mitigate the harms of policing in poor and communities of color. However, this interest and investment has also generated new questions. What gives us the best chance of making long-term systemic changes to policing? Will recent funding patterns encourage organizations to give up more substantial long-term gains for short-term flashier victories, such as putting more cops of color on police forces or introducing new training requirements? Will the recent burst in energy get co-opted by the state or broken up by counterinsurgency efforts under the Trump administration? Or is what has emerged in recent years representative of a new era for the movement against the violence of policing?

Erica R. Meiners: I find this both an incredible and dangerous moment for abolitionist organizing in the US. Reforms of different aspects of the PIC are being celebrated, but we must ask, what do these re-forms achieve? I will just highlight two areas where I have observed a shift: first, news articles and other often mainstream media [that are] critical of the sex offender registry are gaining some momentum, and, second, access to education for people in prison (and those formerly incarcerated) is now on the agenda of some major philanthropic and political stakeholders. Yet, closer scrutiny illustrates why these two re-forms are increasingly visible to the public. For example, many current articles on the "sex offender"—critiquing the high number of young people on the registry, including the "Romeo-Juliet" relationships that are criminalized—are in fact a recirculation of an old criminal justice trope: the system occasionally does harm to the innocent. Simultane-ously, the increased energy around access to education for people in prison—particularly by wealthy and restrictive-enrollment postsecon-dary institutions—is occurring at a moment when the wider public value of postsecondary education is under greater scrutiny.

While some prison and sentencing reform is on the table, these [suggestions] generally do not address the root causes and risks that are deepening rather than shrinking our collective material and af-fective investments in a carceral state. This moment has the potential to provide radical openings to talk about what really makes chil-dren safe from sexual violence—as a quick example, meaningful and comprehensive sexual health education and ending poverty are two clear ways to dramatically reduce child sexual violence—and to dis-cuss access to quality and free public education for all. Some days I believe that abolitionists can leverage the openings created by this political moment toward more radical ends that create more free-dom and do not leave anyone behind.

What can get us there? Perhaps it sounds too empty for some, but this reformist moment is a strong reminder of the importance of ongoing political education and collective movement assessment, which would strengthen a generalized abolitionist politic amongst our movements. We must continue to create spaces inside and outside of our movements for this work. What are some current strategies, cam-paigns, and practices that activists are participating in that strive to-ward an abolitionist future? What is the role of reform in this process?

Rachel: Thinking specifically about the abolition of policing, many of the ideas currently circulating about how to change the way policing is practiced—even from more radical elements of the movement—have closely mirrored plans that are already being discussed by law enforcement agencies at all levels of government: body cameras, independent prosecutors, or increased data collection on police stops. In some cases the proposals are reiterations of standard remedies already in play, such as civilian review or community oversight boards, improved training, or community policing. In other cases there are recommendations that seem to miss the point, such as stopping "for-profit policing" or requiring police departments to hire more people of color or more local residents.

Despite these shortsighted responses to the violence of policing, there are also many promising proposals. For example, I'm excited about Critical Resistance Oakland's Oakland Power Projects,[4] a local project to help seed community capacity building to reduce reliance on policing. I'm also excited about policy campaigns, like Youth Justice Coalition's 1 Percent Campaign,[5] which demands a shift of resources from policing to communities, as well as work by organizations such as the Malcolm X Grassroots Movement and National Day Laborer Organizing Network, both of which have developed different kinds of self-defense strategies and manuals that I think are promising.[6] All of these examples expand our ability to think creatively about alternative means of keeping ourselves and our communities safe without relying on law enforcement, regardless of whether or not the people involved understand them as abolitionist campaigns. While none of these projects immediately eliminate all aspects of the PIC, they offer affirmative incremental measures that lead us in the direction of a world free from the violence of the PIC without extending its life, scope, or legitimacy. And these are just a handful of the many promising projects out there right now.

I think using all available strategies is essential for working toward an abolitionist future. While some abolitionists take the rigid stance that working with legal or policy realms is anti-abolitionist by its very nature, I think it's possible to imagine legal strategies that increase imprisoned people's ability to fight the PIC from the inside out and chip away at prison regimes in a way that erodes them and their power. It is important to note that there have been policy wins

that have incrementally created more space for abolitionist possibilities. The campaign against the use of civil gang injunctions in
Oakland, for instance, was successful because it integrated grassroots
organizing, legal defense, policy advocacy, and cultural work. All four
aspects were balanced toward winning the demand; without legal
defense of people named, or continued pressure on local lawmakers,
the organizing strategy would have failed.

That said, neither legal nor policy remedies alone will move us
towards abolishing the PIC. Those strategies are only useful abolitionist tools when used in service of meeting organizing goals.
When legal or policy approaches begin to set the course rather than
working symbiotically with or following grassroots organizing, they
tend to entrench the PIC, even (or maybe especially) when those
approaches are aimed at reforms.

Cultural work of all sorts is also essential to fighting for abolition. Because none of us have experienced a world without the
PIC, we need help imagining what an abolitionist future could be
like. Visual art, performing arts, film, creative writing, and theater
are all vehicles that spark our imaginations and create space to ex-
periment as we work our way toward abolition. For this work to
move from theory to practice, however, it is best developed in relationship to organizing.

Erica: In Chicago, abolitionist politics continue to be challenged
by the ongoing violence of policing. Those who survive its extreme
forms—being burned by radiators, shot, suffocated, beaten—sometimes define retribution and justice within the confines of criminal
prosecution. Of course, this notion is also often held by the general
population, where solutions to the violence of policing are found in
the very laws the police are mandated to uphold. Yet, as Rachel often says, the only way to reduce the violence of policing is to reduce
contact with police. More cameras on police won't help.

I reiterate the need for ongoing political education in our movements. We have little space and time set aside for unlearning, for
admitting something didn't work, for assessing the costs of using
particular tactics, and for learning from and archiving these discussions. I think about my own work against the school-to-prison-pipeline, for instance. I supported this framework of associated

movements and tactics—including policy reforms—for a decade, because it offered a framework and important policy goals and new practices to ensure that young people and teachers were not feeding the PIC. Slowly, however, the tools and language developed by communities, teachers, and young people were co-opted by the criminal justice system itself. Simultaneously, the work to ensure that young people were not criminalized in schools began to operate in isolation of broader anti-PIC and abolitionist projects. For example, the rationale for organizing in schools only concerned youth rather than targeting the broader structural issues of surveillance, policing, and the PIC itself. In other words, the rationale for removing police from schools was because young people did not deserve to be policed. But what about their parents? Or when they turn eighteen years old?

From this and other experiences, where and when possible, I always try to ask questions I have learned from others, such as:

1. Who benefits from this campaign, initiative, reform, form of resistance? Who doesn't, and why?
2. What are the logics, languages, and "commonsense" discourses that initiatives validate and/or reinforce? Are these logics liberatory or punitive?
3. Who is working on this initiative? Who is not? Why us? Why now?
4. Is this something that we, or others, will be organizing to undo in five years because it is used to cage or dehumanize people?

For example, when "family reunification" emerges in migrant justice discussions, queer challenges to the traditional family model supported by the state make visible the heteronormative logics that anchor these campaigns. When children, students, or mothers are elevated as more deserving of justice (less harsh sentences or conditions of incarceration) than those categorized as "sex offenders" or "violent criminals," questions arise about how these categories function as proxies for innocence or guilt. For me, a crucial part of developing an abolition politics is a commitment to identifying and critiquing the wider PIC, and its ties to white supremacy, while working on a specific campaign or a project.

What are some of the pitfalls and limitations you have observed in abolitionist organizing? How can we effectively organize beyond reform and toward abolition?

Erica: I think fragmentation—by which I mean focusing on one issue at a time, in isolation of its connections to broader systems of domination—is a major challenge. I borrow a comrade's analogy of playing the "whack-a-mole" game to describe the crisis-mode organizing we are often in: working to stop a new prison construction, to defeat a bad law, to support an individual, raise money for bail, stop an execution, show up at court. We are forced to engage with a specific manifestation of the PIC in the immediate present and often do not have the time to interrogate the conditions, contexts, or histories that produce individual crises we seek to respond to. Of course, we can't take on all of its manifestations at once, but do we have an analysis of the wider context? And beyond dismantling the PIC, how can we build movements that are more than reactive? What helps us to imagine and build understandings of community and safety beyond borders and surveillance?

For example, I think about my collaborative work in building access to educational programs for people in prison. How can our goal be to create excellent education programs in a prison when there is shrinking access to quality public postsecondary education and skyrocketing student debt across the country? Who wants a future where the only free quality public education in the US is available for people in prison? Building an abolitionist analysis into the creation of education programs in prison pushes for these linkages and creates new sites of organizing and new coalitional possibilities.

The current reformist logic concentrates on "chiseling away" at the PIC, either to save those deemed worthy or with the belief that chiseling over time will dismantle the system altogether. If our abolitionist practice does not consider the underlying structures that make immigration detention, policing, mass incarceration, and other manifestations of the PIC possible, then we not only keep moving from "mole to mole" without a defined political direction, but we also normalize the system itself.

Rachel: I agree with Erica that considering only one aspect of the PIC at a time makes us more vulnerable in ways that can hurt our overall ability to gain or create the kinds of things that ultimately help us live more healthy, self-determined lives. If, for instance, one only thinks about imprisonment without considering how patterns of arrest or sentencing impact how and why people wind up in cages, then their work to improve conditions of confinement or decrease the current prison population can easily be sidestepped or undone by the system. It could similarly create new penalties or sentencing practices that might drive even more people into imprisonment than another's efforts could release.

What I'm suggesting is that we be responsible to educate ourselves about how other aspects of the PIC impact our work and that we be in conversation with people focusing in other areas. My interest in preventing the violence of policing requires, for instance, that I pay attention to who is being imprisoned and on what grounds. I benefit from paying attention to trends in sentencing (both efforts to lock more people up and to let more people out) and to changing patterns in probation and parole. I think it's important to pay attention to who is being targeted for surveillance through what means and under what justification. Having our independent efforts coalesce into a larger effort also helps prevent our work from being atomized, isolated, and easily picked off. Especially for people fighting for abolition, staying strongly connected to a broader movement prevents us from being isolated as fringe, extreme, or irrelevant.

Erica: In addition to fragmented organizing, another pitfall is the invocation of concepts and language that deepen divides. One of the principles I learned, which was reinforced by Critical Resistance, is to not use the state's binary and essentializing language: "violent offender," "recidivism," "criminal," "at risk." These terms don't help us understand the complexity of harm and make it almost impossible to imagine and build transformative practices of community accountability.

Whenever I go to court to observe or to support someone, I am struck by what is rendered impossible to say or do. The law inscribes oversimplified binaries, and once we enter that system, it is nearly impossible to escape legal categories of guilt and innocence, perpetrator and victim, and so forth, and yet we know, from our loved ones and families, that these categories are inadequate. People who commit harm also experience harm, and the people we love are never defined by the worst thing they have ever done.

Even in the so-called worst of the worst situations, existing research demonstrates that some people who perpetrate sexual harm often have themselves experienced sexual harm. In other words, people classified as "perpetrators" are also often "victims." Research also tells us that our criminal legal system often does not offer a resolution for those who have experienced sexual harm. In fact, it is often re-traumatizing and ultimately does not act in the survivor's interests. Yet these are the scripts and there is very little space for nuance and complexity.

Ten Strategies for Cultivating Community Accountability

■ Ann Russo

M y commitment to prison abolition grows daily in part because I see the possibilities for responding to abuse and violence without relying on punishment, shame, and more violence. The possibilities lie in building communities where community members—be they friends, family members, coworkers, or neighbors—rely on one another to heal, to intervene, to take accountability, and to transform abuse and violence. That's the essence of community accountability as envisioned by INCITE! Women, Gender Non-Conforming, and Trans people of Color Against Violence and by Creative Interventions.

Community accountability can create communal support for those who are affected and/or collectively interrupting, challenging, stopping, and shifting abusive behavior and the underlying systems that support it. The key is working collectively in community rather than relying on external authorities and systems of oppression. It is not a formulaic set of responses but grows organically in relation to the specific people and relationships involved. And like transformative justice, it seeks to address the underlying power systems that ultimately form the root causes of violence.

I work with the Building Communities, Ending Violence project based at DePaul University. We create spaces to build skills and expand our imaginations for community accountability and transformative justice. We engage in peace circles to build community, share stories of resilience and resistance, and create support and accountability. We create strategy sessions to brainstorm, imagine, and practice communal responses to everyday violations. And we

use creative arts for communal healing and transformation. Here
are ten strategies we use to build skills and capacity for community
accountability:

1. **Shift from "What can *I* do?" to "What can *we* do?"** When faced
with abuse or violence, people often are not sure what to do. Instead of feeling the burden of responding solely on your own, gather
with others connected to the situation—family members, friends,
neighbors, coworkers, peers, and so on. Recognize that each of us is
impacted by the abuse/violence whether we are directly involved or
not and that collectively our experience, knowledge, and skills could
shift the situation. Together we can commiserate, analyze, strategize,
and take action.

With a "we," energy shifts and possibilities multiply—more
support, ideas, and capacity. Each person has a unique role to play to
shift any situation; some might be in a good position to support the
person harmed, whereas others might be in a better position to cultivate accountability with the person causing the harm. Some might
have material resources to offer, others might organize community
support, and still others might offer perspectives on the underlying
roots of the violence. With more people, any situation can shift toward healing, accountability, and transformation.

2. **Strengthen communication skills**. I've been in many groups that
have fallen apart over conflicts connected to abuse and violence. We
often did not have the skills to address the problems nor shift the
dynamics. And because the problems were not addressed from the
beginning, they deepened. Fear of conflict prevents intervention—
we talk ourselves out of it, rationalize it, and decide to ignore it.

Making a commitment with people in our families, peer groups,
and organizations to practice direct communication about everyday
conflicts can create a solid ground for addressing more egregious behavior. Being open, honest, and direct about how we experience and
witness one another's behavior can prevent the escalation of abusive
power relations and can create more just relationships within our
communities.

3. **Practice collective support.** Rather than think about support as
something you individually provide to someone else, think about it

as something that is collectively created. Build a supportive community by gathering in circles to share stories, struggles, resources, and strategies for resistance and resilience.

The Building Communities project shifted the format of Take Back the Night at DePaul from a "speak-out" to support circles a few years ago. Rather than individuals speaking in front of audiences, people gathered in small circles to share stories of trauma, resilience, resistance, and self-care. All had a chance to tell our stories, whether we identified as someone who had experienced violence, witnessed it, or been impacted by it. At the end of the event, rather than feeling the collective trauma of one another's stories, participants left feeling like part of a supportive community that each of us could contribute to and be hopeful about the possibilities for support, change, and transformation.

4. Share relationship experiences and resources. Create intentional spaces to share the ins and outs of relationships. When we invest in one another's relationships, we are inclined to take accountability for support and intervention when problems arise. The potential for someone to isolate someone else for abuse becomes much more unlikely in such a community.

A few years ago, when a friend was struggling in an abusive relationship, a group of friends gathered to support her and one another. We realized that the abusive treatment of our friend had affected our relationship with her and with each other. Rather than trying to get her to leave or stay, or to label her relationship as "abusive," which she was reluctant to do, we created a collective space for connection and support. Using a circle process, we shared our own stories of relationships, those that felt more beautiful and loving as well as those that included emotional, physical, or sexual violence. No one became the expert or judge of her or anyone else. Instead of giving lectures and advice, we told stories and commiserated. As a result, our friend talked about her relationship and her hopes for the future without the pressure of feeling forced into a decision. Instead of becoming more isolated and separate, our friendships deepened in response to the situation. And we agreed that whatever the future held, we would be in it together, not alone.

5. Build a shared vocabulary. Create spaces to build a shared language on what positive, loving, and caring relationships look and feel like as well as those that include mistreatment, abuse, and violence. Often the terms we use—"domestic violence," "rape," "stalking"— call up legalistic definitions that require definitive lines of demarcation. They make it hard to talk about the everyday messy ways that mistreatment and abuse live out in our minds, bodies, and hearts.

Creating a shared vocabulary can shift us from debating whether an experience is "bad enough" to constitute abuse, for example, to being able to address negative behaviors without having to fit into the state's definition. As a result, we don't wait until a situation escalates to a more threatening level before addressing it. For instance, there are times when rather than using the term "domestic violence," my friends name dynamics of possessiveness, jealousy, manipulation, and isolation as worth addressing early on in relationships.

6. Practice taking accountability. If taking accountability for harm became a daily practice, rather than solely something that we demand of others in egregious situations, then taking accountability would be less fraught with guilt, shame, defensiveness, punishment, and retaliation. It would create more compassion for one another when we make mistakes, when we speak and act in harmful and oppressive ways (intentionally or unintentionally), or when we contribute to harm in some way. And it would make it easier to admit wrongdoing.

When I have hurt my friends or loved ones, I too have suffered and felt isolated. It helps immensely to have a space to talk with others to gain understanding and to figure out ways to make things right. There are few spaces to talk about the harms we've caused and the systems of oppression in which we've been complicit. Mostly it seems that when confronted, we try to prove that we are not responsible—to prove our "innocence." Or we try to blame others or claim that we are the real victims. Making it a practice of taking accountability and creating a supportive space where we can talk about our actions or complicity would go a long way toward creating more justice in our everyday interactions.

7. Create space to create concrete accountability steps. In this society, accountability is often synonymous with punishment, shame, or retaliatory harm. What if it became synonymous with taking responsibility for harm, making things right, and being willing to understand, change, and transform the harmful behavior and its underlying motivations? What would accountability look and feel like then?

It's a great practice to gather together to brainstorm concrete action steps we might imagine for taking accountability for harm. In the strategy sessions of Building Communities, some common accountability action steps for abuse in intimate relationships are taking responsibility for the destructive and painful impact of abuse, stopping the behavior, respecting the wants and needs of the person being hurt (including separation, ending the relationship, request for no contact, etc.), getting support to address underlying issues (for example, mental health or substance abuse issues), learning about abusive behavior and its impact, and being willing to check in with community members about accountability steps. And through role-plays we practice what it might look like for friends or family to communicate these action steps to one another. This builds our skills and capacity for building accountability into our relationships.

8. Practice everyday interventions. When we witness small- and large-scale violations, our core reactions may be to fight back, to flee the scene, or to freeze and feel immobilized. All of us have stories of when we have regretted our core reaction to witnessing abuse or violence. We may have overlooked it, minimized it, felt helpless in the face of it, or responded aggressively and made the situation worse.

Shifting our core reactions requires skills and practice. Building Communities creates spaces to share stories of small-scale violations where we wanted to respond differently and where we then collectively imagine and practice alternative responses. Role-playing these responses builds skills and expands our capacity for interrupting, disrupting, or responding to violence. A couple of years ago, after participating in Building Communities, Ending Violence, a student intervened in an evolving bar fight. After experiencing an initial reaction to flee, he decided to get a few of his friends to help him, and they de-escalated the fight by diverting people's attention away from one another toward addressing something on the television screen. This distraction shifted the energy within the group and the fight ended.

9. Create collective analysis and action on the roots of violence. Often we respond to oppressive behavior as if it's located within the individual rather than being linked to broader systems.

Understanding the social roots of violence makes us aware that the problem is larger than any individual and that we are all implicated in the structures that cause the problems. This provides us with the ability and responsibility to work toward transforming the roots.

For example, when a friend was being harassed and stalked by an ex-partner who had been emotionally and verbally abusive, a group of us discussed the roots of his behavior and the obstacles to intervention. We recognized that many people may view the ex-partner's behavior as a private personal problem, even common to heterosexual relationships, because these relationships are structured by patriarchy and capitalism. We also agreed that many people may not recognize such behavior as immediately threatening, because there was no physical violence, and so they may minimize the risks. Steps to dismantling these roots might include making our intimate relationships open to communal conversation (e.g., Far Out), building critical consciousness about the impact of sexism and misogyny on relationship dynamics, and expanding our understanding of the violence of emotional and verbal abuse.

10. **Practice, practice, practice.** To me the possibilities for cultivating accountability within our communities are endless, but what it really takes is building skills through practice. With practice, we are more prepared with ideas for intervention. Most importantly, an emphasis on practice reminds us that a situation may not always turn out the way we expect; it will more than likely be messy, and there's no one answer. Yet it's through the experience of trying out our ideas that we learn what's possible.

Section 4

Building Resistance for the Long Term

I n 1977 in the Washington State Penitentiary in Walla Walla—a prison for those the state considered men—incarcerated members of the George Jackson Brigade organized a group, Men Against Sexism, to end sexual assault and to challenge homophobia in the prison. With tactics borrowed from ongoing feminist antiviolence movements, and by forming alliances with outside and local anti-prison LGBTQ organizations and the Seattle chapter of the American Friends Service Committee, they created "safe cells" in the prison, interrupted and protested homophobic religious services and prison personnel, created and circulated a prison newsletter (*The Lady Finger*), and coordinated and trained people in "militant" self-defense.

Several years later, the Lesbian Avengers, a group of early 1990s direct-action antiviolence activists originally based in New York City, showed up in teams, sporting T-shirts with their logo of a lit bomb and the "We Recruit" slogan, to publicly confront men who harmed women. Avengers arrived unannounced at the worksites of specific men, with noisemakers and chants, to out them as rapists, child abusers, sexual harassers, and homophobes. The Avengers— which at its peak had fifty-five chapters—staged actions against the inherent racism and homophobia of policing; supported release campaigns for women imprisoned for defending themselves against abusive partners or husbands; and built some of the earliest online tools, like the Unbash Map Project, to circulate the names and locations of men who harm women.

Over the last year alone, in our own backyard of Chicago, hundreds of thousands have flooded the streets to challenge the violence of policing in Black and Latinx communities; the causally endemic xenophobia, racism, and sexism of the current federal administration; and more. Groups have emerged—such as the Chicago Community Bond Fund and #nocopacademy—to demand what was almost unthinkable five years ago: a call for the end to the money bail system and to fight the establishment of the proposed $95 million police training academy (at a moment when public schools are closing and teachers are being laid off).

Men Against Sexism, Lesbian Avengers, #nocopacademy—in hard spaces, against formidable odds, people coalesce, creatively organize with the tools at hand, and imagine and demand what might appear unimaginable, impossible.

We invoke these organizations, a sliver of the many, to situate this section on building resistance and to claim our lineage. Mobilizations against long-term sentences, we argue, must be tethered to this radical history of everyday people organizing for freedom—inside and outside the prison. Our work is not only to challenge the inhumanity of caging people indefinitely but also to imagine, demand, and build more loving and free communities.

Calls for the radical redistribution of power and resources are not without risk. When those marked as less than fully human challenge the repressive status quo, they become direct and open targets: Michael Brown, shot dead by police in the streets of Ferguson. Assata Shakur, hunted with a bounty on her head. COINTELPRO.

Flawed and partial, accompanied by staggering losses, and almost always erased or gentrified in the historical record, resistance is ever present.

By Any Means Necessary
Reflections on Malcolm X's Birthday—What If What's Necessary Is Awe-Inspiring, Unconditional, Militant Love?

■ adrienne maree brown

> *We declare our right on this Earth to be a man, to be a human being, to be respected as a human being, to be given the rights of a human being in this society, on this Earth, in this day, which we intend to bring into existence by any means necessary.*
>
> —Malcolm X, 1965

Today I am reflecting on the meaning of "by any means necessary." Yesterday was Malcolm X's birthday, and I think of his voice saying those words. At the time he said it, I believe he meant it as it is commonly understood: that Black people must be prepared to take up arms, if that is necessary, to defend our communities and liberate ourselves from the weight of white supremacy.

For me, the meaning has evolved as I experience more and more of this world and its layers of oppression. There is a plethora of internal and external dangers to the soul; it is so hard to keep your integrity intact—especially if you long for change—if the current world disappoints you or makes you furious.

I feel like it has become easy for us to occupy our rage without moving into action. It has become easy for us to get angry and self-righteous without really asking what is needed in that moment.

What if what's needed isn't sexy, intimidating, or violent? What if what is needed is forgiveness? The kind of forgiveness that seems unimaginable, miraculous, holy, unattainable—like forgiving those who hurt you and hate you, like building relationships with those who kill your children? What if what is necessary is trusting people beyond their mistakes and shortcomings, trusting their best intentions? Are we strong enough to default to trust at a community level?

What if what is necessary is learning to see family where you have seen enemies? What if what is necessary is not strategy, not plans, not dollars—just unconditional love? Are we able to be that militant? I want to be militant enough to admit I am changing and growing and don't know the answers.

My sister is about to have her second child, which has me contemplating and researching birth and labor again. After the shooting of seven-year old Aiyana Stanley-Jones by Detroit police last week,[1] I was thinking of how quickly you can violently kill someone versus how long it takes to create and birth someone. I find a small but awe-inspiring hope in the realization that giving life and love is harder work than taking it. Giving life and love and forgiveness and creating family—those are the behaviors to engage in to step into the miraculous.

As we strive to free ourselves, to uplift ourselves, to transform ourselves and our communities, let us consider what "by any means necessary" looks like in practice for us now—especially if the outcome is unknown, immeasurable, and unconditional; even if the means, at this moment, is militant love.

Loving Inward
The Importance of Intimacy

■ Jermond "JFresh" Davis

What does it mean to be intimate? Most folks think intimacy is limited to sexual relationships. However, once you become intimate with yourself, you experience your relationships anew. A long-term intimacy with oneself is a dedication to long-term growth.

Being inside this time helped me realize I was neglecting myself: I did not value my existence. If I had a more intimate relationship with myself, I would never have been riding in a car with a gun for protection. I would not have been living in fear, relying on a weapon for protection. I was driven by fear.

My relationships with loved ones have suffered as I've sat in a foreign land while fighting for my freedom. I've saved my life in here, but I've also taken myself away from my children and their mother. My kids are affected by the absence of my intimacy. The mother of my kids now has to pick up my slack, and more pressure is placed on the grandparents. When the mother of my kids decides to move on to the next lover, and my infants' call another person "Daddy," I blame my absence.

I wonder: if all of us inside these prison walls had embraced intimacy by practicing self-love, would we be caught within this slaughter? It was our failure to do so that resulted in our being locked up.

Somewhere I neglected intimacy, and inside these walls intimacy is placed even further on the back burner. Everything around this place is hardened; intimacy becomes a sign of weakness. But most of us are victims who victimize others instead of tending to our wounds. In order to genuinely heal, we must embrace ourselves and one another. This is how we stop the cycle.

Intimacy must be continuously prioritized for the long term. It must be the platform of our understanding of ourselves. We must develop a practice of being intimate with ourselves, loving more, finding more value, understanding more, growing and shedding more, feeling more and pushing less. When we unconsciously neglect our best selves, we fall into a pattern that eventually builds unwanted forces. But when we are intimate with ourselves, accepting our infinite complexities, the possibilities become endless. I am talking about healing ourselves: coming out of a colonial/slave mentality by loving ourselves and ending modern-day slavery. Being intimate with myself so I can create more safe spaces is a means to independence. When you become intimate with you, you are resilient, powerful, and full of love.

"Making the We as Big as Possible"
An Interview with Damon Williams

■ Alice Kim

Damon Williams is codirector of the #LetUsBreathe Collective. Alice Kim met with Damon at the collective's new Breathing Room space, a Black-led liberation headquarters for arts, organizing, and healing on Chicago's South Side. She spoke with him about his evolution as an activist, the forty-one-day occupation of Freedom Square, and the work of the #LetUsBreathe Collective.

Alice Kim: *Can you talk about how you became involved in the Black Lives Matter movement and organizing against police violence?*

Damon Williams: Some of the roots of wanting to be an active change agent go back to when I was little. In the mid-nineties my mother and her girlfriends started an investment club, because they were lower- to mid-level professionals, mostly clerks or secretaries or HR-type jobs, maybe a lawyer or two. They'd all found themselves really financially illiterate. My mother had been working almost two jobs consistently since she was fifteen; she was twenty-nine when I was born. She had me and my sister and realized that she had nothing to show for all of this labor. A coworker gave her financial magazines, *Better Investing* and *Black Enterprise*, and told her to read them every month. And she started just absorbing this knowledge in terms of concepts of economics and finance. One of the magazines recommended starting a collective, like a capitalist co-op, and so that's what she did. I was at the kitchen table, starting to get a lot of knowledge and financial literacy from age five. In '99 my mother started a youth investment club, which was a different structure and more individualized and more about the education than actual dollars and cents—teaching kids about the stock market mostly and investing in assets and generational wealth,

217

entrepreneurship, cooperative economics. I became a co-teacher with her.

Alice: *And you're still doing that with your mom?*

Damon: Yeah. It's something that's hard to do consistently, and I feel a lot of turmoil and contradiction. I used to wear suits when I was little. A young Black boy from the South Side, talking about delayed gratification and stocks. It was a thing that would get on the news. The way that it was distributed and marketed—kind of like I was a poster child for neoliberal capitalism—is something that I had to critique later as an adult.

Alice: *When did you start critiquing that capitalism? How did you go from there to here?*

Damon: I was in high school during the Obama election, and I started to come into some liberal politics, you know. Or let's say progressive, at least. I went to a private school from fourth to twelfth grades, so they knew me and they knew this story about me investing into big business. And a social studies teacher just asked me, not in a challenging way, "How do you deal with the fact that you are such a liberal?" She pointed out that those things were in contradiction. Outside of school, I started to look and find stuff on YouTube and watching speeches or old clips or the *Black Power Mixtape*. I grew up at an all-Black private school, an independent school, but very much like Martin Luther King–esque. And I learned a lot of Black history, but it wasn't about resistance and radical movements; it was more about inventors—that kind of history. But then I was starting to get deeper into my hip-hop poetics and rapping. When I first heard Kendrick Lamar, that brought something out of me. He had this song called "High Power," where he was referencing Huey Newton and Bobby Seale, and I knew the names and I knew those were people that should be icons to me. I knew about Fred Hampton and I knew the Black Panthers existed, but I couldn't tell you the distinction between who was Eldridge Cleaver, who is Stokely Carmichael. But I knew that these are all my people.

Alice: *So you learned through self-education, really.*

Damon: That's how it started. And when I was in college, there was no core requirements, so I was able to shape my entire four-year curriculum. My general question was, "Why do the south and north sides of Chicago look so different?" I followed that question, no matter what class I was in, and my studies led me to learn about institutional racism and the lineage of Black liberation movements and resistance movements in America. I realized that my heroes were anticapitalists. For my freshman tutorial, which is the only required class of all four years, you have to take the tutorial and it could be about anything. Mine was about feminism and neo soul women. And so I'm learning about Jill Scott, Erykah Badu from the trajectory of the jazz and blues tradition. But the first thing we did before we even got to [any] music was listen to an Angela Davis speech. This was first-term Obama; this was the fall of 2010. So, without being harsh about it, she's trying to encourage us to be critical in that moment when we were so intoxicated with hope. The point that she made and said very clearly is "you cannot be antiracist without being feminist," and just the matter-of-fact, very logical way I heard that, there was no resistance in my body to the truth of it.

Kristiana [Colón] is my big sister, but we weren't political partners growing up. That wasn't the nature of our relationship at all. I saw her plays, and we definitely had in-depth conversations, but we weren't talking explicitly about feminism. But I was receptive, and so that moment and then self-education really got me to figuring out statistical understandings of why Black people are at the bottom in the histories and also the social formations that are connected to that. As I'm learning about housing segregation, I'm learning about really how white supremacy has hoarded and then passed on wealth through inheritance and, like, has exponentially grown the profits of slavery and colonial conquest and then redlining. At the same time, I was becoming an artist and being around the YCA [Young Chicago Authors] and having a community of folks; we were kind of all about that shit. All of this was happening through college. My sophomore year, me and Kristiana developed a hip-hop poetics duo, April Fools, making songs and videos and producing a lot of events. I'm nineteen, and she's probably like twenty-five, twenty-six, and she had been establishing herself not only as a poet but really coming into her own as a playwright and being part of a theater company. From her leadership and through our partnership, I was learning how to shape and create space and make events that were really successful.

Alice: *And so you graduated in 2014, and in fall of 2014 Ferguson happened.*

Damon: Exactly right. My final paper in May of that year was this research project on the Black Power movement and the theoretical contradictions in learning about revolution in a canonized, theoretical way. That then led to the show *Lack on Lack* [Damon and Kristiana's one-act play] and our central claim—even if we couldn't fully articulate it through the show—was that these violent systems of dominance tied into capitalism have this assumption of scarcity. Scarcity is needed for markets to operate and for there to be profit, and that scarcity is not actually true to our reality. There is not a shortage of food in the world; there's not a shortage of water in the world—it's the distribution. There is an abundance of resources and love, which you can also call labor, and it is something that actually brings value to not only goods but to human interaction. Through love and through cooperation with the actual physical resources we have, we see that there is an abundance; if we extrapolate, we make the *we* as big as possible. We had a great reading that July, and then Mike Brown died in August—August 9th.

Within four or five days of stories on Twitter about teargassing and the repression and violence that the protesters were experiencing so close, Kristiana felt this fervor to actually respond and put together the Let Us Breathe initiative. I wasn't like, "Oh, yeah, like Ferguson, let's go do it," but then I saw the response to what we were organizing—we started a GoFundMe campaign that I thought was gonna be like a small thing so that our can wouldn't be empty, and then it ended up getting ten thousand dollars in a few days. With that responsibility and those resources, it pushed things forward. I thought, *If nothing else, I can be the driver.* But then it became just figuring out how to navigate the space, how to be appropriate stewards of the resources, and how to humbly support and to engage in relationships with the people whose fight this is—whose home and whose community this is—without stirring things up or making it about us. We thought it was just gonna be a weekend. I didn't go down there like, "Oh, no, I'm organizer." I didn't even really know that language yet. But through that experience, we partnered with the Lost Voices, a group of young people who ended up camping out on the main thoroughfare, where protests were allowed for fifty-two days. That was the transformation. Meeting them and seeing that it wasn't what I was used to—it wasn't the college kids doing it for the résumé, it wasn't church folks, it wasn't [Al] Sharpton, it wasn't a bunch of post-Occupy granola-crunchin' backpackers, right? It was Crips and Bloods and it felt like home. It felt like the change that I wanna have on my city. It felt like that same family; that same dynamic was happening.

Alice: *How would you describe the evolution of Let Us Breathe from that initial initiative to where you are now?*

Damon: Our first protest—the first time we brought them [Lost Voices] up here—was Columbus Day, so it was around October 13th of 2014, only two months after Mike Brown was killed. We did a march that went to the Columbus statue and then went in at the end of the Columbus parade downtown, and then the next thing that we did was much bigger.

We partnered with BYP [Black Youth Project 100] on Black Friday that same year. We called for a boycott on the Mag [Magnificent] Mile and renamed it "Brown Friday," trying to connect capitalist spending and consumerism to the death of Mike Brown into police violence into the prison-industrial complex. We marched on Mag Mile, and it was a really long march too, from Mag Mile to Wicker Park to the Walmart on the West Side. Five, six miles. A six- or seven-hour day. But you know, at one point we had a thousand people, but hundreds stayed throughout the whole thing. That really changed us, and we started doing more things like that—showing up to the VLA [Village Leadership Academy] joint that went to the juvenile detention center and every week being a part of some type of action. And so we then kind of start to figure out our niche of not just being artists, and not just being rhythmic and artistic while we're protesting, but actually having our direct actions be almost artistic performances as well.

Alice: *How do you consciously do the work of organizing around one issue and then make connections to other issues? I'm thinking about Freedom Square, which wasn't solely about having an occupation and protesting Homan Square [a Chicago police "black site" interrogation facility], or police violence, or Blue Lives Matter; it became—as you describe it on the Let Us Breathe website—"a laboratory in the politics of abolition." And so the occupation itself went beyond direct action.*

Damon: I can go back into the story of the transition from doing antagonist disruption to more community centered, love-based disruption, which is not to shut down your traffic, which is not to chant the chants that we're angry about, but let's have a barbecue. But instead of it just being a barbecue where it's kind of just us, let's put this on wheels and have our sound system not be for chants but for traditional cookout dance music, Frankie Beverly days, like the "Cha-Cha Slide" and stuff. And then give out food. And make space for the arts by having a traveling open mic, so your corner can be then a stage and we're bringing the audience to you. We'll perform, and anybody who is here can sign up and perform.

Alice: *How was that received?*

Damon: It was really beautiful, and I think that is how we started being able to do the Breathing Room series, and Freedom Square came from those actions. Because the goal really was first around [Chicago Police Detective] Dante Servin, right? So it was about getting those petitions signed.

And we're just realizing some of the contradictions: this happened in a park where people know her [Rekia Boyd, who was shot and killed by Servin] or knew about it, or maybe did not, which is just as sad almost. And there had been little to no engagement of the actual neighborhood where it happened. And some of that is just about capacity, but some of that is some things we really have to wrestle with in terms of our positionality as movement builders. There are real reasons, real fears, real limitations, real insecurities, real internalizations of class privilege that allow us to not be in direct communication with the people most impacted by systems of police violence and incarceration.

To be able to do it in a way that felt impactful was where our model came from, to be more inward facing. So it's not like, "We need not to stop talking about the cops and take care of us," but more like, "No, we need to be taking care of us through talking about the cops." And then things just start happening organically. We started getting food donations and then having the [food] wagons, and now we're adding the service of giving out resources on top of just political information cards or petitions. And then it was like, "Okay, we're passing out food, but we're walking past all this other garbage. We need to have garbage bags to clean it up." We didn't come and say, "Oh, we gonna come and do a community service day." But we got a hundred people with us, and gloves and bags for the garbage, and just symbolically what cleaning up then does to a community. "What you all doing?" And the answer is not "come to our church" or "come to our cookout." The answer is "We're here about getting rid of the police. We're here about this young woman." But also, "We wanna abolish this system." Some of the criticism of the first year was that all these kids are doing is yelling. "What are they doing? What are they doing? They're just yellin' and mad." But it's like, "No. We're talking to our people." And so that model basically led into the Breathing Room series, which was a way to create space in a new way.

Alice: *So you essentially took the principles of the Breathing Room to Freedom Square?*

Damon: Right. Freedom Square came about organically, because the first thing—the first real commitment—was a one-day action collaboration with BYP. I was a member of BYP, which is also part of this story that's really important. BYP was where I learned what organizing is, and how structure and consistent coordinated processes are needed to build an organization. BYP was the foundation for all of us in real ways, through high-risk actions when we were able to propel the city over the last couple of years. Becoming a member and then becoming the cochair in 2016 put me in an interesting position. We were in active conversation, recognizing we can't keep protesting city hall and downtown, and the only people around us are photographers from the [Chicago] *Tribune* and the cops.

We also want to be more engaged with our people, and this building of Homan Square had not been addressed by, like, a Black-led resistance at this point. So we're doing that in coordination with a national movement, which was a lot of response to the uptick in action after Philando Castile and Alton Sterling's deaths. The goal for the day was to engage the community. Freedom Square was the lot across the street from Homan Square, and so we're gonna do our thing in that lot, passing out books, open mic, food, some political education workshops, six to seven tents which were symbolic workstations to engage people on the things that we want instead of this building.

Alice: *And the initial idea was to engage the community for a day?*

Damon: Yeah. The only thing we committed to do was to do a block party. And as a way to then take the pressure off people when the arrest warrants come, once they said, "We're gonna arrest people in the street," well, then, we can come to this lot and still be present and still continue to gather and engage. Members of Lost Voices were in town for the first weekend, so there was just, like, some real kindred connection supporting this. And as we're playing with the idea of tents, a few people internally said, "I'll come in, I think it's a cool idea, I wanna do it," but really it was two young girls from the block who saw we had tents and really wanted to talk about it. They'd been having so much fun and was singing on the microphone and just playing, and it was them who said, "Ya'll comin' back? Ya'll stayin'? Can I stay with ya'll?" And we were like, "Yeah, okay. We can't do it right now, but we'll come back in two days and do another block party, and if we can, we might be able to stay." And then we thought we were gonna get kicked off the lot within a day to four days, and we thought we were just gonna be holding down the space, right? We didn't know that so many artists would come and help make the space beautiful.

Alice: *Freedom Square captured so many people's imagination through the occupation and the tent city.*

Damon: When the young people were so invested and wanted to sleep in the tents, and they wanted to wake up in the tents and go back to sleep in the tents, it quickly turned into a twenty-four-hour youth engagement, which then stretched our capacity and definitely put us in a riskier position. But then also I think that solidified and expanded the strength of what we were doing. Regular people just saw us taking care of the kids. And so if you ever make a community center without a community center, or just through perpetually being responsive and just keep believing in this philosophy of abundance that "we have what we need to create what we want if we cooperate and distribute our resources in a loving, equitable way." Then it just expanded.

Within two to three days—because people didn't know who we were and because we didn't have signs up saying like, *It's torture happening across the street*—people started to just come, and we'd have larger conversations about abolition and use this space as an example. We started having so many conversations with people who were just like, "What's this?" "Can I get a plate? What ya'll here for?" and "Oh, yeah, I was in there." That story kept happening in a way that became really emotional. There was one day where I talked to a seventeen-year-old and said, "Well, yeah, we're here for, you know what happens in there?" And he's like, "Yeah, I was in there, my homies in there, they beat people up with phone books." He'd be saying, "All of this happened the summer I'm seventeen." And later that evening, a man who looked fifty, but from the timeline he was anywhere from thirty-five to forty, I talked to him and he said, "I was in there when I was seventeen." So there's the generational scope and seeing it in one day, right?

By talking to people, at least in the immediate circle right around there, [we learned] there's no household that somebody doesn't have a one-degree personal connection with either an uncle, cousin, aunt, somebody that has been affected by torture. And then you're trying to really internalize what that means for generational trauma. We were across the street from arguably the most violent symbol of state violence in the country. I don't know of anything that is worse than a black site that is connected to the CIA and tortures people by the thousands over a generation.

Alice: *You all held Freedom Square for forty-one days. What were the key lessons learned from that occupation?*

Damon: It's really hard to answer that question, 'cause the lessons were really infinite. I learned so much just like from hour to hour that it was brain overload. It changed everything about my constitution, understanding of myself and the world around me. One thing is, I don't think we talked about housing in relationship to all of this concretely enough. You know, we did not set out to shelter folks, but just, again, being responsive and always critiquing our internal contradictions, us as people with homes who have extra tents, who are talking about radical justice, really have no right to turn away a person who's sleeping on a bench across the street, right? So now that we've put ourselves out there, there's somewhat of a responsibility, so now we are incidentally dealing with homelessness and addiction. We need to figure out how we talk about that in relationship to policing or relationship to incarceration, much more tangibly and concretely and start figuring out solutions. Having land and the ability to shelter yourself and have autonomy over that is always at the crux of the changing of institutions. The people, whether it's the serfs or the peasants or the slaves, having land and having a home that is yours and not someone else's, that they're granting you access to, or you're paying for access to, that you can be kicked out of—this is at the root, and it's something that we really need to go much further to address.

Alice: *One last question: Why the arts? What about the roles of arts, culture, and creativity and imagination in your organizing?*

Damon: We all need our creative processes flowing in order to imagine what is the way we replace violent punishment, you know? But also we need community, and so outside of the explicitly political, we need to be able to share space in a way that is generative and regenerative, and nothing does that like the arts. It's a necessary tool more than like, "We good" or "We got here and we painted and now we have a banner." We need to be in the room together and not just for an objective or for a campaign or for a linear project like, "Now we won and now we can dissolve," but we need to build for generations.

The way to get kids to stay is to give them paint and paper to let them make a mess, even if it's not a piece that we're framing. It's just that activity. Once we were struggling in Freedom Square when people's capacity drained or the work wasn't the sexy new thing—it was more just like a day-to-day-type thing; it was harder to mobilize people to help us program activities. At a certain point, all we could do was give young people paints and paper, and that would be a way to keep us gathered. To keep the energy from roaming into the alley, to roaming down the block, we'd dance or freestyle. We need collective consciousness; we need community. It is essential.

Schooling and the Prison-Industrial Complex

■ People's Education Movement Chicago: Erica R. Davila, Mathilda de Dios, Valentina Gamboa-Turner, Angel Pantoja, Isaura B. Pulido, Ananka Shony, and David O. Stovall

A s schools and prisons become parallel institutions, practical and material tools in our communities are needed to resist and rethink our relationship to the US prison nation. We are educators, community workers, and parents who believe that building transformative learning spaces is not a path of least resistance; it is a call for educators to cultivate authentic solidarity and relationships with families, communities, and students aimed at ending the prison-industrial complex.

In this essay we listen to youth writers who are affiliated with Free Write Arts and Literacy, a project based in Chicago that engages incarcerated and court-involved youth in the performing, visual, and literary arts. By designing creative space for their students, incarcerated and court-involved youth "become the narrators of their own stories and the authors of their futures" and in turn, the project supports young people in "developing educational and career opportunities that reduce recidivism."[1]

For more than seventeen years, young people from Free Write have been using their writing to illuminate their lived experiences; the authors of this essay draw on writings developed in Free Write to better understand system-involved youth. As youth are thought to be "removed" from the system, we rarely take into account the long-term residual effects on their educational opportunities, mental health, and employment once they are released from a juvenile detention facility.

Young people's experience and voice must be considered when providing viable options to resist state-sanctioned violence in the form of imprisonment. By listening to young people, the authors seek to highlight a different perspective on what is commonly known as the "long term."

Redefining Incarceration

In his poem "Trust," Angel Pantoja's words are a call to action, specifically to teachers and educators to center their students with a "pedagogy of love."[2]

Trust

People doubted she could teach us poetry,
calling us underdogs at best,
but Ms. Arthur believed in us,
knew we could surpass any test.
We ignored her at first, drifting off in class.
But there was no evading her.
Short shot of black espresso, she woke us up, had us writing by
    the mass.
Concisely like she said, straight to the point like a haiku.
She ain't waste no time or syllables on nonsense.
Genuinely cared in the process, always listening to what we
    shared as if it were already a poem recited in the air.
We learned to tell our truth this way, unafraid to be ourselves.
Even learned new words like "resilient," "metaphor" and
    "simile."
One day she told me,
"It's not the dog in the fight, but the fight in the dog."
Trust me, she would've spit the truth in this minute, and in it
    you might've found yourself.[3]

Decreased Educational Opportunities

Countless research projects have demonstrated the lack of educational opportunities for youth of color and low-income families, which fuels

the perception that they are deficient. Michelle Alexander explains in
The New Jim Crow that this marginalization leads to many youth
being victimized by the project of mass incarceration.[4] As educators
in Chicago, we have witnessed many youth, as young as eleven years
old, fall into the traps of mass incarceration: increased surveillance
through the use of blue-light cameras mounted on neighborhood
light poles, proliferation of metal detectors and pat-downs in schools,
and the establishment of policies that mandate all students use clear
book bags. These policies and procedures, which are closely aligned
with the county jail and other detention centers, send a message to
our youth: they not only lack safety, but they also are expected to
misbehave and are perceived as being predisposed to criminality. Our
schools position youth as the problem rather than the global markets
that bank on the arrest and detainment of their very bodies. This can
be seen through the increase in school-based police officers, Chicago
Police Department (CPD) satellite processing stations in schools,
hyperdisciplinary policies, and the criminalization of youth who try
to reenter education spaces post-incarceration. The report *Handcuffs
in Hallways* describes several surveillance programs that collect un-
regulated data on our students and place it into sophisticated databases that use undisclosed algorithms to identify so-called criminals.
Surveillance systems include the city of Chicago's Strategic Subject
List, gang audits, and over forty-five hundred cameras that are monitored by the CPD Crime Prevention and Information Center.[5] A
recent report by the Institute for Research on Race and Public Policy
highlights the disproportionate ways Black and Latinx students are
disciplined and processed into the school-to-prison-pipeline. According to their report, "Black students accounted for 76.9% of all ex-
pulsions (253 out of 329) in Chicago Public Schools during 2015–2016
even though they accounted for only 38.9% of student enrollment."[6]
Not only are Black and Latinx students pushed out of our classrooms
at alarming rates, but reports of their misconduct are more likely to
be elevated to police notifications.

The Sentencing Project reports that "the rate of growth for female imprisonment has outpaced men by more than 50% between
1980 and 2014." Girls represent "a high portion of those who are
confined for low-level crimes such as status offenses and technical

oregationdictionary

violations, behaviors that would not be considered illegal if committed by adults."[7] Schools are feeding our children to the carceral state and investing heavily in policies and systems that do not improve safety or the academic advancement of youth.

As an alternative to the school-to-prison-pipeline, we call on educators to break the silence and humanize our children who suffer under the project of mass incarceration. We need to work with preservice and in-service teachers to help them gain an understanding of our unjust and dehumanizing prison nation. Teacher education programs do not prepare teachers to talk about marginalization, criminalization, and mass incarceration in their classrooms—and this needs to change. There are certain schools where it is the norm for children of color to go in and out of detention centers, and these youth are often framed as misbehaving, unfit, and deserving of this punishment. Despite research showing that these youth do not commit more crime, they are surveilled at higher rates. For example, Joshua Rovner found that "black teenagers are far more likely than their white peers to be arrested across a range of offenses."[8] Recently the city of Chicago hired one thousand additional police officers as a response to street crime while closing many public schools (forty-nine in one school year alone) and laying off thousands of teachers. Decisions by the police department and school district speak to a perception that our youth need to be monitored and controlled, not educated and empowered. We need to shift this representation and frame the larger prison-industrial complex—a system that profits from locking up a disproportionate number of young Black and Brown people living in poverty—as unfit for our young people and our communities.

For youth who have served time, institutional barriers abound when they are looking for opportunities upon reentry to mainstream society. Depending on their conviction, students may not even be allowed to go back to their respective schools, especially given the plethora of charter schools across the nation with enrollment policies that exclude this group of youth. Furthermore, when students are allowed to return to their schools, they are often labeled by school staff as "criminal" and perceived as "disposable." These perceptions can lead to youth being incarcerated again and again. Teachers and administrators should be aware of this context and work harder to provide quality mental health services, culturally relevant curricula, and humane disciplinary policies. We need to recruit and support transformative teachers who are ready to engage and empower these students—and all students—as learners.

This is not an attempt to blame educators, many of whom sacrifice and push themselves to meet their students' needs. This is an attempt to reflect on what are we pushing toward. Often educators are not aware of their own internalized biases and perceptions of power, control, and punishment, and they perform and internalize dynamics of crime and punishment. Consequently, educators use tools and practices that disproportionately marginalize Black and Latinx young people, as well as other people of color in our schools.

As educators, community, and family members of system-involved youth, it is imperative that we engage texts and narratives of those most impacted by incarceration.[9] Their own words and stories can lead us on a path toward disrupting the imprisonment of our youth. Jaren H.'s poem below calls out the hypocrisy of a system that fails to spend a dime on recreation centers and school funding while "you can lose your life in a flash." It eloquently makes a broader call to invest in our communities.

Excerpt from "Modern Day Slavery"

So how dare you criticize
the loss of people's lives
always talking about the crime
but you ain't even spent a dime
to open up new rec centers
or even school funding
all the gang leaders locked up
probably ain't never coming
back to these streets, so they can't tell us nothing
like why would I listen to you
if you ain't getting no money
and I think it's funny how Obama from Chicago
so it got me wondering
like if y'all ain't give me nothing

how I'm gonna make it to something
but my ambition, my grind, and loyalty gon' make me shine
they think I lost my mind
but I'm just taking my time
my Grandma told me, "Boy, just be patient."
but how long have I been waiting?
With these dreads in my head
their perception of me is Satan
but I'm God-fearing, Lord knows I'm gon' make a billion
these streets already showed me you can lose your life in a flash
and be the next pack in the blunt that somebody 'bout to pass.[10]

Residual Effects on Employment and Mental Health Outcomes

Without interventions, experiences, or opportunities that may lead young, poor youth of color toward productive paths, they are funneled into the criminal legal system. We know that youths' educational trajectories are stifled as they come into contact with the criminal justice system and incarceration; therefore, it is not surprising that, as a consequence, incarceration has negative effects on their employment prospects. Employment opportunities are especially challenging for those who have less schooling, mental health issues, and substance abuse issues. These issues, coupled with the social stigma of incarceration and criminal records laws, make it difficult for young people to get jobs after incarceration.[11] In addition, approximately one-third of incarcerated youth require ongoing mental health care, and many more, almost 66 percent, meet criteria for mental health diagnoses. Jails and detention centers serve as "dumping grounds" for young people with mental health needs, while funding for community mental health facilities continues to diminish.[12]

The poem below by Barrett C. provides a window into the psychological toll of incarceration on one particular youth. For some, incarceration is the place where the first signs of depression, self-harm, and thoughts of suicide first emerge.

Stress

Nobody knows until one's in jail.
It all starts when the judge declares no bail.
Straight to your cell without saying goodbye.
Waving to your loved ones as they cry, cry, cry.
Worrying about your child or a letter from home.
Not to mention residents of all kinds
          wanting to bust your dome.
Stress so high you can feel the growing rage;
Like a wild blue-eyed wolf locked in a cage.
The pain of stress is only a reminder I'm still alive;
But I can do without all this freaking jive.
They say stress can cause you an early death.
If this is true, I'm on my last breath.[13]

Many young people, like Barrett, do not receive the care they need while incarcerated, even as their mental health deteriorates. In fact, a vast majority of young people who are incarcerated develop posttraumatic stress disorder (PTSD). Trauma scholar and psychiatrist Judith Herman suggests that "complex PTSD" more accurately describes the repeated trauma young people face when incarcerated, which "can result in protracted depression, apathy and the development of a deep sense of hopelessness as the long-term psychological costs of adapting to an oppressive situation."[14] Upon release, many young people bring home traumas created or exacerbated by their experiences of incarceration that continue to reverberate throughout different areas of their lives.

As women, particularly women of color and mothers, continue to be one of the fastest-growing populations in prison, families are deeply affected. Given these disparate effects on incarcerated youth, it behooves us as educators to acknowledge and engage in educational practices with youth as if their lives depend on it, because in fact they do.

A Call to Action

We recognize that prison advocacy and justice work can be over-whelming, especially for folks who are struggling within their close circle of family and friends who are targets in the project of mass incarceration. But we boldly urge those very people and our allies to reflect on what their sphere of influence is and can be. Your sphere can be as small as your household, but the influence can be powerful and much needed. Particularly for those in schools and educational spaces, your sphere is wider and its actions have the ripple effect necessary to make the critical transformations to stop mass incarceration. Practicing transformative educational justice for our students is not a path of least resistance. We work against the conditions and machinations of oppression, incarceration, and domination that permeate throughout all of our educational institutions. Articulated in the voices of system-involved youth, we call on educators to cultivate authentic solidarity and relationships with families, communities, and students. As educators, we must lean into the humanity of our youth, investigate the conditions of mass incarceration, and engage in acts of healing in their lives and communities.

Resources

The following resources make up an initial list of suggestions for people who are interested in historical and contemporary analysis of incarceration, the current work happening in prison abolition, and emerging alternatives to incarceration. We encourage a continued commitment to reflect, practice, and empower our students to undo oppressive systems that are often resourced by our own communities through our tax dollars and our silence.

A Tale of Three Cities: The State of Racial Justice in Chicago Report: A 2017 report by the Institute for Research on Race and Public Policy at the University of Illinois at Chicago that examines competing public narratives about Chicago to assess what the challenges and opportunities are for the city's residents today. http://stateofracialjusticechicago.com/wp-content/uploads/IRRPP_StateOfRacialJusticeReport.pdf

Citizens Police Data Project: This online portal produced by the Invisible Institute, whose mission is to enhance the capacity of citizens to hold public institutions accountable, contains data, analysis, and multimedia resources.
https://invisible.institute/police-data

"Curricular Seeds in the Spirit of Liberatory Education": Essential questions, activities, and resources for educators and community organizers to use in spaces of learning and empowerment. Collected from presenters at the People's Education Forum: Healing in Education, Resilience in Action.
http://tinyurl.com/yalmjem3

Defund Policing, Fund Schools and Communities: Teachers for Social Justice (TSJ) 15th Annual Curriculum Fair: Led by teachers, TSJ is an international organization with chapters in many communities working to partner schools and communities. This video provides a summary of the event.
www.youtube.com/watch?v=ADCKla71Lro&feature=youtu.be

Free Write Arts and Literacy: This program offers workshops in writing, art, and music to incarcerated and court-involved youth. Free Write supports students to become narrators of their own stories and the authors of their own futures.
http://freewriteartsliteracy.org

Handcuffs in Hallways: The State of Policing in Chicago Public Schools: This February 2017 report from the Sargent Shriver National Center on Poverty Law provides important data and context about juvenile injustice in the Chicago Public School system and the cost to our children and city.
http://povertylaw.org/files/docs/handcuffs-in-hallways-final.pdf

The Peace Diet Program: Curing Violence with Food: This program endeavors to stop violence before it happens by intervening at the root of human behavior: the brain.
https://www.indiegogo.com/projects/the-peace-diet-program
-curing-violence-with-food#

Sounding the Alarm: Building the Climate & Culture Our Students Need. This June 2017 report from Educators in Excellence provides a model for creating healthy classrooms in one of the largest urban school districts. https://e4e.org/what-we-do /policy-solutions/sounding-alarm

#SurvivedAndPunished: Survivor Defense as Abolitionist Praxis: Contains educational, art, and media resources focused on supporting survivors of domestic violence and dismantling all state-sanctioned violence. https://view.publitas.com/survived-and-punished/toolkit/page/1

Trauma and Families: Fact Sheet for Providers: A set of guidelines supporting children and families, publihsed by the National Child Traumatic Stress Network. http://www.nctsn.org/sites/default/files/assets/pdfs/family _systems_factsheetproviders.pdf

Uprooting the Punitive Practices of New York's Parole Board

■ Mujahid Farid

Across the nation there is growing concern that much of the progress made in the past five years to educate the federal government on the harms associated with mass incarceration will be significantly turned back. Donald Trump's ascension to the presidency fuels that concern.

However, Trump's counter-progressive platform does not have the power to silence a movement whose time has come. Because the vast majority of incarcerated individuals are in state prison systems, not the federal system, the primary focal point for challenging mass incarceration must be at the local and state level and at policies championed by so-called progressive politicians who long precede Trump.

Nationwide and local coalitions of formerly incarcerated men and women have been pushing a bold vision for justice and transformation for decades. Notably, in New York State, organizations and groups have been hard at work, creating and developing coalitions and coming out of their silos to address the crisis of a punishment paradigm that has threatened the health and well-being of New Yorkers and their families and communities since Governor Nelson Rockefeller's administration.

Today, groups like the Challenging Incarceration coalition, which is made up of more than sixty organizations and issue-based campaigns, are demanding that Governor Andrew Cuomo and leaders of the state legislature join the movement to transform New York's racist carceral state and the rise of the newly emboldened conservative right by championing policy that ends mass incarceration, state violence and torture, racism and identity-based oppression and empowers all New Yorkers, not just those who are convicted of nonviolent drug offenses.

As a start, the governor could take steps to uproot the punitive practices of the state Board of Parole, which continues to annually deny release to thousands of people—many of whom are elders—despite the incredible extent to which they have transformed over time.

I myself was denied by the board nine times, adding an extra eighteen years to my original fifteen-years-to-life sentence, despite my having already earned four college degrees—two bachelor's and two master's—before my first interview with the board.

To continue to deny people parole based on one immutable factor—the nature of the original offense—without regard for their life-changing transformations is to follow the lead of the new president, not combat him. State and local organizations and individuals will not abandon inclusive reform efforts until the governor and legislature act accordingly by changing the composition of the Board of Parole; passing the Safe and Fair Evaluations Parole Act (A.4353/S.3095A) which, among other things, requires that incarcerated people who are denied parole be told what corrective actions they need to take; and championing incarceration-related policy that ensures New York remains a steadfast leader in the dawn of a new and uncertain day.

The on-the-ground work being done by organizers and advocates on the state and local levels will not be uprooted by a new presidential administration, but it remains to be seen whether it will be embraced by the governor and his peers. If the elected leaders of our state wish to rout the rise of the nationally occupying radical right, they must join the local movement seeking to penetrate its punitive roots.

Ban the Box and the Impact of Organizing by Formerly Incarcerated People

■ Linda Evans

The impacts of organizing by formerly incarcerated people have yet to be adequately acknowledged but can be seen in three primary areas:

1. Organizing has affected our personal development.
2. It has impacted our families and communities.
3. It has influenced the direction and content of local and national social justice campaigns.[1]

On the personal level, organizing builds self-confidence and self-worth. Through training and workshops, we gain new skills necessary to building political power. By analyzing our experiences, we learn how to think more critically and deeply. By joining others in common cause, we break out of personal isolation and begin to see ourselves as part of something larger than only ourselves.[2]

When formerly incarcerated people get involved in social change, it affects the quality of life for our families and communities. Many of the problems facing us when we are released concern our families: child custody, child support issues, family reunification, housing, employment, education. When we begin to confront these problems collectively and work toward community-wide solutions, conditions can change. Additionally, the increased self-confidence and self-worth that we gain through organizing is valuable to our family and community. Since people in prison are predominantly people of color, learning how to organize also disrupts generations of powerlessness and alienation and increases the political power of communities of color as a whole.

When the opinions of people who have been in prison are noted and taken seriously, the debate around any criminal justice issue is affected. Organizing by formerly incarcerated people has changed the direction and content of national criminal justice campaigns. For example, it was formerly incarcerated women who protested law enforcement policies of shackling pregnant women during transportation and labor. Young people subjected to arbitrary inclusion in gang databases demanded and won ways to remove their names. Men and women lifers in prison have started a campaign to reopen LWOP (life without parole) sentences. Because of our direct experience living in cages, our participation affects and improves any proposed solutions.

One of the most successful organizing campaigns initiated by formerly incarcerated people is a broad antidiscrimination campaign known as Ban the Box.

The Origins of Ban the Box

Ban the Box got its name from a particular box that appears on most employment forms, as well as applications for housing, college, public benefits, and the right to serve on a jury. It's the box that reads, "Have you ever been convicted of a felony?" While the wording may change slightly from application to application, the result is the same: a barrier is created for people who want to work, educate themselves, provide for their families, and lead healthy, productive lives. Imagine yourself caught in a situation where authorities require stable housing and a job before you can reunite with your children, yet you are barred from affordable housing and turned away at every job interview because of your past conviction.

Ban the Box is a campaign to end *structural discrimination*—that is, discrimination directed against everyone who has a past conviction, without consideration for individual circumstances. Ban the Box is a powerful tool in equalizing opportunity, ensuring that people get a second chance to put their lives together. It reduces the blanket discrimination that shuts millions out of jobs, shelter, education, and participation in the democratic process. And it's a key step in acknowledging the humanity of all people, regardless of past behavior or mistakes.

The Ban the Box campaign began in 2004 in the San Francisco Bay Area. It was initiated as a project of All of Us or None, a grassroots group of formerly incarcerated people dedicated to winning full restoration of our rights after our release from prison and to ending the discrimination faced by those with criminal records.[3]

Between 2003 and 2005, All of Us or None organized six Peace and Justice Community Summits where formerly incarcerated people spoke out about the barriers to success they face when returning home from prison. The purpose of the summits was to promote solutions to these problems, and hundreds of community members attended each summit to listen to the testimonies of formerly incarcerated people. Elected officials and other community leaders served on "action panels" tasked with implementing recommendations made in the testimonies. One of the most common issues raised was the need to end all forms of discrimination based on conviction records.

Employment discrimination is perhaps the most pervasive of all problems facing those returning from prison, largely because it has such far-reaching effects. Employment is necessary for people to achieve stability in their lives, and it is usually a requirement for parole or probation. Banning the box—removing the "criminal history" question from job applications—is one way to give formerly incarcerated people equal opportunity, allowing them to compete for jobs on the basis of their skills and qualifications.

All of Us or None initially decided to focus on public rather than private employment, because we agreed that community pressure would be most effective within the public sector, where elected officials have an obligation to represent and respond to their constituents. We also hoped that banning the box in public employment would set an example for private employers.

We soon became aware that in 1998 Hawaii had already adopted a statewide law in this regard, and it applied to both public and private employers. We also learned that a Ban the Box campaign very similar to ours was starting up in Boston. But beyond that, we were entering unexplored territory, ready to tackle an enormous problem.

The San Francisco Campaign

Working from an analysis of local governments, and the fact that the majority of All of Us or None's early members lived in the San Francisco Bay Area, we decided to focus first on San Francisco. The Peace and Justice Community Summit had brought several hundred people together to build awareness of the problems encountered by formerly incarcerated people. A smaller core group of around thirty people started to strategize about how to move our demand forward.

From the very beginning, we faced many challenges. All of our members were new to the policy world and had little experience with government structures or processes. Additionally, when dealing with elected officials, lawyers, social service professionals, and many others, we often needed to deal with deeply entrenched prejudice against formerly incarcerated people.

Because the right to work and the right to housing are human rights issues, we first approached San Francisco's Human Rights Commission (HRC) for guidance. Staff members at the HRC were extremely helpful and gave us great advice about how government works, including the fact that altering existing employment policy would require hearings in front of the Board of Supervisors and Civil Service Commission in addition to the HRC. When an HRC hearing was held on the issue of banning the box, we mobilized formerly incarcerated people to attend. We prepared ourselves to testify about the difference it would make to ban the box in city employment. For most of our members, this was the first time they had ever spoken publicly, and it was a unifying, confidence-building experience for all of us.

Next, All of Us or None wrote a resolution describing the barriers people face when coming back from prison, calling on the San Francisco Board of Supervisors to remove the conviction history question from the initial application for public employment. We worked for many months to get this resolution passed: testifying at meetings, circulating a petition in the community, creating flyers, and talking on radio shows.

Finally, in early 2006 we appeared in front of the Board of Supervisors. We had publicized the meeting widely because we wanted the supervisors to see the magnitude of the problem and how many people supported Ban the Box. Staff and clients from drug treatment centers, criminal justice organizations, halfway houses, reentry agencies, civil rights allies, and many community residents showed up to pack the room. Although we had met with several supervisors before the vote, we weren't sure what the final outcome would be. But we won the vote! The Board of Supervisors issued an official resolution requiring the human resources department to remove the box from city employment applications.

But our job wasn't over in San Francisco. We worked with the city's Department of Human Resources to hammer out "best policy practices," including a matrix to determine the job-relatedness of specific convictions. Through this process, we learned when to compromise and when not to. For example, supervisors had recommended changing the language of our resolution to delete any mention of physically removing the conviction history question from the application. We changed other language to appease them, because we knew it was imperative for the resolution to call for physically removing the box, or it wouldn't happen.

As organizers, we all learned how crucial it is to be knowledgeable and prepared with facts and figures when working with government officials. Many of our members discovered that regardless of education or past experience, we could all learn how to read and analyze public policy. That lesson was tremendously empowering for all of us.

On January 24, 2006, we held a press conference on the steps of city hall to announce the final adoption of Ban the Box. Many of our members, along with allies in city government and other elected officials, attended. We wanted press coverage so that more people would know of these changes and be able to benefit from them. But press coverage was sparse locally, with no national press coverage at all, so we knew we had hard work ahead to publicize our success. Still, we celebrated a victory that had been won by hardworking formerly incarcerated people from all over the Bay Area![4]

The Movement Grows

The first Ban the Box successes were hard-won. Many of us were inexperienced as political organizers or public speakers. We didn't know how to write a resolution or draft a law. The learning curve was steep. But we were in the struggle for the long term, and our movement started to accrue victories.

All of Us or None chapters developed around California—Los Angeles, San Bernardino, San Diego, East Palo Alto, Sacramento, and Long Beach—as well as across the country in places such as San Antonio, Texas. We shared strategies with similar groups such as the Better Way Foundation (Connecticut), the Ordinary People's Society (Alabama), Voice of the Ex-Offender (New Orleans), A New Way of Life (Los Angeles), and Ex-Prisoners Organizing for Community Advancement (Massachusetts). As the groups multiplied, we connected with one another and shared strategies and resources. All of Us or None created a Ban the Box Toolkit and made two organizing videos that were widely shown.[5] Many new chapters and other groups began local Ban the Box campaigns.

Formerly incarcerated people wanted to take responsibility for the direction of the Ban the Box movement. We realized it was crucial that we speak for ourselves rather than relinquish leadership to others such as lawyers, politicians, and well-meaning nonprofit allies. But people who had been advocating on behalf of former prisoners were often reluctant to share leadership and access to resources. Allies in nonprofit organizations had spoken on our behalf for years when we were their legal clients or recipients of their social services. Now we asked them to support us in speaking for ourselves. Many felt their jobs were threatened, since one of our demands was that criminal justice reform organizations should be willing to hire formerly incarcerated people. Others believed that our histories of being in prison somehow stigmatized us permanently and that we didn't have the skills necessary to speak with elected officials. It has taken years for traditional policy advocates to accept us as equal partners, much less leaders of social change, despite the specific and effective solutions we have recommended in policy discussions.

One way we sought to influence the discussion was to educate ourselves about issues of language. When referring to people who

have been incarcerated, we choose language that affirms human
dignity. Gone are terms such as "ex-con," "prisoner," "inmate," or
"ex-prisoner"—all words that define a person as an embodiment
of their past mistakes. Instead, terms that refer to us as people—
"people in prison," "people on parole or probation," "formerly incarcerated people," or "people with a conviction history"—describe
a condition we share with others. This choice of language has been
integral to the Ban the Box movement, a way to fight the stigma we
encounter in our daily lives.

Building alliances between grassroots activists, nonprofit advocates, social service professionals, lawyers, and elected officials has
been critical to the success of Ban the Box campaigns. Gradually,
people from very different backgrounds have learned to talk together
and respect one another. As we broke through prejudice and stereotypes, formerly incarcerated people began to be recognized as experts and leaders, and we became more effective advocates for Ban
the Box and other campaigns as well.

In the fifteen years since the launch of the San Francisco movement, Ban the Box campaigns around the country, led by formerly
incarcerated people, have taken on four areas of deep structural discrimination: employment, housing, education, and voting.

Employment for All

Georgia

The movement to Ban the Box in Georgia was notable for being
led largely by women. In 2012 the campaign began with a meeting
of several grassroots groups: Women on the Rise, an organization
of formerly incarcerated women; 9 to 5 Atlanta, a group advocating
for women in the workplace; the Solutions Not Punishment coalition, a social justice organization concerned with police abuse and
the rights of trans people and sex workers; and Atlantans Building
Leadership for Empowerment (ABLE), a faith-based multiracial
coalition of congregations, unions, and grassroots groups. All of
these groups had members who were directly affected by employment discrimination based on conviction histories.

The coalition trained and mobilized formerly incarcerated

people and their families to speak at public hearings and attend one-on-one meetings with Atlanta elected officials and Fulton County commissioners. Through this process, the campaign built strong relationships with several commissioners, and formerly incarcerated people built confidence in their political abilities.

By 2014, members had drafted a model Fair Chance Ordinance and worked with Fulton County's human resources (HR) department to create an inclusive policy. Although advocates pushed for the ordinance to include private vendors and contractors, the final law fell short of this goal. Political in-fighting may have been the reason for this setback. The commissioner who originally sponsored the ordinance had been working closely with community representatives. Suddenly another commissioner introduced his own, weaker version of the bill and orchestrated its quick passage. This taught activists to beware of competing politicians who may use Ban the Box for their own purposes.

The women of 9 to 5 Atlanta pressured Mayor Kasim Reed, starting in 2012, until he ordered the city's HR department to remove the "conviction history" box from employment applications in 2013. But organizers knew this was insufficient—there was no executive order, no legal ordinance, no additional provisions to protect applicants. So formerly incarcerated women in Women on the Rise and 9 to 5 worked with city council members to improve the initially inadequate policy. Using their personal stories and expertise, they convinced council members to strengthen key provisions.

Since the Fulton County and Atlanta victories, organizers in Georgia have also banned the box in at least six more counties and five additional cities.

Ohio

The Ohio Ban the Box movement started with the personal employment struggle of one formerly incarcerated man. In 2010 a man came to the Ohio Justice and Policy Center (OJPC) asking for legal assistance. After being released from prison, he had been accepted into an electricians apprenticeship program. He had graduated number one in his class and passed the civil service exam to become an electrician for the City of Cincinnati. But he was removed from the pool of qualified applicants on the basis of his twelve-year-old criminal record. OJPC realized that in order to address this man's situation it was necessary to ban the box.

To this end, OJPC partnered with the AMOS Project, a faith-based social justice organization, and the Ohio Organizing Collaborative, a statewide group with members in every major city, which works on issues such as climate change, minimum wage reform, and ending mass incarceration.

The effort made swift progress because of the support of these already existing organizations and networks. The campaign was spirited, with formerly incarcerated people and their allies attending and, when necessary, disrupting meetings to get attention for proposed changes. After activists disrupted one Civil Service Commission in Cincinnati, they marched to Mayor Mark Mallory's office to deliver hundreds of petition signatures. In 2010 Cincinnati became the first city in Ohio to ban the box.

With a strong, broad base of activists working around the state, the Ohio coalition won Ban the Box reforms in sixteen cities and counties. In 2015 John Kasich, the Republican governor of Ohio, signed into law a Ban the Box bill that applied to all public hiring—city, county, and state—in Ohio. All of these victories are a testament to the power of collective organizing work.

As of August 2017, twenty-nine states have banned the box for public employment. In nine of these states, the law also applies to private employers.[6] In addition, over 150 cities and counties have banned the box.[7] Due to the success of the Ban the Box campaign, over 223 million Americans now live in areas that have adopted fair chance hiring policies. That's over two-thirds of the population of the United States. Millions of lives have been affected for the better as barriers to gainful employment have fallen.

Eventually a national Ban the Box in Employment campaign grew out of the many local and state efforts. In 2011 many organizations and individual formerly incarcerated people met in Los Angeles and adopted a national program, agreeing to move forward as the Formerly Incarcerated and Convicted People's Movement (FICPM).[8] The existence of a national program and structure has helped further Ban the Box organizing goals.

In 2015 FICPM, the National Employment Law Project, and the PICO (People Improving Communities through Organizing) National Network launched an initiative urging President Obama to issue an executive order to Ban the Box in hiring for all federal jobs and contractors. The initiative was supported by over two hundred national, state, and local organizations, and by twenty-seven senators and over seventy members of the House of Representatives. John Legend, musician and celebrity activist, supported the campaign by creating videos highlighting the stories of formerly incarcerated leaders.

In November 2015, President Obama issued an executive order directing the Office of Personnel Management to delay inquiries into conviction history until later in its hiring process. Additionally, the president issued a challenge to private business owners: the Fair Chance Business Pledge.[9] Over three hundred private employers have signed this pledge as of November 2016.

Ban the Box in Housing

Because housing is such an immediate and crucial need for those coming out of prison, formerly incarcerated people have launched Ban the Box campaigns for fair chance housing. Prior to these campaigns, federal Department of Housing and Urban Development (HUD) policy was founded on "one-strike evictions," meaning when any family member was arrested, the entire family could be evicted from public housing. Millions of people with past convictions and their families feel the weight of being excluded from housing. More and more people with records end up homeless because they cannot reunite with their families living in public housing. Children suffer continuing separation and damage when returning parents are unable to reunite with their families.

Ban the Box campaigns in housing have demanded that the conviction history question on housing applications be eliminated until the final stages of consideration and that only tenancy-related convictions be considered. It has been extremely difficult to win the support of private landlords, but some cities have adopted fair chance policies for subsidized and public housing.

San Bernardino, California: Time for Change Foundation

Many women come out of prison with no place to call home. They want to reunite with their children and families but have no way to do so if they are homeless. At Time for Change, homeless women and their children are provided safe and sober housing, family and individual counseling, financial planning classes, and a true sense of community. Application processes at Time for Change do not eliminate people because of past convictions, and people coming out of prison are welcomed and encouraged to participate.

The Time for Change Foundation was started in 2002 by Kim Carter, a formerly incarcerated woman who wanted to help others like herself. The foundation's mission is clear from its slogan: "We Call it Home, Others Call it Hope." Besides gaining safe housing and crucial survival services, women at Time for Change are encouraged to develop leadership skills. Many take part in a speakers training program and participate in advocacy campaigns. Hundreds of women and children have lived in Time for Change transitional homes and have been supported by its programs.

In 2012 Time for Change ventured even further into solving the problem of homelessness, becoming a nonprofit housing developer. They designed and constructed Phoenix Square, in San Bernardino, an affordable housing project for very low-income families. A seven-unit apartment complex was extensively renovated and leased out. More housing and community space will be developed, and a solar-paneled parking structure and community garden are planned for the future.

Since 2014 Time for Change has also partnered with HUD in administering the Homes for Hope project. This project places homeless families directly into their own apartments, even when they face institutional barriers like conviction histories, bad credit, or previous evictions. Through this program, families receive supportive services, learn how to maintain stable housing, and then assume the lease when they are ready.

New Orleans

Since Hurricane Katrina struck in 2005, New Orleans residents have faced a severe housing crisis. Today, over seventeen thousand families, most of them African American, are on the waiting list for public housing. And poverty is so widespread that one in four households in New Orleans receives rental assistance from the government.

This housing crisis is even worse for people with conviction histories. Louisiana incarcerates more people per capita than any other state.[10] Huge numbers of families in New Orleans include family members with conviction records. Among African American men in New Orleans, one in seven is either in prison, on parole, or on probation.

In 2013 Voice of the Ex-Offender (VOTE) issued a report on housing in New Orleans titled *Communities, Evictions, and Criminal Convictions.*[11] This report, written by formerly incarcerated people, became the starting point for organizing to change New Orleans' public housing policy.

VOTE members formed a housing rights coalition with a diverse group of organizations, many of which had formerly incarcerated people in their membership or on their staff. The coalition's members were a great resource for firsthand expertise about the solutions needed in New Orleans public housing.

The coalition initiated discussions with the Housing Authority of New Orleans (HANO). HANO was notorious for evicting whole families for criminal activity, even when no arrest had occurred and where the alleged activity was not even attributed to a household member. The coalition organized in the community and wrote a proposed model policy to HANO that would change how it considers conviction history.

Because of this ongoing public pressure, HANO issued a draft of a Criminal Background Policy Statement and held a public hearing in January 2013. This represented a major shift in policy, largely won by the advocacy of formerly incarcerated people and their family members. The coalition mobilized people to attend the hearing and wrote a detailed critique of the draft policy statement. HANO responded to community concerns by issuing a revised policy that incorporated some of their suggestions. Due to the organizing efforts by formerly incarcerated people in New Orleans, housing opportunities have improved for those who need it desperately.

Inland Empire: Starting Over Inc.

Many formerly incarcerated people conquer addiction, embrace sobriety, and want to help others. In 2002 Vonya Quarles, a formerly incarcerated woman in Riverside, California, got sober and stable, then opened up her home to others facing the same obstacles she faced when she left prison. Starting Over Inc. began as just one house in 2002, but now it has grown to five homes with the capacity for fifty-five residents. People can stay up to eighteen months, and are encouraged and assisted in finding other housing, but they are never kicked out. One woman stayed for four years. She was eventually hired as a house manager and left Starting Over only because she was finally convinced that someone else needed her bed.

Starting Over is the home base for the Riverside chapter of All of Us or None. Riverside is an extremely conservative area. Every single county supervisor is a Republican. But despite this conservative climate, All of Us or None members worked with the city's public housing authority to improve public housing access for people with records. They convinced the housing authority that people coming out of prison or jail into transitional housing should be added to a pre-existing "preference list." This preference list allows homeless people with underage children to go to the top of the waiting list for affordable housing. Prior to All of Us or None advocacy, people living in transitional housing were excluded from this list because they were already "housed." All of Us or None successfully argued that transitional housing is by nature only temporary and that residents of transitional housing should be eligible for the preference list. Otherwise, after they leave transitional housing they would be homeless.

At first the director of the Riverside Housing Authority was reluctant to engage in discussion with All of Us or None and resistant to any suggestions from formerly incarcerated people. After this director's retirement, however, housing authority staff became much more receptive; it now supports All of Us or None recommendations at the housing commission.

Ban the Box in Education

What are the ways a criminal conviction creates barriers to higher education? Imprisonment itself is a barrier. Few prisons or jails have on-site college programs, so people in prison rarely have the opportunity to take college classes. Correspondence courses may not be available or approved by prison administrators, and they are expensive. It's very difficult to obtain books and research materials necessary for college-level work in a prison setting.

After release from prison, a conviction history is a barrier for admissions to many colleges and universities. Over six hundred colleges use the Common Application, a standard application used by undergraduates to apply for admission to member colleges, which includes questions about past convictions. Some schools require students with conviction histories to provide copies of their criminal record and to complete additional admissions essays. Many formerly incarcerated students are discouraged by these questions on the application and abandon their plans to attend college. Removing the conviction history question from college applications has been a focus of Ban the Box student activism.

The limits of the campaign to Ban the Box on college applications are ever present and quite clear. In September 2017 the *New York Times* featured the story of Michelle Jones, a remarkable woman who was accepted into—and then rejected from—a highly competitive PhD history program at Harvard University after serving twenty years in prison. (Harvard has removed the conviction history question on applications to graduate programs.) Two professors questioned her acceptance into the program, stating that she had not revealed enough about her past crime. Harvard administrators decided that accepting Ms. Jones might cause resentment among rejected applicants or parents of students and could create negative news coverage on conservative media outlets. So Harvard rescinded its offer to Ms. Jones; however, she will be pursuing her PhD at New York University, one of several other universities that recruited her for their doctoral programs.

The barrier for Ms. Jones was not the box but long-embedded prejudices against people with records and the public's reluctance to embrace us. The director of graduate studies for Harvard's history department criticized administrators for rescinding Michelle's admission, saying, "Is it that she did not show the appropriate degree of horror in herself, by applying?"[12] Another history professor asked, "How much do we really believe in the possibility of human redemption?"

Ms. Jones's story is not unique, though it has received unusual publicity. In Seattle, Tarra Simmons completed law school, but the Washington State Bar Association denied her the right to take the bar exam. (On November 16, 2017, the Supreme Court ruled that she *could* take the exam.)[13] Dwayne Betts, a Yale Law School graduate, was initially denied admission to the Connecticut Bar, despite having received numerous awards and passing the state bar exam. Betts's subsequent, successful appeal of this grievous decision is a tremendous achievement; his extraordinary efforts are in response to the stigma and prejudice that formerly incarcerated people must mobilize against.

State University of New York

Formerly incarcerated people and their allies in New York formed the Education from the Inside Out coalition to push the State University of New York (SUNY) system to remove the conviction history box from its admissions application. Cofounders included College and Community Fellowship and JustLeadershipUSA, both organizations founded by formerly incarcerated people. The coalition researched the use of conviction history records in college admissions and urged universities and colleges to remove the box altogether.[14] They also produced a short documentary film titled *Imagine a World without the Box*.[15]

The Inside Out coalition also drafted legislation to Ban the Box on all college applications used in New York, which is still pending. But most of the energies of the coalition were directed to Abolish the Box at SUNY, the largest university system in the United States, with sixty-four campuses serving 1.3 million students.

The coalition brought their Abolish the Box campaign directly to the SUNY Student Assembly, which decided to support Abolish the Box after much debate. At their April 2016 meeting, hundreds of

student senators voted to support a resolution urging admissions officials to ban the box. Their resolution recommended that "criminal history screenings should only be implemented after a student has been
admitted, and that they should never be used to revoke admission."[16]

Six months later, with pressure from the Student Assembly,
SUNY's Board of Trustees voted to ban the box in their admissions
application. It was the first time a university system reversed its decision to screen for conviction history and remove the question from
its admissions application.

To this day, however, questions about past convictions have not
disappeared completely from the SUNY system. Students are still
asked to disclose felony convictions if they seek campus housing, if
they want to participate in clinical or field experiences, and if they
apply for internships or study abroad. Education from the Inside Out
members and other SUNY students have vowed to continue the struggle until all discrimination based on past convictions is eliminated.

Louisiana

The Louisiana Prison Education Coalition helped write and advocate for a bill that would ban the box on all public university applications in the state. Eloquent testimony from formerly incarcerated
men and women convinced lawmakers to pass the bill unanimously.
State universities requested a compromise allowing questions about
convictions for rape, stalking, or sexual battery during the admissions process, with the right to appeal if a student is not admitted
because of a conviction. In June 2017 this bill was signed into law by
the governor, John Bel Edwards, making Louisiana the first state to
ban the box on college applications.

Ban the Box in Voting

In the 2016 presidential election, a full 2.5 percent of the voting
age population were denied their right to vote because of a past
conviction—over six million potential voters.[17] Yet Donald Trump
became the forty-fifth president of the United States because of
a scant 77,744 votes in Pennsylvania, Wisconsin, and Michigan.
In Florida, Trump won critical electoral college votes because of

a 113,000-vote margin—in a state where over 1.7 million people are barred for life from voting because of their conviction history, including 21 percent of the state's African American voters. Just before the election, Virginia governor Terry McAuliffe was accused of trying to influence the election by extending voter eligibility to 206,000 people with past convictions. (The Virginia Supreme Court forced him to rescind this blanket policy after Republicans brought a lawsuit.) Whether the conviction is for a felony or misdemeanor, this strategy of voting prohibition is known as "criminal disenfranchisement."[18]

Denying people their right to vote because of a past conviction has become a partisan strategy to win elections. Criminal disenfranchisement happens not as a part of the punishment for a specific crime but also when state constitutions disenfranchise everyone who has certain types of convictions or incarceration. With one in three people in the United States having a conviction record, criminal disenfranchisement has become a massive threat to representative democracy in our country.

Only 23 percent of the people disenfranchised because of felony convictions are in prison or jail. The majority are living, working, and paying taxes in their communities after fully completing their sentences or while on probation or parole. Because voter eligibility laws change often and differ widely between states, many formerly incarcerated people don't know their rights or may lose their right to vote simply by moving from one state to another.

In recent years, criminal disenfranchisement has become an important tool of voter suppression strategies that target people of color and people from poor communities. Republicans have been ruthlessly curtailing the right to vote in every state where they can. Their efforts at voter suppression through felony disenfranchisement have significantly affected voters of color. In the "swing state" of Florida, over 10 percent of the adult population is barred for life from voting because of a felony conviction. One in five Black Florida residents belongs to that group.[19]

Often it has been the grassroots organizing of formerly incarcerated people working with civil rights organizations such as the American Civil Liberties Union that have pushed for voting rights restoration. Formerly incarcerated people have run voter registration campaigns in most states. They have also filed legal challenges to expand and clarify voting rights for people with past convictions.

Voting rights restoration is a growing movement. Twenty-seven bills have been introduced in fifteen states to restore voting rights for people with past convictions. Maryland's legislature overrode a governor's veto to restore the rights of forty thousand state residents. As of this writing, Kentucky's legislature is deadlocked over a law to automatically restore voting rights. Formerly incarcerated people are involved in these fights and determined to win restoration of their right to vote.

Conclusion

Ban the Box is only one of many organizing initiatives led by formerly incarcerated people. National organizations are forming to increase our effectiveness. For example, the National Council of Incarcerated and Formerly Incarcerated Women and Girls has recently emerged in an attempt to build unity and national political power.[20] Formerly incarcerated people are sharing model legislation and campaign strategies. We are collaborating to increase our influence and visibility via Twitter "Power Hours" and social media campaigns. Our movement is growing, and we are becoming more effective, more powerful, and more determined. Having endured long-term imprisonment and discrimination, we are emerging as a political force because of our dedication to long-term organizing.

Coming out of prison, we are often isolated from one another because parole conditions prohibit us from associating with anyone who has a conviction history, including family members. We face many challenges in restarting our life on the outside. Formerly incarcerated people who become involved in organizing for positive social change often find this activism to be a crucial piece in building a new, meaningful, connected life.

For some, activism is a natural outgrowth of the work they did while in prison. Organizing by formerly incarcerated people has its roots in decades of activism by people behind bars. In the 1960s many Black prisoners connected to the civil rights struggle and organized for their own human rights in prison. In the 1990s women in federal prison organized around health and medical issues. Many of these prison organizers continued their organizing once they were released.

Collectively, formerly incarcerated people are daring to speak in our own voice, as people directly affected by the criminal justice system. As we work to improve conditions for ourselves, our families and communities, and the nation as a whole, we are transformed in the process. With each win, each loss, each lesson learned, we grow as people, becoming more effective agents in our work toward a more just and humane world.

#CLOSErikers

■ Janos Marton

As the director of policy and campaigns at JustLeadershipUSA, Janos Marton managed the nationally renowned campaign to #CLOSErikers.

On March 30, 2017, following a year of intense pressure from the #CLOSErikers campaign, New York City mayor Bill de Blasio announced that closing the long-troubled Rikers Island jail complex would become city policy. Since Rikers Island opened eight decades ago, it has been marked by violence, corruption, lawsuits, and blue-ribbon commissions seeking to reform it. Rikers Island's imperviousness to reform is what led to the formation of the #CLOSErikers campaign. The campaign is led by JustLeadershipUSA (JLUSA), a national criminal justice advocacy organization committed to "cutting the US correctional population in half by 2030." As an organization we believe that "those closest to the problem are closest to the solution," and we seek to elevate the voices of formerly incarcerated leaders in the policy conversation.[1]

Consistent with JLUSA's values, since its outset the #CLOSErikers campaign has been focused not only on shuttering a jail complex but also on dramatically reducing the number of New Yorkers in city jails and empowering communities that have been most harmed by Rikers Island. During the past year and a half, JLUSA has employed various strategies such as community organizing, coalition building, public demonstrations, social media activism, and policy advocacy to advance a highly sophisticated campaign that has changed the landscape of criminal justice in New York.

When the #CLOSErikers campaign began in April 2016, it was met with widespread skepticism, in part because Rikers has been an intractable part of the New York City criminal justice system for decades. In researching the history of Rikers Island, we found that the island's torturous legacy precedes even its use as a jail. The island is named for the slave-owning Riker family, whose most notorious descendant, Richard Riker, ran the New York City court system in the early nineteenth century. As a member of the "Kidnapping Club," he and others would capture free Black men and sell them back into slavery in the South. The Riker family later leased the island to the military during the Civil War—the first time it was used as a jail—and then sold it to New York City in the late nineteenth century when work on building a large-scale jail complex began. The jail opened in 1935, replacing New York's original penal colony, Blackwell's Island. In August 2017, in the midst of a broader local and national conversation about Confederate monuments in public spaces, the #CLOSErikers campaign held a protest to remind New Yorkers of this history.

#CLOSErikers "Richard Riker" billboard, David Etheridge-Bartow, 2017

Since #CLOSErikers launched on the steps of city hall in April 2016, the campaign has used a variety of approaches to raise awareness about the horrors of Rikers and to mobilize communities for change. First, we engaged in community organizing: identifying people directly affected by Rikers and developing them into leaders. Second, we built a coalition of more than 170 organizations committed to closure, looking beyond the established partners in the criminal justice field to include faith, labor, public health, and environmental justice groups—all of whom will help us shape the community-based solutions needed to move past a strictly punitive criminal justice system. Third, we shaped the narrative about Rikers Island with creative events like the Richard Riker action, which included a dramatic one-thousand-person march to the foot of the Rikers Island Bridge in September 2016, creating a viral digital GIF in December 2016, and in June 2017 surprising Mayor de Blasio at his local gym to hand him a copy of a report on closing Rikers that he publicly acknowledged not reading. Finally, all the attention we generated wouldn't have counted if we hadn't had serious policy goals that we were trying to advance along the way, including bail reform, speedy trial reform, and investments in supportive community-based programs to keep people out of the criminal justice system. The publication of the influential Lippman Commission Report in the spring of 2017 was essential to moving policy makers toward our point of view.

There are many reasons we believe the #CLOSErikers campaign has been successful, but the most important has been its focus on communities most impacted by mass incarceration. Our members have created a movement rooted in values, where political compromise is not an option. Their leadership has shown New Yorkers that they must recognize the humanity of people locked away in what the campaign refers to as a "torture island" sitting just a few feet from LaGuardia Airport. A mere nineteen months after this campaign was launched, we have succeeded in building a powerful coalition, educating New Yorkers, and influencing policy makers. The campaign has not been without challenges—the grueling nature of this type of campaign is not easy on individuals—and in future campaigns we intend to develop more sustainable practices.

Today the campaign to #CLOSErikers marches on. Even though closing the jail complex is now the official position of New York City government, how long that will take is a matter of political debate, and we still need to pass a number of local and state-level reforms to significantly decarcerate New York. We have been excited to see renewed energy for jail closure campaigns across the country, and JLUSA itself launched several municipal closure campaigns in 2018.

A Mother Confronts Chicago Police Torture

■ Mary L. Johnson

Chicago's history of police violence is all too familiar for Mary L. Johnson, a pioneer in the struggle against Chicago police torture. On August 28, 2015, at the "Reparations Now" exhibition at Chicago's Uri-Eichen Gallery, Johnson shared a deep and powerful account of her life as an activist. The text of her talk, below, has been edited for length.[1]

Hi warriors, because that's what I consider people who are willing to stand up and fight. Wherever there is a struggle, I will get in it. Because I feel like if you want justice, you got to be willing to fight for peace, and peace includes all of us. . . .

The thing that got me, my son was beat up in the park. He came and told me about the police jumping on him and I saw his face scarred up. And I went and filed a complaint. I learned then that the police don't only get you when you're bad; the police can get you when you're good, and you better not say anything about it.

By me reporting to the police what they did to my son, they targeted him after that. See that's the lowdown way they can destroy him, and all of us.

So I was feeling very bad. I started disliking all them white folks that I liked so much. 'Cause everywhere I went, I had to give my story to a white person. I saw all of them as being in charge. And I resented them so 'til I rode the bus and I'd see a white person looking at me and I'd roll my eyes 'til they'd turn their head. I said to myself, *Don't you even look at me, all the stuff you is.* But then I came to realize that if I was a person of color and I didn't realize what was going on, why do I think they knew? They had been brainwashed also.

They separated us so we wouldn't know what was happening to one another. I got a lot of white friends, they like me, but they don't live near me. They march with me and talk to me, but when we go home we part our ways. So that keeps us divided.

I learned to speak up and talk about what was going on because I was really mad with white folks. Police, Santa Claus, and Jesus. All of them. Because they had hurt my son and it was constantly going on. They told him they was gonna jam him—that's what they say and they put a case on him; put him in the penitentiary at seventeen years old. See, everybody in control is people that don't look like me.

So, I started feeling sorry for myself, but I was driven by my love for my son. I say, *I'm gonna expose these son of a guns*. If there's anybody out there with any kind of backbone, they gonna have to learn: until you overcome your fear you're not even living.

It's not a good feeling when you can't help your young ones. You see the cats how they go after their kittens? Well that's the way I was. I wasn't satisfied until all of them was at home. And I got that one that's still in the penitentiary framed up for something that he didn't do.

As long as my son's doing life, I'm a lifer. I'm a lifer. The whole penitentiary knows he didn't do that. The guards know he didn't do it! But guess what? They target him, they thought they was gonna shut my mouth. They say, "We'll give her something. We'll send him to Tamms!" He didn't even have a ticket! He didn't go because of the fact he was such a bad inmate. They put him there because they knew how powerful he was and the kind of mind that he had. And then another reason they put him there—they knew his mother was still out here running her mouth about justice. Everywhere they ask me to come and speak, I do it. ·

I got an invitation to go to death row and I got in, in spite of the rules. I was walking up and down death row. And when they saw me, they said I reminded them of the mother they hadn't seen in years, I remind them of the sister they left behind. It was such a feeling for me 'til I couldn't miss going. I was going every month. I got addicted to it because I saw the good that I was doing for those guys.

I couldn't help my son, but I could help somebody else's. I went because I cared. I'm an only child. I don't have any brothers or sisters and my mother died when I was four. And when I saw those guys, they needed me. And people say: "Well, where's the mother? Where are they parents?" You be their parents!

I realize, all the time I was growing up, I was in basic training for what I do now. I'm a foot soldier. I'm the one that make the way for the others to come through. See we're in battle. We're in a battle to be fair. I don't want you feeling sorry for me, because I am Black and strong. . . . How would you feel if this was your son? How would you feel if they took your child? You know, just like they did during slavery. Take them right out of arms.

They take our sons, they beat them, and what can we do about it? Tell them to stay in the house and don't go out? That's not fair. That's not right. Sympathy, no I don't need sympathy, but now *empathy*. Put yourself in my position, how would you feel? When we work together we can do beautiful things.

See it's sad when our children are out there trying to make a living and the first thing they talk about is them wearing their pants down low. The first time I saw pants pulled down like that, guess what they was doing? Standing being searched by the police. That's when I saw their pants down like that! And I lived on the North Side for about fourteen years, I never saw police searching white kids like that. I never saw them being humiliated. So how can you know it's happening to mine if I don't say something?

I'm still working on my son's case, but I'm not too busy to try to help other people. I got some news, y'all gon' make history with this case, and I'm looking for my son to come out and get a chance to dance with his mother again.

Pelican Bay Hunger Strike
Building Unity behind Bars

■ Claude Marks and Isaac Ontiveros

I n 2011, prisoners in California—led by those in the control units of Pelican Bay State Prison—organized a hunger strike to demand an end to the torturous conditions of solitary confinement. Two more strikes would follow, with over thirty thousand prisoners taking united action in the summer of 2013—both in isolation and in the general population of nearly every California prison. The strikes reflected significant shifts in political consciousness among prisoners and their loved ones. The violence of imprisonment was further exposed by demands and heightened organization from within the cages. Prisoner-led collective actions and growing public support have changed the political landscape dramatically.

The organization of hunger strikes in 2011 surprised many, especially the CDCr—the California Department of Corrections and Rehabilitation (the lowercase *r*, preferred by most prison writers, derides the Orwellian use of the word "rehabilitation")—the media, and much of the public.

Current prison organizing continues a historic legacy of struggle. Among prisoners, the strikes of 2011–13 were compared to the Attica Prison uprising of 1971. Shortly before that rebellion, prisoners at Attica refused to speak or eat in the facility's chow hall, paying tribute to Black Panther Party member and California prison movement leader George Jackson, who had been assassinated at San Quentin State Prison on August 21. Jackson was a skilled and effective leader who connected the human rights demands of prisoners to revolutionary ideas both globally and in the streets. He argued with powerful clarity that racist and exploitive power relations could and should be changed through political and military struggle, and that Black liberation was achievable as part of an international struggle to destroy imperialism. Within the prisons, he built unity across racial lines—thinking that a unified prison movement could succeed in winning basic human rights both within the cages and in oppressed communities. While the state obviously found Jackson's ideas and example extremely dangerous, many prisoners and community members found them a clarion call for action.

On September 9, 1971, Attica erupted. Led by prisoners affiliated with the Nation of Islam, the Black Panther Party, the Young Lords, and the Five Percenters, the rebellion seized control of several large areas of the prison and issued a manifesto demanding, among other things, better health conditions, an end to political persecution of prisoners, and a right to organize or join labor unions (these demands were very similar to the Folsom Prison manifesto written in California in 1970). After four days of negotiations, New York governor Nelson Rockefeller ordered that the prison be retaken, and in the ensuing brutal military assault, thirty-nine people were killed by state police and prison guards.

While Attica is one of the most remembered uprisings, between the late 1960s and the early 1980s there were over three hundred prison rebellions across the United States, including those at the Oklahoma State Penitentiary in 1973 and the Idaho State Penitentiary in 1972–73, the August Rebellion in 1974 at Bedford Hills Correctional Facility for Women in New York State, a 1975 demonstration at the North Carolina Correctional Center for Women, and one at the Penitentiary of New Mexico in 1980.

In response to these militant uprisings, prisons developed unprecedented strategies of repression and isolation, and for a time resistance took less dramatic forms. Yet prisoners were still inspired to resist. In one example that took place in 1995, women in California state prisons initiated a class action lawsuit against genocidal health-care conditions, and successfully organized family members and allies across the state to support them.

Prisoners in California in 2011–13 organized against the very policies, strategies, and technology that had been put into place to neutralize the rebellions of previous decades (both inside and outside prison), such as solitary confinement, gang validation (which includes the criminalization of George Jackson's writings), and the gutting of educational programming. In turn, prisoners used strategies similar to those of the previous era: collective direct action, multiracial unity, and building strong support and solidarity networks on the outside.

The prisoners issued five core demands that called for an end to the prisons' use of long-term solitary confinement, gang validation, and collective punishment and pressed for better food and access to educational programming on TV. Following fruitless complaints and attempts to negotiate, the hunger strikes ignited the political energies of tens of thousands of imprisoned people in a majority of California prisons; they also sparked life into a vast solidarity network led by prisoners' families and loved ones, former prisoners, and anti-prison organizations. The strike was multi-pronged. It included a legal, legislative, and mass media strategy, as well as organizing prisoner-led solutions to violence on the inside. Support for the strike was broad and international. Imprisoned people—from those held in detention centers in Washington and Texas, to prisoners in Georgia, Ohio, Illinois, and Guantanamo, to Palestinian political prisoners held by the state of Israel—all took inspiration from and expressed solidarity with the strike.

From the outset and over the course of three mass actions, the strikers were clear that their demands could be met by honest negotiation and moderate reforms. Todd Ashker, a leader in the Short Corridor Collective at Pelican Bay, explained, "Our struggle adheres to the principles of the Constitution and International Treaty Law and is inspired by all oppressed people's demands for human rights, dignity, respect, justice and equality—the demand to be treated as living beings."[1] In turn, the CDCr took an entrenched position; they dismissed the legitimacy of prisoners' concerns, retaliated against strike participants, targeted the strike leadership, harassed prisoners' loved ones and supporters, and launched a generally harsh and fear-mongering public relations campaign.

Maintaining a collective stance, prisoners who had spent over ten years in isolation filed a class action civil lawsuit in federal court in May 2012, charging that their being held in solitary confinement constituted a violation of prisoners' Eighth Amendment rights against cruel and unusual punishment. To date, the CDCr's attempts to dismiss and defang the suit have been unsuccessful.

Reminiscent of George Jackson's call forty years ago to "settle your quarrels [and] come together," in 2012 California prisoners issued an "Agreement to End Hostilities." In it they declared, "Now is the time for us to collectively seize this moment in time and put an end to more than 20–30 years of hostilities between our racial groups," encouraging prisoners to resolve their differences, for prison officials one of the most feared developments.[2] An anonymous prisoner characterized the agreement as something that creates new horizons for prisoner unity, beyond the demands for an end to long-term solitary and validation: "The inclusion of the Agreement to end race-based hostilities to our struggle against California's solitary confinement policies represents a qualitative leap of the insight of all prison nationalities, and unites us beyond the fight to free ourselves from CDCr's torture units."[3]

Two other prison leaders, Kijani Tashiri Askari and Akili Castlin at Tehachapi prison, enlarged upon this by writing that when it comes to power, "our exemplary conduct has made CDCr completely powerless over us, as we have successfully taken away the fodder that used to fuel their political rhetoric in labeling us the 'worst of the worst.' Our unity now qualitatively threatens the political, social, and economic stability of the CDCr."[4]

Key to organizing direct support and solidarity efforts for the strikes, including spreading the word about the "Agreement to End Hostilities" in communities across California, were the family members and loved ones of the prisoners leading and participating in the strike. The prisoner action also had the inspiring effect of renewing connections between prisoners and their families, who grew from being personal supporters to participants and new leaders of the movement against solitary confinement and the wider anti-prison movement.

The hunger strikers made it clear that they also wanted to help shine a light on the conditions of isolation in women's prisons, which too often are even more invisible and ignored than those in men's prisons. In January 2013, California Families Against Solitary Confinement—founded by hunger strikers' loved ones and

overwhelmingly led by women of color—mobilized as part of a coalition organized by the California Coalition for Women Prisoners,
bringing hundreds of community members from across the state to
protest the devastating impacts of overcrowding at Central California Women's Facility in the Central Valley city of Chowchilla.
Medical care had significantly deteriorated, and there was a dramatic increase in women being thrown into isolation. Overcrowding
in women's prisons has aggravated mental health issues, causing an
increase in the number of mentally disabled people in the special
housing unit (SHU), even though this is the worst place to put them.
In recent years there were several preventable deaths and numerous suicides at Califonia Institution for Women (CIW) in Corona.
None of the deaths have been made public by the prisons, although
they clearly signify a state of crisis.

April Harris, imprisoned at CIW, described conditions there
around the time of the protest: "We have women dropping like
flies and not one person has been questioned as to why. . . . I have
been down almost 20 years and I have never seen anything like this.
Ever."[5] The hunger strikes helped to address the too often ignored
struggles of imprisoned women (now close to 115,000 in the United
States) and trans people against solitary confinement and other violent prison conditions. Many women and trans prisoners also refused food in solidarity with the overall demands emerging from the
leadership in Pelican Bay.

An energized movement was critical to supporting the 2013
strike—coordinating mass support, maintaining good communication among prisoners, and developing a strategy to give voice to
those inside despite their isolation and lockdowns. The solidarity
effort was able to establish a relationship with the United Nations
special rapporteur on torture and was also able to convince key California state politicians to recognize the legitimacy of the strikers' demands and to hold special public hearings on solitary confinement.
This solid work undermined the CDCr's entrenched position and
supported the prisoners when they decided to suspend the strike in
order to support the public hearings.

In the mass media, in the communities, and even among
elected officials, the conditions, uses, and devastating effects of

solitary confinement—along with the term itself—were pulled from out of the shadows and thrust into the spotlight. In turn, the California prison regime did everything in its power to suppress the strike, retaliate against its participants, target and neutralize its leadership, regain an upper hand in public opinion, and reconsolidate its control, even at the cost of making concessions and changes to its policy. Todd Ashker reflected on the historic impact of the strikers' mass actions:

> I personally believe the prisoncrats' efforts to turn the global support we have gained for our cause against us will fail. . . . CDCr rhetoric indicates desperation; a very concerning desperation in the sense that it is demonstrative of CDCr's top administrators' intent to continue their culture of dehumanization, torture, and other types of abusive policies and practices. . . .
>
> 1.) Our key demand(s) remain unresolved. The primary goal is abolishing indefinite SHU and Ad.-Seg [administrative segregation] confinement, and related torturous conditions therein; the abolishment of the debriefing policy; and meaningful Individual Accountability."[6]

At one time the leaders of the strike were all in the same prison at Pelican Bay. The Pelican Bay State Penitentiary SHU Short Corridor Collective was originally made up of Todd Ashker, Arturo Castellanos, Sitawa Nantambu Jamaa (Dewberry) and Antonio Guillen; and members of the Representatives Body were Danny Troxell, George Franco, Ronnie Yandell, Paul Redd, James Baridi Williamson, Alfred Sandoval, Louis Powell, Alex Yrigollen, Gabriel Huerta, Frank Clement, Raymond "Chavo" Perez, and James Mario Perez (as of September 2013, when prisoners suspended the third hunger strike). The CDCr has since dispersed the leadership by sending some people to other SHUs, including Tehachapi and Corcoran prisons. These prisoners largely remain in isolation, despite some of them having been sent to the prison's general population. According to the prisoners themselves and those in close contact with them, rather than suffering a complete collapse in leadership and unity, the prisoners have reorganized and reconstituted an inclusive structure by bringing more people into representative and leadership positions in these other prisons. Their ability to organize and build new leadership has defied the CDCr's attempts to demobilize and demoralize the struggle.

What the CDCr is peddling as a reform is a step-down program (SDP). The SDP claims to offer an "incentive-based, multi-step process that affords offenders placed in a Security Housing Unit (SHU) due to validations and/or documented Security Threat Group (STG) behaviors ["STG" replacing the word "gang" in policy] the opportunity to earn enhanced privileges and to demonstrate the ability to refrain from STG behavior, with the ultimate goal of release from the SHU."[7] The SDP consists of five steps. Typically steps 1 and 2 take a year to complete, although in some cases they can be completed within six months. Steps 3–5 each take a minimum of a year to complete. Each step imposes benchmarks on prisoner behavior and participation. A person may be placed in any step or may be released to the general population at the SDP review board's discretion. The best scenario that the average person placed in step 1 can anticipate is that it will take at least four years before they are released from the SHU to the general population—assuming that this is ever even a possibility. A prisoner can be bumped back by administrative discretion with no due process. Informing on fellow prisoners is also an element of the SDP. Most of those who led the strike have refused to go along with the new program. Mutope Duguma at Pelican Bay says, "We have been able to examine, evaluate and investigate the STG and SDP policies and we unanimously reject them, because simply put, they are more of the same. They empower the previous policies that we were initially peacefully protesting."[8]

The CDCr has also tried to use the SDP as a response to the class action civil suit—hoping a dispersal of plaintiffs would nullify their claims and standing as a class within the courts. However, the courts ruled that despite being dispersed, prisoners who met the criterion of ten years or more in isolation continue to have standing in raising constitutional questions about prolonged isolation.

Conditions for prisoners and their families, particularly following the strikes, are very serious. As Duguma says, "CDCr has turned up its attacks, making it worse for each and every prisoner and his or her family. New regulations on personal property and

on 'obscenity'—actually censorship, a direct attack on free speech—
have been implemented, and the proposed regulations to use canine
searches of visitors—a direct attack on our families—are not yet approved but are in effect 'on a temporary basis.'"⁹

Since 2011, imprisoned people living in some of the worst conditions imaginable have been able to organize and take collective action.
They have created unity around agreed-upon goals and have coordinated multiple strategies using diverse tactics. Prisoners understand
that their fight, like most freedom struggles, is long term. They have
built alliances with different movements, peoples, and communities.

The CDCr's primary goal is to maintain control and legitimacy—using whatever means. The state of California may be forced
to offer some concessions given the advances made by the prisoners'
struggle. Some individuals will experience improved conditions, but
we would do well to remember the warning of political prisoner
Jamil Al-Amin (speaking then as H. Rap Brown) offered at a 1968
rally to free Huey P. Newton: "We tend to equate progress with concessions. We can no longer make that mistake."¹⁰

The strike of 2011–13 and the unity reflected by the coordinated
action of thirty thousand prisoners will continue to embolden those
at the center of the struggle and, with the support of our families and
communities, will empower ongoing challenges to the violence of
imprisonment, policing, and social inequity. The strikes have helped
to generate national movement against solitary confinement, joining
together people inside and outside prisons in many different states.
Several states have pending legislation against long-term solitary
confinement. Most importantly, public consciousness is shifting to
understand that it is torture and must be ended. As one of the state-
ments from prison hunger strikers at Pelican Bay said, "This struggle
has contributed to progressively changing attitudes in society and
prisons. Our collective efforts have repeatedly exposed the state's
contradictions and sparked the People's appetite for freedom and
new social relationships."¹¹

◆

Prisoners' Demands[12]

1. **End Group Punishment & Administrative Abuse** – This is in response to PBSP's [Pelican Bay State Penitentiary's] application of "group punishment" as a means to address individual inmates' rule violations. This includes the administration's abusive, pretextual use of "safety and concern" to justify what are unnecessary punitive acts. This policy has been applied in the context of justifying indefinite SHU status, and progressively restricting our programming and privileges.

2. **Abolish the Debriefing Policy, and Modify Active/Inactive Gang Status Criteria** –

- Perceived gang membership is one of the leading reasons for placement in solitary confinement.
- The practice of "debriefing," or offering up information about fellow prisoners particularly regarding gang status, is often demanded in return for better food or release from the SHU. Debriefing puts the safety of prisoners and their families at risk, because they are then viewed as "snitches."
- The validation procedure used by the California Department of Corrections and Rehabilitation (CDCR) employs such criteria as tattoos, readings [sic] materials, and associations with other prisoners (which can amount to as little as greeting [them]) to identify gang members.
- Many prisoners report that they are validated as gang members with evidence that is clearly false or using procedures that do not follow the Castillo v. Alameida settlement which restricted the use of photographs to prove association.

3. **Comply with the US Commission on Safety and Abuse in America's Prisons 2006 Recommendations Regarding an End to Long-Term Solitary Confinement** – CDCR shall implement the findings and recommendations of the US commission on safety and abuse in America's prisons final 2006 report regarding CDCR SHU facilities as follows:

- End Conditions of Isolation (p. 14). Ensure that prisoners in SHU and Ad-Seg (Administrative Segregation) have

regular meaningful contact and freedom from extreme
physical deprivations that are known to cause lasting harm.
(pp. 52–57)

- Make Segregation a Last Resort (p. 14). Create a more
  productive form of confinement in the areas of allowing
  inmates in SHU and Ad-Seg (Administrative Segregation)
  the opportunity to engage in meaningful self-help
  treatment, work, education, religious, and other productive
  activities relating to having a sense of being a part of the
  community.
- End Long-Term Solitary Confinement. Release inmates
  to general prison population who have been warehoused
  indefinitely in SHU for the last 10 to 40 years (and
  counting).
- Provide SHU Inmates Immediate Meaningful Access to:
  i) adequate natural sunlight [and] ii) quality health care
  and treatment, including the mandate of transferring all
  PBSP–SHU inmates with chronic health care problems to
  the New Folsom Medical SHU facility.

4. Provide Adequate and Nutritious Food – Cease the practice of
denying adequate food, and provide wholesome nutritional meals
including special diet meals, and allow inmates to purchase additional vitamin supplements.

- PBSP staff must cease their use of food as a tool to punish
  SHU inmates.
- Provide a sergeant/lieutenant to independently observe the
  serving of each meal, and ensure each tray has the complete
  issue of food on it.
- Feed the inmates whose job it is to serve SHU meals with
  meals that are separate from the pans of food sent from
  kitchen for SHU meals.

**5. Expand and Provide Constructive Programming and Privileges
for Indefinite SHU Status Inmates.**
Examples include:

- Expand visiting regarding amount of time and adding one
  day per week.

- Allow one photo per year.
- Allow a weekly phone call.
- Allow Two (2) annual packages per year. A 30 lb. package based on "item" weight and not packaging and box weight.
- Expand canteen and package items allowed. Allow us to have the items in their original packaging (the cost for cosmetics, stationary [sic], envelopes, should not count towards the max draw limit).
- More TV channels.
- Allow TV/Radio combinations, or TV and small battery operated radio.
- Allow Hobby Craft Items—art paper, colored pens, small pieces of colored pencils, watercolors, chalk, etc.
- Allow sweat suits and watch caps.
- Allow wall calendars.
- Install pull-up/dip bars on SHU yards.
- Allow correspondence courses that require proctored exams.

**Signed by
Todd Ashker
Arturo Castellanos
Sitawa N. Jamaa (s/n R. N. Dewberry)
George Franco
Antonio Guillen
Louis Powell
Paul Redd
Alfred Sandoval
Danny Troxell
James Williamson
Ronnie Yandell
. . . and all other similarly situated prisoners

The Lil' Paralegal Who Could and the Birth of a New Law

■ Patrick Pursley

This is a story of hope against all odds. From my prison cell, fighting a natural-life sentence, I helped introduce a law that eventually freed me after twenty-four years of a wrongful conviction.

More than twenty years ago, I was a petty criminal, in and out of prison, and basically a troubled young man. I thought I was a rebel, a radical, because I read a few books and would rage against the machine, and by that I mean I did a lot of complaining about the "system." Every once in a while, someone would tell me, "If you don't like the system, then work to change it." At the time, I wasn't wanting to hear that. Twenty years later I would find that working within the "system" was my only realistic shot at freedom.

It's October 2006, and I'm now a prisoner at Stateville Maximum Security Prison. While going to the chow hall one evening, during the month of Ramadan, I'm suddenly pulled out of line by the infamous Warden McCann. "What are these?" he asked as he stared at my neck.

"Those are prayer beads, sir," I replied.

"Are you allowed to have them?" he asked.

"Yes, sir," I firmly responded, like a private at attention being grilled by a drill sergeant.

Warden McCann eyed me up and down, trying to figure me out and replied, "I don't like your attitude."

There's an officer hanging out of the window of the gun tower with a shotgun in front of me and close to one hundred people eating in chow hall when I decide to open mouth and insert foot. Without missing a beat, I respond, "We don't like your attitude either, sir.

You have brought much misery and suffering to the land." I knew instantly those were not the words I should have said.

That sarcastic stunt got me tossed in the hole for six months. I was stripped of almost all of my property with the exception of a pen, paper, and books. I was supposed to be alone in there, but I soon found out that the thousands of roaches and other unknown bug "cellies" would keep me company. As I looked around my new temporary home, I noticed there was ice on my walls but no extra blanket or clothing. It was going to be a long and painful winter. All I had to keep me warm was a steely determination to get out of prison and help my children. While in segregation, I got a letter from my oldest daughter explaining that she had been the victim of a violent crime; she wrote that she wished she had never been born. I was tormented by her words and worked even harder, doubling my efforts for freedom. The problem was that no matter how good of a jailhouse lawyer I thought I was, in my case, I was still getting nowhere fast.

For years before my time in the hole, I'd been fighting my case. In 1993 I was tried and convicted of a stick-up murder. The facts of my case were this: an eyewitness said that I wasn't the shooter; I had an alibi; the crime scene depicted tennis shoe prints in the snow, not the combat boot prints belonging to me; pictures of tennis shoe prints were going in the opposite direction than what the state claimed. I was arrested based on the word of a crackhead who also had pending charges and to whom the police paid $2,640.00.[1] Most importantly, I had my own independent ballistic experts whose testing demonstrated that the gun I owned did not match the bullets found at the crime scene!

In my 1995 appeal the pictures of the tennis shoe and bullets came up missing. At my insistence, my appellate defender obtained the ballistic pictures, but instead of using them in my appeal or giving me a copy, incredibly, he sent them back to the state's attorney's office![2] It took me eight years and a stack of pleadings, filling six legal boxes, to get those pictures back. No one cared, though. During my trial the state's expert witness testified that their agency didn't even use the ballistics photographs and identification in trial testimony. But in 2000 I read an article in the *Chicago Tribune* that showed otherwise.[3] The Illinois State Crime Police crime lab did, in fact, have a camera on their microscopes, and they were implementing IBIS (Integrated Ballistics Imaging System), a national network that uses digital imaging to match guns to crimes. This system was also used in the DC sniper case. By this time, I had pretty much exhausted my appeals; no court cared a whit about anything I had to say. I had a lot of experience as a paralegal in helping others, but, like a stereotypical jailhouse lawyer, I couldn't get myself out of prison. I had nothing to lose, so I tried to get gun testing under the new DNA law in Illinois, which stated that forensic testing not available at the time of trial can be sought to prove innocence. Since the IBIS network wasn't around in 1993, I petitioned the court to retest the gun using computer matching. I was denied, but the appeal court threw me a bone: because the law, as it stood, didn't allow for gun testing, the law would have to be amended first. I now had hope!

There was one problem, though. I was one of many people in prison trying to get free, but with no money, no power, no support, no lobby, and no political connections. I wrote letters to lawmakers, to no avail. I even sued Attorney General Lisa Madigan, my old judge, the state's attorney, and Governor Rod Blagojevich, trying to get the law changed and access to new ballistics testing. The federal courts deemed me a "frivolous filer" and hit me with "three strikes" to bar future litigation without the three-hundred-dollar filing fee up front. Undaunted, I went back to state court, because no matter how many times you are told no, all you need is one yes! Of course, my next suit was again dismissed, but I appealed and the appellate court threw me another bone. They ordered that the gun, bullets, and ballistic pictures be preserved by the state. Hope!

I knew that if I was to have any real chance of getting out, I needed outside help. I was sending out letters every week to lawyers, professors, and lawmakers. I was largely being ignored, and those who did respond said they couldn't help. This went on for years. In the cold winter of 2006, while sitting in the hole for six months, I wrote an article for *Stateville Speaks Newsletter* arguing that Illinois law needed to keep up with current technology and that the use of IBIS should become available for a post-conviction petition so a defendant could establish actual innocence based upon new ballistics testing. It turned out that the editor of the newsletter, Bill Ryan, a prison reform advocate, had contacts in the Illinois legislature, where he floated my idea and it was made into a bill. By some miracle, before Governor Blagojevich got fired and cuffed up, he signed the bill into law in October 2007. Perseverance!

I filed a petition in 2008 under the new law, and the Center on Wrongful Convictions at Northwestern Law School and Jenner & Block, a private law firm, took my case. In the circuit court the trial court dismissed my petition, denying my request for a new gun test. Thankfully, my legal team was in it for the long haul, and on appeal we won. They ordered the gun test I had been chasing for almost fifteen years. Reading the court order was bittersweet: the appellate court summed up all my efforts to get the gun tested on just one page. I felt the sting of tears well up in my eyes and thought about how it made no mention of my kids growing up without me, or the anger my son has toward me, or how the streets claimed my daughters. There was not a word of my grandkids not knowing me and no mention of how I had been fighting for fifteen years for a gun test that would take fifteen minutes. But the reality was, this was a miracle and I was thankful!

The new gun test did not connect the gun to the murder. Further, through IBIS we now know that the gun used in the crime for which I had been wrongly convicted had been used in another crime while I was locked up. My case set a precedent that will hopefully help countless other people prove their innocence, just like DNA testing has done.

Eight years later I would get an evidentiary hearing that resulted in a new trial. Five experts testified during that 2016 hearing. The visual evidence based on ballistics testing was the linchpin in the case. My experts tested the bullets and shell casings in seven different spots at 120-times magnification, and they presented large digital prints that clearly showed the gun didn't match. For their part, the state had tested the bullets and casings in three spots at 20–40 times magnification and had submitted blurry photos claiming the shell casings matched the crime scene. The prosecution now admitted the bullets did not match, but instead of making any concession, they claimed that although the bullets did match in 1993, they no longer matched due to degradation or mishandling.

Since 1993 I've been saying I'm innocent; since 1999 I've been pursuing new gun testing. My word and ballistic photos were largely ignored. The same gun test I asked for in 2000 was not granted until 2011–12, when I fought for a change in the law and was blessed with the attorneys I now have (as they say, "Pro se gets no play").

I may have won this round, but the battle rages on, because the state filed an appeal, which means this can go on another two years. While I'm finally free on bail after twenty-four years of a wrongful conviction, the ballistics testing and visual evidence will continue to be questioned simply because they are an extension of me.

To those fighting the good fight, even when things seem against the odds, never give up! You can take it from me: the little paralegal who could.

Playlists and Liner Notes

Over the four months that artist and architect Andres L. Hernandez worked with a group of incarcerated artists—all serving long-term sentences—they listened to and talked about music as they made art. In the isolated space of a prison, music has connected the artists to memories before incarceration, times remembered with both joy and pain. The idea of creating "playlists for the long term" emerged from the conversations. The following excerpts are songs and liner notes from playlists developed by the artists.

George Gomez

Sangre de Indio
by Banda Machos

Sangre De Indio is a song that gives me courage and strength every time I play it. It's a song of great emotions with pride and honor as it glorified my parents' indigenous bloodline.

Dreaming of You
by Selena

Selena instantly reminds me of my loving mother because she loves all her music. But this song in particular connects me to the time when my daughter was not in my life and how, throughout those years, I had many dreams of her.

De Esta Sierra a Otra Sierra
by El As de la Sierra

This song takes me back to my youth days and my sister's schoolgirl days when my father helped her prepare and memorize this song for our yearly Cinco de Mayo festival that our school always celebrated.

Rest in Peace
by Brownside

I like to replace the word "carnal" (brother) to "jefe" (father) because this song describes exactly how sad I feel about my father's passing. R.I.P. "Jefe." I know we will see each other again because I will be there someday.

No Sunshine
by Kid Frost

Lyrics: "If you don't want to do no time, you better take time to try to draw the line or you are going to be the next fool in line doing time."

People of the Sun
by Rage Against the Machine

Lyrics: "Since 1516 minds attacked and overseen now crawl amidst the ruins of this empty dream. Their borders and boots on top of us. . . . the spirit of Cuauhtémoc alive and untamed . . . the vulture came to try to steal your name . . . this is for the people of the sun, it's coming back again."

(Powerful words to me.)

Smooth
by Carlos Santana

When I was in junior high school, a teacher of mine was deeply in love with this artist. She always played his songs and the more I listened, the more I liked them. This song takes me back to her classroom.

Nieves de Enero
by Chalino Sanchez

This is one of many songs that I like about Chalino. Chalino Sanchez has deep roots in my family tree. I grew up listening to his songs with my dad, uncles, cousins, brothers, friends, neighbors, and so on. Chalino Sanchez's songs have helped me a lot with my time in prison.

Cuando Volverás
by Aventura

Lyrics: "Me duele corazón de tanta penas. Por favor llame un doctor y que vuelva mi morena. Te extraño dia y noche sin cezar y el pensar que estás con otro me a tormento cada dia mas. ¿Cuando volverás? ¿Cuando volverás? Dime morena si hay otro en mi lugar. ¿Por que? ¿Por que? ¿Me haces esto mujer? Si siempre yo te quise."

Daniel Scott

Hypocrite

by Kendrick Lamar

The song exposes the root of white supremacy and points to gang banging as its fruit. It teaches the hypocrisy of abhorring racial discrimination yet perpetuating Black-on-Black violence.

War

by Bob Marley

This sends chills down my spine. It exposes the root of the world conflict and wars. It prescribes a solution: Rid the planet of white supremacy and its inherent caste system.

Assassination

by Dead Prez

"Cops ride by in the streets and blow my friends way, I try to smoke enough lah to take my sins away . . ." There's so much pressure on the Black man in America to stay alive. Upon every turn, he's under threat of assassination at the hands of systemic racism spearheaded by the police. We self-medicate to take the edge off.

I See God in You

by India Arie

This is the solution to ALL human conflicts. We have to recognize honor and respect all human beings, because supreme consciousness is the divine force within us all. Such recognition, honor, and respect kills white supremacy, discrimination, and oppression.

You're Always in My Head
by India Arie

This beautiful song reminds me of the ever presence of supreme consciousness we call God. It reminds me of the "still small voice" leading me through life's twists and turns. It reminds me to see God in EVERYTHING.

Purge
by The Game

This was a timely song released during the height of urban unrest, in response to police assassinations of Black men captured on camera. This gift from my fellow Blood brother and Comptonite also offers a solution for the perpetrators of police brutality, child molestation, and racism: Purge!

Guiltiness
by Bob Marley

Evil against the oppressed will not prevail. The guilty instinctively know that justice demands an accounting of the dirty deeds "the system" perpetuates against the righteous. Bob Marley sounds the prophetic pronouncement "woe to the down pressors, they eat the bread of sorrow, woe to the down pressors, they eat the bread of sad tomorrow—oh yeah!"

Redemption Song
by Bob Marley

Ultimately the oppressed are victims of mental slavery from which we must be emancipated. Once we download the right knowledge and put it in motion, we will redeem ourselves and resurrect from the grave of ignorance.

Elton Williams

Little Wing
by Jimi Hendrix, Stevie Ray Vaughan

They take it to another level of sound, adding that missing touch of soul, making it a mainstay in blues history and a legend. In the lead guitar's riffs, anguish is expressed with unfiltered intensity, while the somber tones of the bass deliver your heart to experience the depths of loneliness and solitude.

I Touched a Dream
by The Mighty Dells

The lonely person calls to mind all that he's lost due to his extended absence from society. His lover severs their bond, moved to part ways, leaving him bereft of all he once held most precious. The smoothly delivered lyrics highlight that lonely hearts need to be wrapped up in the security of each other, shielding him from the ravages and rough nature of his present condition. This affords him at least half a chance to maintain and hold onto that better nature within himself or that part of the man that needs and knows how to love.

Statue of a Fool
by David Ruffin

Misunderstanding leads to the proclamation "somewhere there should be, for all the world to see, a statue of a fool made of stone." This song is a clear message for a man who has finally come to grips with his reality. In all the time that's passed, he has engaged in sincere contemplation of his situation and circumstances. He's weathered the emotional storms and conquered the first leg of his journey. He accepts the cause of his condition (himself) and, in that acceptance, he gives himself the opportunity to forgive himself and move on to what life has next in store.

What Becomes of the Brokenhearted

Jimmy Ruffin

This song testifies to the lonely person's understanding of his condition and speaks aloud the question that weighs so heavily upon his heart and mind. In those musings, he spies a glimmer of light and that light inspires hope and that hope leads him to dream.

I Want to Make You Glad

Main Ingredients

This tells of the lonely person's desire to find and bring a smile to the face of a woman who has suffered as bitterly as he has; to love her and show her that she is worthy of being loved.

Oceans of Thoughts and Dreams

The Dramatics

This song carries on the theme of the dream, as the dream morphs into memories. The lonely person can't help recalling what love was like in days past, hoping to find such affection with the woman who would fill the pages of the book of his life with scripture that would outlast the ages.

Guess Who's Back in Town

Heaven & Earth

This song tells the story of the lover's return to love-land and the end of a journey from heartache to hope.

Section 5

Litanies for Survival

n September 2016 the Formerly Incarcerated, Convicted People and Families Movement (FICPFM) held their first conference in Oakland, California. The conference, the first of its kind in the United States, drew more than five hundred people, among them several contributors in this book, including James Kilgore, Albert Woodfox, and Kathy Boudin.

FICPFM, which grew out of gatherings of formerly incarcerated and convicted people in Alabama and California in 2011, calls mass incarceration "a national program overwhelmingly reserved for people from low-income communities, overwhelmingly imposed upon Communities of Color" and recognizes that "the current criminal justice system has never worked for people of color, poor people, or our community, and ultimately this system predicated on racism and torture should be dismantled."[1]

Partner groups included for this historic conference included grassroots and national organizations such as Legal Services for Prisoners with Children, A New Way of Life Reentry Project, All of Us or None, JustLeadershipUSA, College and Community Fellowship, Voices of Experience, Women on the Rise, National Alliance for the Empowerment of the Formerly Incarcerated, and Release Aging People in Prison.

This kind of coalition building—between incarcerated people, formerly incarcerated people, and the families and loved ones connected to people inside—is lifted up here. Through vivid and impressionistic entries, the wide-ranging consequences of the long term are made immediate. In this section we read stories of anguish, isolation, resourcefulness, and constancy.

What is most remarkable is the immediacy of each contributor's offering. These narratives emerge from the complex "dailyness" of the long term, illuminating difficulties and possibilities that are ongoing. Each entry offers radiant insight—kindling to imagine and make way(s) for more peace, more thriving, more justice.

Section 5 takes its title from Audre Lorde's poem "Litany for Survival." In a clear and steady voice, the speaker in Lorde's poem gathers a very particular *we*—those of us "standing on the constant edge of decision / crucial and alone." The speaker sees us. The speaker is us. Marginalized and resilient, living through fear, seeking futures "like bread in our children's mouths." The poem commiserates, defies, comforts; it registers lamentation and sounds and resounds triumph. "We were never meant to survive." And yet we do.

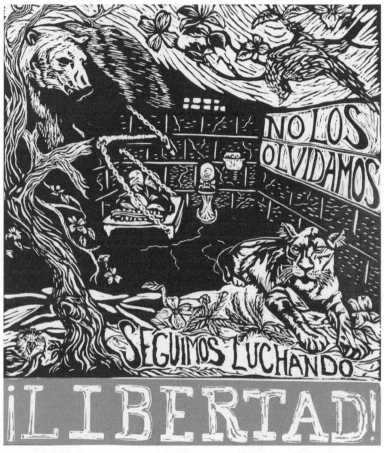

No Los Olvidamos/We haven't forgotten you, linoleum block print, Thea Gahr, 2010

Whole Foods, Black Wall Street, and My 13-Inch Flat-Screen TV

■ Andre Patterson

It was "Groundhog's Day" at Stateville prison—that is to say, another redundant night. I sat on the top bunk in my small concrete box, head scraping the low, paint-chipped ceiling, cursing my two-hundred-dollar, 13-inch flat-screen television. The TV defiantly cut off every few minutes, despite my chastising finger mashing the power button and my verbal assault on its character: "Piece of crap!" I'd only had it for a year. The joint had sold me a lemon. I was going to have to buy a new one already.

I made a quick mental calculation of how long it would take me to save up to two hundred bucks working my kitchen job six hours a day, seven days a week for twenty-eight dollars a month. That's minus the roughly ten to twelve dollars I must mandatorily spend on personal hygiene products each month. It added up to a long, slow process. My mind switched from financial independence to beggar mode. Which one of my loved ones would have pity on me and sponsor the exorbitant cost of my penitentiary life?

It was five o'clock, and I was chasing the news like most prisoners do around this time every night. We shake our heads at the rampant violence plaguing the neighborhoods we left behind while hoping to glimpse a familiar dilapidated building or vacant lot, despite the atrocity that might have occurred there, in order to experience that moment of nostalgia.

In between my bogus TV's blackouts, I caught a report about the grand opening of Whole Foods smack-dab in the middle of Englewood, an economically depressed neighborhood on the South Side of Chicago. News cameras captured the reactions of ecstatic residents briskly moving through the aisles, taking in all the new product choices. A reporter interviewed a grateful Black entrepreneur who beamed over the fact that their product was being featured on the shelves. Major business had come back to Englewood. The people were hopeful; their savior had arrived.

But I was conflicted in my enthusiasm. On the surface it looked like things could be turning around for this neighborhood. The arrival of what's considered an "upscale" grocery chain, bringing with it a hundred new jobs. The shiny new store would potentially attract more companies, resurrecting the Sixty-third and Halsted business district. On the flip side, when monoliths like Whole Foods knock on the door of a neighborhood like Englewood, it is often a signal of an influx of wealthier residents. Gentrification. White people intent on reclaiming prime real estate abandoned decades ago in the frenzy of what is referred to as "white flight." This frenzy kicked off in Englewood in the early 1960s, when Black folks were legally allowed to encroach into what had been a white neighborhood, and white residents fled to the suburbs in response.

What would be the angle of this store, often referred to as "Whole Paycheck," to lay roots down in a location blighted by poverty, unemployment, and violent crime? Would the new jobs provide livable wages that would improve the quality of life for residents rather than just enough to get by?

I began thinking about self-determination: the "free choice of one's own acts or states without external compulsion" and "the determination by the people of a territorial unit of their own future political status," as defined by the Merriam-Webster dictionary. When I was growing up, it seemed like everyone around me was shuffled along by "external compulsions" to one dead-end low-wage job after another. They had to pay the rent, which had just been raised again; make sure the kids were clothed and fed; pay off bill collectors, who hounded them daily; and in some cases, support incarcerated family members. I watched my dad disappear every day, just when the sun was flirting with the horizon, and resurface after dark to eat, shit, go to bed, and have nightmares of doing it all over again the next day. All that this afforded him was a cramped, musty basement apartment where he, my little brother, and I shared the lone bedroom while my stepmom lived on the couch. Throughout my childhood and into adulthood, I resided in various aggregates like this that included my grandmas, aunties, and uncles. They would all follow the same cycle, crawling on top of each other, scrambling to get to jobs that barely kept them afloat, returning home to screen phone calls from bill collectors.

In hindsight, I wonder what kept a family unit like mine dependent on each other, pooling our meager resources for food, clothing, and shelter without any visions for advancement. The only steps any of us took in the direction of a better quality of living was to go to the corner store to buy a lottery ticket or the corner bar to sell cocaine. Why not come together to start a business, purchase property, or invest in our education so we could potentially secure stepping-stones out of this depressing existence?

Throughout school, my teachers often said the same thing about me: "Andre is very smart and capable of doing the work; he just doesn't seem to put in enough effort." Or something to that effect. I had fallen into the mode of doing just enough to get by with no vision of a future for myself. How did this happen and how did I get here? In my imaginings, my family—a resilient bunch that overcame the challenges of post-slavery reconstruction—descended from those who started Black Wall Street, a thriving, independently Black-owned commercial community in Tulsa, Oklahoma. But on June 1, 1921, the Ku Klux Klan, with the assistance of the US military, rained fire from the skies over this prosperous community, destroying thirty-five city blocks, leaving ten thousand people homeless and sending over eight hundred to local hospitals. This unprovoked attack caused my ancestors to lose hope and to pass down a fatalism that now plagues everyone in my immediate family.

Some say that the condition of poor Blacks is perpetuated by a cycle of dependence. But what if the city invested $10 million (the amount that Chicago government invested in Whole Foods) into local Black businesses instead? Rather than paying for an outside entity to come in and potentially wipe out surrounding smaller businesses that can't compete, investment in local businesses could create an economic base with shop owners and residents reinvesting in their community.

If Englewood were to become more like Black Wall Street, kids (like I once was) could witness, firsthand *and* long term, what self-determination looks like and envision different futures. Maybe it wouldn't have been so easy for a guy like me to relinquish responsibility for my life, make a seamless transition to prison, and now as a thirty-seven-year-old man, depend on others to provide my food, clothing, shelter, and a 13-inch flat-screen TV.

Life on the Registry

■ Tammy Bond

As someone who is required to register as a sex offender for life, I know I will experience a lifetime of limitations— limited housing, limited employment (if you're able to obtain it), limited travel, limited holiday participation, limited family involvement, limited aspirations.

Housing

After I was released, I was displaced from my home because there is a preschool in a church across the street from my house. Illinois law prohibits people on the registry from "living within 500 feet of a school, playground, or any facility providing programs or services exclusively directed toward people under age 18." I've never attended the church across the street or realized that it even had a daycare. I never saw children being dropped off or picked up. I know now that the preschool is only open three hours a day and I worked during those hours. If that preschool wasn't in that church, I could have stayed in my house.

For me, adequate, legal, and affordable housing was almost impossible to find. For three months I lived with a close friend, continued to pay the mortgage on my empty house, and finally found a place to live. And I am one of the lucky ones! Very often, landlords and rental property managers (if you're fortunate enough to get this far in the search process) perform background checks. When "sexual predator" appears in big, bold, red letters under your picture on the registry (like mine does), odds are you're not welcome. But I'm getting ahead of myself. Even when I found a place that I could afford that might be willing to rent to me, it had to be approved by local authority that it indeed meets the sex offense guidelines for residency (was it near a private home daycare, a church with a daycare, a park, a trail, etc.?). This process took days, sometimes weeks, and many times the landlord was not willing to wait to rent it to me. And other people on the registry, who don't have even my limited resources, have other challenges finding housing: multifamily dwellings and homeless shelters can house only one person on the registry, if any.

Limited Employment

While a criminal background makes finding employment hard, being on the registry can make it next to impossible. Employers fear loss of patronage or possible liability if they employ people on the registry. I have a résumé that is chock-full of educational and employment experience. Initially I sought jobs in my areas of expertise: education and clerical positions. I've been called for second and third interviews. Yet I never get the job. Was I passed over because I am on the registry, or was the person chosen a better fit for the position? While I could be wrong, my guess is the former. After I could not find work in my field, I applied to jobs in the service industry: fast food, retail, and waitressing. I never received any calls. I applied to numerous positions. Surely I was suitable for one of them! "Leave your college experience off your résumé," I was told. Yet I was forty-six years old and most of my employment experience is professional. Who finally hired me? Another formerly incarcerated person, who started a small telecommunications company, and my local state representative, who is committed to criminal justice reform.

Limited Travel

Under the Fifth Amendment, citizens have the right to travel freely. However, registered sex offenders must do our homework before any travel. Registration requirements and restrictions vary by state and even across some municipalities. Ignorance of the law is no excuse. Several states require me to register if I visit, and their restrictive zones may differ greatly from those of Illinois. For example, they could prohibit me from being near any church (with or without daycares) and all bus-loading zones. I must notify my local authority of my plans to travel and provide an itinerary upon my return. Do

I dare mention overseas travel? In many countries a person on the registry may be denied entrance. I can fly to a country and be turned around and required to immediately exit. Last year former president Obama signed the International Megan's Law, which allows a "marker" to be placed on the passport of people who are on the registry. More stigma.

Being on the registry is a violation of privacy—forever. For people who are fortunate enough to be removed from the registry, even after their faces and information are removed, their status as a person who committed a sex offense is still obtainable online to anyone who wants to google their information, including potential employers, potential partners, and curious neighbors.

Being on the registry is banishment. When people hear that I am a registered sex offender, most people assume I am a vile, untreatable inhuman who no longer deserves a place in society. I'm banned from going to parks, although my conviction has no bearing on my conduct in a park. I am prohibited from specific kinds of jobs that require licensure, even if the occupation has no bearing on the offense I was convicted of. I cannot babysit my own family members, because I cannot be with persons under the age of eighteen without supervision. I'm barred from attending sporting and extracurricular activities that take place on school property or in parks. I often feel banned from reaching my full potential, and many times I feel helpless to do anything about it. I've learned in my three years on the registry that it's possible to exist and have some semblance of normalcy, but it definitely isn't living a life of endless possibilities nor is it redemptive.

Contradictory Notes on a Question
Harrison Seuga on What It Means to Be Free, Stay Free, and Free Others

■ Roger Viet Chung

Harrison Seuga was tried as an adult at the age of seventeen and was sentenced to seventeen years to life in prison. After twenty-one years behind bars at San Quentin State Prison, he now serves as the reentry director for the Asian Prisoner Support Committee located in Oakland, California. Roger Viet Chung, a core member of the committee, spoke with Harrison and asked him to share his experiences and thoughts. The following is Roger's summary of that conversation..

While prison programs often emphasize individual determination and self-discipline, Harrison Seuga encountered many limitations and contradictions in being and staying free that were outside of his control. His parole experience was not just as a form of supervision but as an extension of the prison itself, except without the basic material needs often provided while locked up—for example, medical care. Being paroled to a region with a high cost of living, such as the San Francisco Bay Area, meant having access to culturally relevant resources that would allow him to experience freedom in meaningful ways; on the other hand, being situated in that area presented problems when it came to housing and employment. The new routines that came with daily life on the outside were stressful. Many times, Harrison's parole officer showed up at his home at early hours or when he was at work. The anxiety of always feeling supervised, coupled with the anxiety of the daily things free folks consider mundane, such as riding public transit, tempered his feelings of freedom during his parole.

Many of the practices of survival Harrison learned on the inside had to be unlearned on the outside, and this further complicated his freedom. For him, survival on the inside first meant becoming physically imposing in order to avoid predators. Yet adopting a threatening form of masculinity not only created problems when interacting with people inside the prison; it also presented particular difficulties in interactions with women. For Harrison, just the presence of women in prison introduced danger—he knew he could get a 115 (a disciplinary ticket inside the prison) if he was perceived as "eyeballin'" someone the wrong way. In prison Harrison felt he had to become more antisocial to avoid punishment, and this became something he needed to unlearn after his release.

At prisons with higher levels of security, survival also mandated that he participate in racial segregation and associated racial antagonism. Challenging his deep mistrust of other groups transformed Harrison. He focused on unlearning such feelings while still incarcerated by building a trusting community that would defend him and that he in turn would defend. After parole and release from prison, he was not allowed contact with this trusted community, posing yet another barrier to experiencing and practicing freedom. Harrison has committed his life to supporting the freedom of his family and families like his.

Working with and within the system that held him prisoner for two decades comes with many challenges. Harrison, who describes himself as an abolitionist, is keenly aware that his life narrative can easily be co-opted into a story that may suggest that prisons are effective in rehabilitation. He is concerned that his reentry work "sanitizes the problem" of incarceration, but he is even more concerned about the folks inside coming home, even if it means living in contradiction.

"Strugglin', Strivin', and Survivin'"
An Interview with Damien, Carlthel, and Elizabeth Brent

■ Sarah Ross

Damien, Carlthel, and Elizabeth Brent are siblings of Larry Brent, who is serving twenty-five years on a murder charge for which another man has confessed. Larry, Elizabeth, and their father, Larry Sr., are artists in the family. Sharing art techniques and critiquing one another's work has kept them engaged over the long years of Larry's incarceration.

Sarah Ross, also an artist and one of Larry's former teachers, facilitated this conversation over several emails with Elizabeth and her brothers in the summer of 2017. The title of this interview comes from a common expression in Larry's letters. Elizabeth says, "It's something Larry has always included in the closing of every letter he's ever written us."

Sarah Ross: *How old were you when Larry was locked up? And do you remember how Larry being incarcerated was talked about or described to you?*

Damien Brent: I had just turned thirteen when there were talks that the police were looking for Larry, and it was sad and scary because my brother who I idolized couldn't come around. I remember thinking, "They have everything all wrong; my brother will come home soon," and every day, for the first two years, I prayed and cried every day, hoping and wishing it was a mistake and he was released. This last portion of the question has me in tears as we speak. I was followed by the police every day for nine months to and from school, and they would verbally abuse me, saying, "Where's your murderer, gangbanging brother?" and I wouldn't respond, and [I'd] go to school and all the students and teachers talked about my brother, saying he's

America's most wanted. Those are my memories.

Carlthel Brent: I was three years old when Larry was locked up. My only memory of him outside the walls was when the police took him out of our home. People just said that he gotten mixed up with the wrong crowd and had to go away for some time but didn't know how long. The neighborhood feared him and my family.

Elizabeth Brent: I was two years old when Larry was arrested. I only have two memories of Larry before he was in prison. I remember him sharing a room with my brother Mario, always playing his music loud. The other memory is of him playing chess, and even that is a blur. Other than that, my earliest memory of him is just visiting him and seeing how happy he always was to see us, and remembering how happy I was to see him and how tight he would always hug me.

Sarah: *What do you remember about visiting Larry when you were young?*

Damien: My brother was always so happy to see us. It was amazing to see his spirit, and deep down inside we were all dying at the fact that he would spend half of his life in there. I remember during one visit, my mother asked what he wanted from the machine, and he wanted pizza, some pop, and microwave popcorn, because in prison you can't get any of that.

Carlthel: I remember me and my family packing into the car, driving for long periods of times. Once we got there, we were questioned and searched by strangers in a very cold and ugly place. They looked like police with different uniforms. We would sit and talk with him for a few hours but couldn't get too close or touch for too long. The food was very terrible, but we did this every year, sometimes more than once. It was a family vacation. Something stood out each time. I remember in 1995, we had visited Larry at Pontiac penitentiary. My father got pulled over right by the prison, and his license had expired. The police arrested him, towed our car, and left me, my mother, my sister Elizabeth, and brother Damien at the gas station. He told us we had to call a ride from Chicago to pick us up and get my father and the car out of jail. We waited in the hot sun for hours until our rescue from Chicago came and picked us children up. My mom went back to get my father and the car once we arrived in Chicago safe.

Elizabeth: I can't recall the first time I visited Larry in prison, as I was so young. But I remember how serious it always felt when we went to see him. Once arriving at the prison, it seemed so sad to me how there were always so many people there to visit loved ones. I also thought the check-in procedure was sad, because the family would sign it, sit and wait for a while before it was our turn to get patted down, searched, and finally escorted to the visiting area. Sometimes we would wait an extremely long time before we actually got to the visiting room. Each visit with Larry was always a good one as I can remember, just because time was spent talking, laughing, and sometimes drawing together. At the end of each visit, I remember how he'd hug us as tight as he could, and I'd always be almost out of breath from how tight he'd hug me. It was our way of joking around and for him to see if I'd gotten any stronger.

Sarah: *Do you remember friends or family that you could talk to about having a family member locked up?*

Damien: Out of all my friends—they couldn't relate to what we was going through. That's why we strengthened ourselves and kept pushing, because the ones around us turned they backs on him and us, even our own family members, not knowing that the evidence they had was weak. All we needed was a real attorney, which cost fifty K to represent him.

Carlthel: In Englewood, going to jail was a part of life. Everybody had somebody that was locked up; it was no big deal. Just a lot of family and friends forgot about Larry, and he haven't communicated with them since 1994.

Elizabeth: My family always talked about Larry—it's not really something we kept quiet about amongst each other—and I remember talking to friends at school about him too. I do remember that I always had to explain him being innocent to people, and I always felt like they really didn't believe me. As I got a little older, I remember keeping more quiet about him to people unless they were close to

The Long Term

the family, because I was tired of being questioned about him in a negative way.

Sarah: *How often do you talk or write with Larry, and has that changed over time? Can you call anytime, or do you wait for him to call?*

Damien: Larry normally calls me every Sunday or every other Sunday. We talk about sports and what's going on in our lives. What amazes me about my brother is he's still family oriented. Even the ones who forgot about him, he still writes them or asks about them. My brother is so forgiving and has a big heart. It's been twenty-four years that my brother been locked up, since I was thirteen, and I will turn thirty-seven this year. It's a lot of pain that needs to be expressed. Just talking about it now relieved a little of it.

Carlthel: We don't write much; we mainly talk on the phone at least once a month, sometimes more if we are working on an art project together and he need ideas. Since I became a parent, it's harder to write letters consistently, so I keep money on the phone and wait for his call even though it's pretty expensive. Contact is not permitted upon our requests; everything is scheduled and approved by the authorities that hold him captive.

Elizabeth: I started writing Larry when I first learned to write. My parents always encouraged us to write him. We always sent him pictures of family and school events and tried our best to keep him updated on everything. We used to write every two weeks, but in the past few years, we talk on the phone more than writing since I've been able to afford my own phone calls and have become more busy for writing. There is no way to call him in prison; I can only talk when he calls me. Right now, each call is limited to just thirty minutes, and he can only use the phone at certain times of day.

Sarah: *As a family of artists, making and sharing art with Larry has been one important way you've bridged the distance and time apart. When did you first remember sharing art with Larry, and in what ways does it connect you?*

Elizabeth: My earliest memories of Larry's art is his custom birth-day cards he would draw for everyone's birthday, and they always included a poem or nice message that he wrote. He never allowed time to pass without sharing life's special moments with us, especially his younger siblings. Although he was away, he never missed one birthday or major celebratory event, because he congratulated or celebrated us with his art.

Sarah: *What advice would you give to other siblings whose families are locked up, serving long terms?*

Damien: My advice to other siblings is to continue to pray for strength for you and your loved ones, because prison can take a toll on somebody who is lacking strength, support, and prayer. What I mean by that is a lot of people go to prison every day, but everybody don't come home. A lot of guys are losing their life or their minds or come home with bitterness and a hard heart. So stay in tune with your loved ones. If you don't have money to send them, at least have a phone for them to call or send a letter with some pictures. Stuff like that goes a long way.

Beyond Survivor's Guilt
Responding to a Sibling's Incarceration

■ Maya Schenwar

My younger sister has spent much of the past twelve years in jail and prison, serving short, repeated sentences. Each time she's been incarcerated, I've felt a certain amount of "survivor's guilt." I've thought, *Maybe I shouldn't be allowed to be happy if she's behind bars.* I've felt that maybe the responsibility is mine to make the problem go away. Each time, I've "failed." In fact, my sister is in jail right now, and I'm in the process of failing—failing to get her free and keep her free.

Other siblings of incarcerated people tell me they've also experienced this feeling of personal failure. I recently discussed it with anti-drug war activist Nora Callahan, whose brother was sentenced in the 1980s to over twenty-seven years in federal prison on drug "conspiracy" charges. She described feeling a similar sense of restless helplessness—intensified, of course, by her brother's gargantuan sentence.

"There was sibling survival guilt throughout the twenty-five-plus years, even though I was not involved in the 'conspiracy,'" she said. "One of the worst hurdles was dealing with the emotions I had when I realized that there wasn't any justice in the war on drugs—that the government that is supposed to protect us was instead harming us."

The smallest details of daily life took on desolate new meanings.

"I couldn't look at the moon without being filled with sadness because my brother couldn't see it," she said. "Most small joys of life were eclipsed."

I know what she means. I think of my sister when I wake up and am free to take a shower, when I open my refrigerator and choose the food I'll eat for breakfast, when I grab my keys and head out the door unencumbered, when I feel the wind on my face.

I talked with Barbara Fair, a longtime activist from New Haven, Connecticut, whose brother spent seventeen years in prison for a gun possession charge, and asked her what she experienced when he was taken away. She spoke of feeling like her brother was being taken into slavery.

"It's very difficult knowing someone you love is entering a system that will completely dehumanize them . . . a system that places people in steel cages, takes away their name and assigns them a lifelong number, strips them naked while they 'inspect' their body cavities, treating them as though they are completely worthless," she said. "Seeing my brother handcuffed and chained like an animal was especially painful because he is such a gentle soul. Hearing about the transport to a prison hundreds of miles away reminded me of the Middle Passage."

Coping was a difficult and ongoing challenge, Barbara said, and on top of the emotional pain, the cost of phone calls and visits added up overwhelmingly over the years.

However, Barbara's tenacious advocacy—both for her brother and for all marginalized and incarcerated people—helped to get her through.

"As a criminal justice activist for as long as I can remember, I educated myself to the workings of the system and developed close relationships which allowed me to advocate for my brother," she said.

One of those relationships was with Nora, who was also building toward a life of activism. Nora says that after seven years of visiting her brother in federal prison, she found an "effective way of coping." She and her brother founded the groundbreaking November Coalition, organizing incarcerated people and their families to fight back against the war on drugs. They produced a printed newspaper, *The Razor Wire*, which spread news of the drug war and resistance to people inside the walls.

Throughout her brother's seventeen years in prison, Barbara worked tirelessly for grassroots prison reform. She organized with People Against Injustice to oppose the war on drugs, mass incarceration, police violence, and racial inequity in the criminal legal system. She founded the youth mentorship and legislative advocacy organization My Brother's Keeper. She regularly coordinated protests, educational events, and other organizing efforts—all while supporting her brother and other incarcerated family members.

I've learned a lot from Nora, Barbara, and other siblings of incarcerated people who have engaged full force in movements to end the systems that caged their loved ones. I have come to realize that I cannot singlehandedly prevent my sister's ongoing arrests and incarcerations. However, I *can* work to find ways of attacking the problem at its roots—that is, confronting the problem of incarceration itself. I attempt to do this through my writing, my work as an editor at *Truthout*, and my activism. When I'm enraged—about being denied an in-person visit with my sister, about her restrictions while on electronic monitoring, or about her incarceration pretrial on a high bond—I write about it, or commission an article, or participate in an organizing effort to abolish the practice in question.

None of these strategies are replacements for basic self-care or for individual advocacy for our siblings inside. But when my sister calls me and the jail phone service cuts off our call mid-sentence (as it almost always does), fighting for an end to incarceration feels like a way to finish the sentence—and even to finish it with hope.

Though I still feel helpless sometimes, I now know that it's not me who's "failing" when my sister is arrested and locked up. It's the system that's failing—or, rather, it's the system that's doing its job all too well, incarcerating and re-incarcerating vast numbers of people. Challenging that system is one of the most valuable things that we, as family members, can do—for ourselves, for our loved ones behind bars, and for our society as a whole.

Breaking Walls
Lessons from Chicago

■ Alice Kim

O n May 6, 2015, fourteen torture survivors—all African American men—stood up at the Chicago City Council meeting as their names were read aloud by Alderman Joe Moreno, a chief sponsor of the Reparations Ordinance for Chicago Police Torture Survivors. Each one of these men had been tortured by former commander Jon Burge or officers under his command; many had languished behind bars incarcerated for decades as a result of confessions elicited by torture. As the city council unanimously passed a reparations package for the Burge torture survivors, they received a long overdue apology from Mayor Rahm Emanuel on behalf of the city and a standing ovation from the city council.

For Anthony Holmes this moment was a long time coming. He had fallen prey to Burge in 1973 in an interrogation room at Area 2 police headquarters on the South Side of Chicago. There, Burge repeatedly electric-shocked and suffocated Holmes with a plastic bag. Holmes eventually confessed to a crime he did not commit, and his confession, the only evidence against him, was used to convict and sentence him.

"What really hurt me is that no one really listened to what I had to say," Holmes testified at Burge's sentencing hearing in 2011. "No one believed in me."[1] Forty-three years after he had been tortured, the city of Chicago finally began a process to make amends.

I witnessed this historic moment in city council chambers along with hundreds of activists, survivors, and family members who had participated in countless protests, marches, rallies, teach-ins, sing-ins, Twitter "Power Hours," and train takeovers during the previous six months. One of these activists was Mary L. Johnson, whose son Michael Johnson was tortured by Burge in 1982 and is currently serving a life sentence without the possibility of parole (for an unrelated conviction). She was one of the first people to file a complaint against Burge, and for more than three decades she has been unwavering in her efforts to seek justice for her son and all survivors of torture by Chicago police. Like several other intrepid mothers who have been the heart and the backbone of the movement, her early activism helped pave the way for the campaign that successfully organized and won reparations.

In the midst of a hotly contested mayoral election and an unrelenting campaign led by a coalition including Chicago Torture Justice Memorials (CTJM), Project NIA, We Charge Genocide, and Amnesty International USA, with critical organizing efforts from Black Youth Project 100, Chicago Alliance Against Racism and Political Repression, Chicago Light Brigade, and others, Chicago evolved from a city that had covered up the systematic torture of African Americans by white officers—125 fully documented cases—into one taking unprecedented measures of redress for Burge torture survivors.[2] This was the result of struggle and coalition work, not the benevolence of politicians.

When Chicago passed reparations legislation, it marked the first time in US history that a municipality was providing reparations for racially motivated police violence. In 2006, human rights attorney Stan Willis founded Black People Against Police Torture (BPAPT) to galvanize support and leadership in the African American community—he and BPAPT made the initial demand for reparations to heal the long-term trauma of torture for individuals and their families and to obtain redress.[3] Introducing the language, demand, and possibility into the political vernacular of the city was a huge opening. In 2011, CTJM formed to organize a campaign fueled by an expansive vision for justice informed by input from torture survivors, family members, and extensive research on reparations.

When the reparations package came to fruition, in May 2015, it included a $5.5 million fund to provide financial compensation to survivors; curriculum addressing the Burge torture cases to be taught to eighth- and tenth-graders in Chicago Public Schools; a community center on the South Side providing specialized trauma counseling and other services for Burge torture survivors and their family members; free tuition at Chicago City Colleges for survivors and their family members, including grandchildren; the creation of a public memorial; and an official apology from the city. While this legislation is limited in scope, providing reparations only to those who were violated by Burge's torture ring, the legislation offers something else: a new paradigm for addressing the violence of policing. As Joey Mogul, cofounder of CTJM and the attorney-activist who authored the Chicago reparations ordinance, said, "Chicago's approach to systemic racial harm offers a glimmer of a possible future in which the nation as a whole might finally grapple with reparations for the legacy of slavery, Jim Crow, and its direct descendant, mass incarceration, each of which echo through the Chicago Police torture cases."[4]

In particular, for me, there are three enduring lessons from this recent struggle. First, reparations did not come readily from the courts or our elected officials. Despite numerous allegations of torture, for years the city and the courts not only turned a blind eye but also actively covered up the torture claims. While Burge and officers under his command were promoted, their victims faced convictions and long prison sentences, including death row for some. Victories in the long history of struggle in the Burge torture cases came about as a result of the consistent courage of the survivors and their family members, on-the-ground activism, and organized pressure.

In the late 1980s community activists and attorneys demanded an official investigation of the torture allegations and Burge's removal from the police force. In the mid-1990s Burge torture survivors on Illinois's death row organized themselves from their prison cells; they demanded new hearings in their cases and the abolition of the death penalty. In the 2000s, unable to find justice in our own courts, human rights attorneys and activists took the Burge torture cases to the Inter-American Commission on Human Rights and the United Nations Committee Against Torture. From Burge being fired in 1993, to the commutations of all Illinois death sentences and pardons for four members of the Death Row 10 by Governor George

Ryan in 2003, to Burge's prosecution and conviction in 2010 for lying about the torture, justice was sought, demanded, and insisted upon by the survivors and their family members, community activists, and attorneys. The reparations legislation that was passed in May 2015 was the culmination of decades of struggle around the Burge torture cases. "We are committed here in Chicago to 'making' Black Lives Matter," wrote Mariame Kaba, abolitionist organizer and coleader of the #RahmRepNow campaign, in a blog post she composed the day after a powerful Valentine's Day rally in Chicago. "The Reparations Ordinance is one concrete way that some of us have chosen to fight to make them matter. Through this decades-long struggle, we are pre-figuring the world that we want to inhabit."[5]

The second lesson is that justice remained elusive for the torture survivors—even after Burge was convicted in 2010. While Burge's conviction was remarkable because of the court's prior unwillingness to prosecute the perpetrators of torture—which stood in stark contrast to their zealous prosecution of Burge's victims—it ultimately failed to address the systemic harm that was done to the survivors. Moreover, Burge's conviction did nothing to challenge how racism is endemic in the criminal legal system and apparent at all levels of the city's governance. What became increasingly clear was that seeking justice within the confines of the legal system had limited our vision for justice. And as abolition activists in Critical Resistance and INCITE! steadfastly remind us, prisons, even for those whose crimes are as heinous as Burge's, don't offer lasting solutions to violence and injustice.[6]

Left to deal with this glaring reality, the same year that Burge was sentenced, a group of activists, educators, artists, and an attorney came together to form the Chicago Torture Justice Memorials. Our first call to action was to announce an open call for speculative memorials commemorating the Burge torture cases. In essence, through this open call we were asking the public—and ourselves— to reimagine what justice could look like in the Burge torture cases.

CTJM received over seventy submissions, all of which were displayed in an exhibit titled "Opening the Black Box: The Charge Is Torture" in the Sullivan Galleries at the School of the Art Institute of Chicago. The original draft of the reparations ordinance for Burge torture survivors was first introduced to the public on the walls of this exhibit, as was artist and CTJM member Carla Mayer's reimagined Chicago flag with a fifth black star added to the existing four red stars. Later emblazoned on movement T-shirts worn by protesters, Mayer's flag became the iconic image of the reparations campaign.

The ordinance itself reflected the experiences and material needs expressed by the survivors. "I still have nightmares," Anthony Holmes said in his 2011 personal testimony. "I see myself falling in a deep hole and no one helping me to get out."[7]

"We are individuals that have suffered," torture survivor Mark Clements said as hundreds of protesters delivered nearly forty thousand signatures on a petition supporting the reparations ordinance to Mayor Emanuel's office in December 2014. "Each and every day, I suffer. Where is my psychological treatment?"[8]

"I'll be doggoned if this wasn't a war that we were involved in, too, here in the United States," Darrell Cannon said at a torture survivors' roundtable organized by CTJM in 2011. "And we deserve reparations."[9]

Seeking reparations—and insisting on that term even when various aldermen questioned its use as divisive or controversial—meant centering the survivors' experiences as well as the racial nature of this violence. At a time when police accountability is sought by many nationwide through prosecutions, the Chicago reparations package offers a new model of accountability, one providing tangible redress that criminal prosecutions fail to deliver.

The third lesson is that survivors have been central actors in this fight from the beginning. Their self-determination and insistence that their lives matter in the face of sadistic, racist brutality carried out against them by white police officers, a hostile criminal legal system, racist media, and a corrupt city leadership from the mayor on down stand as testaments to the power of people who fight for themselves against seemingly impossible obstacles.

Andrew Wilson, for example, convicted of killing two white police officers, dared to raise his voice and speak out about the torture he had endured. He'd been shocked with electrodes, burned by a radiator, suffocated with a plastic bag, kicked in the eye, and badly beaten. Without a lawyer, he filed a pro se civil suit in 1986 that was later taken up by the People's Law Office, and his case would be pivotal in exposing the systematic torture carried out by Burge and his torture ring.[10]

In his cell at Cook County Jail after he was tortured and arrested, Darrell Cannon used pen and paper as weapons in his defense and provided his lawyer with detailed drawings showing how three officers in Burge's crew took him to an abandoned parking lot and proceeded to shock his genitals with an electric cattle prod and ram what they made him believe was a loaded shotgun into his mouth, pulling the trigger in a mock execution. His drawings were submitted as evidence, and Cannon says that even the psychiatrist for the state's attorney said the level of detail in his drawings indicated that he had indeed been tortured. A vocal leader in the Chicago reparations campaign, Cannon tells his personal story time and time again in spite of how emotionally taxing it is for him. "It's torturous any time I have to talk about this here," Cannon said, "but it would be more torturous if I didn't."[11]

Tortured, convicted, and sentenced to death, Aaron Patterson refused to be silenced. Declaring that his cell was his "war room," he formed the Aaron Patterson Defense Committee and fought fearlessly for his freedom. When he was pardoned by Governor George Ryan in 2003, he jumped right into the activist scene, vowing to fight against police violence and a corrupt legal system.

Calling themselves the Death Row 10, a group of African American men—all of whom were tortured by Burge and sentenced to death—organized collectively. Cofounder Stanley Howard announced the Death Row 10's first rally in the fall of 1998, creating a flyer for the event from his cell by cutting and pasting words from newspaper and magazine articles. Though modest in size, with sixty to seventy family members and activists in attendance, their demonstration managed to get local and national media coverage, and as the *New Abolitionist* reported, that night, prisoners and others nationwide saw mothers and fathers of the Death Row 10 marching around the precinct carrying pictures of their sons.[12] Their efforts, in conjunction with the efforts of their mothers who organized a special meeting with then Governor Ryan, helped shift the tide of public opinion in the campaign for commutations of all of Illinois's death sentences in 2003, a move that would lead to the abolition of the state's death penalty eight years later. Interrupting a dehumanizing narrative that had cast death row prisoners as the worst of the worst, their campaign put a human face on the death penalty. From the abolition of the death penalty in Illinois to reparations legislation, Burge torture survivors have been at the center of these struggles.

The last chapter in this story has yet to be written. There is much more to do in order to create a society based on respect for human rights and dignity; there is much to accomplish in terms of demilitarizing cities, ending police violence, and building the power of communities to control the resources that keep them safe; there is more to organize in terms of linking racial justice with economic and global justice. But to this point the story teaches us a lesson we must never forget: the power of a people who organize and mobilize in the cause of justice can break walls and make history.

Affirmation

Eve L. Ewing

to youth living in prison
after Assata Shakur

S peak this to yourself
until you know it is true.
I believe that I woke up today
and my lungs were working,
miraculously,
my voice can sing and murmur and ask,
miraculously.
My hands may shake, but they can hold
me, or another.
My blood still carries the gifts of the air
from my heart to my brain,
miraculously.
Put a finger to my wrist or my temple
And feel it: I am magic. Life
and all its good and bad and ugly things,
scary things which I would like to forget
beautiful things which I would like to remember
—the whole messy lovely true story of myself
pulses within me.
I believe that the sun shines,
if not here, then somewhere.
Somewhere it rains,
and things will grow green and wonderful.
Somewhere inside me, too, it rains,
and things will grow green and wonderful.

Sometimes my insides rain from the inside out
And then I know
I am alive
I am alive
I am alive

Formerly Incarcerated, Convicted People and Families Movement Platform

■ FICPFM

Punishment persists even for the people who secure release from prison. A complex and devastating patchwork of barriers enacted by a range of actors, including local, state, and federal governments as well as private corporations and public entities, deny people with criminal records access to housing, education, employment, voting, the right to parent, and more. In ten states people with felony convictions can permanently lose their right to vote. Most employers and postsecondary educational institutions require applicants to disclose whether they have been convicted of a crime or even arrested. Criminal background checks often disqualify people from unpaid internships or volunteering at their own children's or grandchildren's schools. Some convictions—for example, for sexual offenses—require paying money and being visible on a public registry for the remainder of one's life. The list of ongoing and punitive consequences after release from prison is endless.

These restrictions—some enshrined in laws and others in discriminatory cultural norms—ensure that most people with records will struggle to survive after their release. Yet groups led by formerly incarcerated people and their families have *always* pushed back against these devastating policies and practices. Because many of these barriers are local—state licensure or voting regulations, for example—most of the organizing has been highly localized as well. One current, vibrant national example of an effective coalition of local grassroots groups that is led by formerly incarcerated people and their families is the Formerly Incarcerated, Convicted People and Families Movement (FICPFM).

FICPFM is composed of a number of member organizations, including the National Alliance for the Empowerment of the Formerly Incarcerated (Chicago); the Women's ReEntry Network (Cleveland); National Exhoodus Council (Philadelphia); Youth Justice Coalition (Los Angeles); California Coalition for Women Prisoners (San Francisco); HOPE (Detroit); Legal Services for Prisoners with Children (San Francisco); Uniprison (blog); Center for Young Women's Development (San Francisco); Women on the Rise Telling HerStory (New York); A New Way of Life (Los Angeles); Riverside Church Prison Ministry (Harlem, NY); The Time Is Now to Make a Change (Philadelphia); Direct Action for Rights and Equality (Providence, RI); All of Us or None; Council on Crime and Justice (Minneapolis); The Ordinary People's Society (Dothan, AL); Center for NuLeadership on Urban Solutions (New York); Transgender Gender Variant and Intersex Justice Project (San Francisco); National Council for Urban Peace and Justice (Pittsburgh); VOTE NOLA (New Orleans); X-Offenders for Community Empowerment (Philadelphia); League of United Latin American Citizens, Council 4994 (San Antonio, TX); Southern Coalition for Social Justice (Durham, NC); JustLeadershipUSA (New York); College and Community Fellowship (New York); and Primary Group Inc. (Las Vegas).[1]

On November 2, 2011, more than three hundred activists as well as formerly incarcerated people and their families came together in Los Angeles to share ideas, establish an agenda, and create a national platform for the FICPFM. The theme of the meeting was "Strengthening Our Actions and Voices through Unity."

In September 2016 this coalition held its first national conference, in Oakland, California, with more than five hundred people from across the United States and abroad in attendance. With welcome remarks from national leaders from two California-based grassroots organizations—Dorsey Nunn, from Legal Services for Prisoners with Children, and Susan Burton, from A New Way of Life Reentry Project—the weekend featured panels and discussion and the ongoing leadership of formerly incarcerated people, collectives, and family members.

The FICPFM's platform is intended to be dynamic, or always in dialogue with organizations and people most impacted. It is presented here in full:[2]

Our Vision

There are tens of millions of people in the United States suffering the collateral consequences of a felony conviction. We are people who have been charged, convicted and branded with an arrest and conviction history. Millions of us have served prison time, and it is estimated that 600,000 people will be released from prison per year for the next five years while millions more will be placed on probation and face the extremely low standards of guilt for a probation violation.

All of us have human rights that are being abused by the criminal justice system. We believe that imprisonment or conviction on a felony charge should not result in a lifelong violation of our basic rights as human beings, either while we are on probation, in prison or as we make the transition from prison back into our communities. We are firmly committed to prioritizing De-Entry over Re-Entry, and oppose the concept of a Rehabilitative Industrial Complex that grows along with prisons. All efforts to educate, assist, and empower our communities should be within the context of eliminating human cages as a mainstream livelihood.

The Formerly Incarcerated & Convicted People's Movement is committed to the full restoration of our civil and human rights. We have drafted an initial platform to develop a common voice, to pursue a common political reality and to secure our common interest. However, we recognize that the current criminal justice system has never worked for people of color, poor people, or our community, and ultimately this system predicated on racism and torture should be dismantled.

Society's reliance on prisons and punishment does not make our communities safer. The warehousing of human beings, mostly people of color, is an unacceptable substitute for social programs. Prisons are not a substitute for mental health care, and jails are not housing for the homeless. We work to develop political power and healthy communities. The criminal justice system is cruelly devastating and disrupting, especially in communities of color. After two generations of the Drug War, the American people are suffering far more than when it began. Over 2 million people are currently locked up [in] United States prisons and jails. Over 2 million children have a parent behind bars, and 10 million children have had a parent in prison at some time in their lives. With the explosion of criminalization in the 1980's and 1990's, we have entire school systems facing the effects of parents being incarcerated or facing the discrimination of a criminal record.

We call on the U.S. to recognize the treatment of ethnic minorities under standards set forth in the United Nations Universal Declaration of Human Rights. We want an end to racial profiling, racial disparities, and the disproportionate imprisonment of people of color. African-Americans are admitted to state prisons at a rate that is 13.4 times greater than white Americans, a disparity driven largely by the grossly racial targeting of drug laws. These punitive drug laws need to be abolished. Women represent the fastest-growing segment of the prison and jail population. African-American women are more than three times as likely as Latino women and six times more likely than white women to face imprisonment.

The dehumanization faced by gay and transgender people is unacceptable, both inside and out of prison; for example, transgender and gender-nonconforming people are six times more likely than others to go to jail or prison. We oppose the institutionalized racism and various modes of discrimination within the courts and prison system, and are working for alternatives to incarceration along with the rights of those inside.

· We firmly believe that it is as true today as it was when uttered by Frederick Douglass "that power concedes nothing without a demand. It never has and it never will." Our platform is being drafted to hold the weight of a movement, but it cannot stand by itself. This platform must be in conjunction with, and supported by, the pursuit of demands by formerly incarcerated and convicted people, our families, and community.

Our Platform

I. We Demand an End to Mass Incarceration

The first goal of changing the criminal justice system is to create and implement alternatives to incarceration, working toward a society where prisons do not exist. We demand the end of mass incarceration and commit ourselves to fighting the notion and the practice of building new prisons, juvenile detention facilities and immigration detention centers.

Mass incarceration does not add to public safety, and diverts real resources from other social needs. We are cognizant that the Prison Industrial Complex is so expensive that it denies society the opportunity to provide basic structure such as children's education, medical care, mental health care, and support for our elders. We commit ourselves to pursuing a new direction, one that ensures genuine safety for our community and transforms "hoods" back into neighborhoods.

II. We Demand Equality and Opportunity for All People

As a basic civil right, we demand equality and equal opportunity with other members of society, both when we have completed our sentences and while living on probation or parole. The lifelong discrimination people with convictions face is a form of double jeopardy that never allows us to finish serving our time.

We demand an end to all forms of structural and permanent discrimination based on arrest or conviction records.

This discrimination is everywhere, like race-based laws once were, and it is not confined to one area of the nation. It is nearly impossible for people with conviction histories to survive and access opportunities for a better life. It is structural discrimination that is embodied in the question appearing on applications for jobs, public benefits, housing, insurance, student loans, and more: "Have you ever been convicted by a court?" The obvious effects of this structural discrimination are extremely high unemployment rates, homelessness, lack of medical insurance and the inability of formerly incarcerated or convicted people to adequately support families and contribute to our communities.

We commit ourselves to "Ban the Box" throughout the United States—to eliminate that question that appears on countless applications (public and private) asking about our conviction history.

III. We Demand the Right to Vote

We demand the right to full democratic participation, inside and outside of prisons and jails. We demand the right to vote while we are incarcerated and after our release, regardless of probation or parole.

The disenfranchisement of people in prison, and people with conviction histories, strips rightful political power from communities of color. We should not be subject to having our rights taken because we simply move from one state to another.

For purposes of political representation and the Census, incarcerated people should be counted in the communities where they lived prior to incarceration: this is where their families live, and where voices of representation should be heard.

IV. We Demand Respect and Dignity for Our Children

We acknowledge that as the result of mass incarceration our children have been rendered vulnerable. Parents are often disappeared into the prison system without any real explanation or particular care of our children.

The practice of fast-track adoptions must end. Imprisonment or felony conviction can result in our children being stolen from us; incarcerated parents should not automatically forfeit their parental rights, and should have the right to be present at all custody-related court proceedings.

Contact visits and overnight family visiting should be universally available, and people should be incarcerated close to their families to facilitate visiting. Teenage mothers in juvenile facilities are often afraid to disclose that they are parents, and thus denied visits with their children.

Parents of U.S. citizens should not be deported, and children should not be deported away from their parents.

We call on the federal and state governments to adopt and implement the Bill of Rights for Children of Incarcerated Parents: protocols that empower our young to have a voice in their own future, and to have a relationship with their incarcerated parent(s).

We demand the right to be involved with our children's schooling, and should not be systematically excluded from being a school volunteer or field trip chaperon.

V. We Demand Community Development, Not Prison Profit

We state clearly that our pain should not be used for economic gain. Prisons have been considered as "economic development projects" for the communities where they are built, typically in rural areas far from where masses of people are arrested.

We oppose the construction of additional prisons, jails, juvenile, or immigrant detention centers, including those disguised as medical, geriatric, or mental health facilities. Privately-owned prisons should be declared illegal. Corporations have been selling shares in prisons and contracting billions of dollars from public funds, and then use a portion of these profits to lobby legislators to ensure the growth of imprisonment.

Price-gouging in prisons must end. Our families have been subjected to ransom and extortion through exorbitant fees imposed by telephone companies, or the online stores we are forced to utilize to send goods into prison and to our loved ones.

Healthy and sustainable economic development will be possible only when the billions of dollars spent on prisons are re-invested into job creation, educational opportunities, and stable housing for all, regardless of conviction histories.

VI. End Immigration Detention and Deportation

Our immigrant neighbors, friends, and family are being deported at an alarming rate in all our communities. During the last 3 years, over 1 million people have been deported, tearing apart families and disrupting our communities. "Crimmigration" is the merging of the criminal justice and immigration systems and it's having devastating results for migrants of color.

Immigration Customs and Enforcement (ICE) is actively organizing law enforcement all over the U.S. to participate in an "ethnic cleansing" program by deporting non-citizens who have minor arrest or conviction histories. "Secure Communities" and the 287(g) program are two of the collaborations between ICE and local police and sheriffs. They require local police to verify immigration status and conviction history, and detain anyone with past convictions of any type for deportation.

Arizona, Georgia and other states have legalized racial profiling and targeting through new anti-immigrant laws. We oppose these racial profiling programs as discriminatory and cruel. Deportation should not be a "collateral consequence" in addition to the sentence imposed for a crime.

VII. End Racial Profiling Inside Prison and in Our Communities

Racism permeates every aspect of the criminal justice system, jails, and prisons. We believe all human beings are created equal, and oppose every effort to divide our community by race. We oppose the practice of racial profiling by law enforcement and the courts in arrests, prosecutions, sentencing, and prison designation.

Racial profiling is closely tied to the increasing use of "gang injunctions" and "gang databases" which target young men of color. The use of the "gang" label is one way that young Black and Brown men have been criminalized. Once labeled a "gang member" and entered into a statewide gang database, a young person is subject to increased police harassment, searches, arrests, imprisonment, and sentencing enhancements.

In prison, this label often results in false gang validations by prison administrations, harassment, pressure to turn informant, and torture if one resists.

We oppose the criminalization of our young people through "gang validation" tactics by law enforcement, whether in the courts through "gang injunctions," in the statewide databases, or by police on the streets and in the prisons. We call for unity in our communities, inside the prison system and on the streets.

VIII. End Extortion and Slavery in Prisons

A person becomes captive to the conditions determined by the guards and administrations when sentenced to prison. One example is the criminal monopoly that runs prison telephone systems. These phone systems are the lifeline of prisoners and families, but the systems charge far more than in the community. The charges include huge profits as well as kickbacks to funds that benefit prison guards. We oppose the extortion that is built into the prison system—telephone charges and restrictions, exorbitant commissary markup rates, the monopoly system for sending prison packages.

Many prison systems now charge prisoners a co-pay for medical visits, which often prevents prisoners from accessing necessary medical care. We oppose these medical co-pays as a barrier to the health and well-being of our prisoners, and reject the "poverty defense" of a system that continues to force more people into custody, with no regard for their care.

The use of prison labor since 1865 is no more than an extension of slavery. Whether it is working on behalf of federal military contractors, state governments, prison farms, or private corporations, people working in prison should receive just

compensation and on-the-job protections. We oppose the exploitation of the labor of people in prison.

IX. End Sexual Harassment of People in Prison

Men, women, LGBTQ and gender non-conforming people,
and children inside the prison system are vulnerable to sexual
exploitation by guards as well as other prisoners. We oppose the
sexual harassment of prisoners by guards, including the extortion of sex, rape, or profiteering from prostitution. Pat searches
of women prisoners by male guards is dehumanizing, oppressive, and exacerbates the many traumas a person has experienced
prior to incarceration. Furthermore, these practices constitute
sexual harassment—we oppose cross-gender pat searches.

Transgender prisoners are subject to particular exploitation, and should be assigned to prison and housing based on
their own gender identification and choice.

X. Human Contact Is a Human Right

Maintaining connections and contact with our families is crucial to surviving prison, and to rejoining our communities as
whole people. We place great value on the ability to visit as a
means of maintaining our families, friendships, and a genuine
relationship with our community.

We oppose out-of-state transfers without consent or concern for maintaining family relationships. Limiting contact
visits should not be used as a form of punishment—contact
visiting and overnight family visiting are the most effective
ways to maintain our relationships with our families and community. Human touch, kindness, and love are a human right.

Recidivism, re-entry and survival are greatly dependent on
a strong positive relationship with families and communities,
and we should not be banned from living with our families.

XI. End Cruel and Unusual Punishment

We oppose the adjudication of young people as adults, and the
designation of young people to adult prisons.

Long-term segregation and sensory deprivation are torture. We demand an end to all indeterminate administrative
segregation or SHU [special housing unit] sentences. All
prisons within the jurisdiction of the U.S. government should

conform to international standards prohibiting torture. En-hanced sentencing structures (such as California's Three Strikes law) should be abolished—they increase sentences beyond the punishment legislated for the crime.

Guards who abuse prisoners become criminals themselves. Such abuse is systemic, not isolated cases, rooted in the power imbalances and personal prejudices that are reinforced by the prison structure.

The criminal justice system wrongfully convicts extremely high numbers of people, and forces thousands into bogus plea agreements because they have inadequate legal representation. People who have been exonerated due to DNA evidence represent a mere fraction of the innocent people in prison. The average case takes years, even decades, to overturn, which shows that the criminal justice system cannot adequately review itself.

We oppose the death penalty absolutely, as the ultimate human rights violation.

XII. We Demand Proper Medical Treatment

Our government should seek to save money by stopping mass incarceration rather than failing to maintain legal and moral standards for those it has chosen to take over full custody and control. The standards of medical treatment for prisoners should not fall below levels of care available in the community, including laws on medical confidentiality, and prisoners should not be charged to access medical care.

All prisoners should have access to adequate and nutritious food, including medical and religious diets. Access to natural light, fresh air, and outdoor exercise are fundamental to health, and should be provided in every detention setting.

Prisons should provide medical treatment by licensed professionals for pre-existing as well as emerging medical issues, including degenerative diseases, chronic and communicable diseases, and gender-specific medical care. Those with specific diseases should not be subjected to discrimination, punishment, or violence.

Women prisoners should not be shackled during the course of pregnancy, and should not be shackled while giving birth.

Prisoners over 55 should be guaranteed retirement from forced labor, and considered for early release. Eligibility for medical parole and compassionate release should be expanded.

All prisoners, including transgender, should be provided necessary ongoing medications. Withholding medications should not be allowed as a disciplinary practice or pressure tactic.

XIII. End the Incarceration of Children

This nation currently incarcerates a million children, half of whom are in for-profit penal institutions. This high number of children in prison exposes the inhumanity of our system's approach to human and community development. The damage done by imprisoning children at this stage of life, particularly for petty crimes and misdemeanors, is irreparable, and continues the direction toward intergenerational poverty and dysfunction.

Sentences of life without parole should be abolished for juveniles and minors.

XIV. Free Our Political Prisoners

Over the past fifty years, liberation struggles and resistance to repression, both in domestic and international relations, have produced a great deal of turmoil. Individuals and groups took actions, or affiliated with others, in ways that were deemed criminal in the U.S. courts of law. This nation was born out of similar opposition to the oppression of their era.

Some of our political prisoners have been incarcerated for over thirty years in response to their acts of resistance—we demand they be released. Many other prisoners have taken action inside prisons to assert their humanity and resist oppression, resulting in new "criminal" cases and prison sentences. We call for a repeal of these retaliatory sentences and for the release of these organizers. The rights to peacefully organize, free speech, and self-determination are universally recognized human rights.

Furthermore, we recognize that certain religious beliefs and spiritual practices face both discriminatory treatment and outright bans, and we re-assert the need for religious freedom within prisons. Religious faith should not be used as evidence of criminal activity, nor as grounds for additional punishment within prisons.

Acknowledgments

The Long Term: Resisting Life Sentences, Working for Our Freedom is indebted to people and organizations that continue to fuel the movements to imagine, build, and practice making another world.

Prison+Neighborhood Arts Project (P+NAP) students and colleagues ensured that this project remained grounded, inspired, and accountable. Aaron Hughes and Anna Martine Whitehead kept the project organized and flowing. Bill Ayers, Harry Backlund, Ryan Griffis, Rachael Hudak, Natalie Moore, Fred Sasaki, Maya Schenwar, and Nikhil Singh offered critical feedback. Julie Fain from Haymarket Books and Jill R. Hughes provided meaningful support and keen editorial acumen. Anya Degenshein, Dawn Teft, Nancy Traver, and Snezana Zabic assisted with editing. Mario Padilla and Isabella Schnapps typed manuscripts. Haerim Lee took amazing photographs of the Survival Kits. William C. Anderson and Home Pro Transcribing in Illinois provided transcription services. Artwork for our book cover was designed by Damon Locks, artist and our collaborator.

P+NAP's organizing committee, including Tim Barnett, Tess Landon, and Damon Locks, provided key support for this project. This project was made possible with financial support from the College of Education at Northeastern Illinois University, Illinois Humanities, Institute for Research on Race and Public Policy at the University of Illinois at Chicago (UIC), Invisible Institute, and Woods Fund Chicago. The Social Justice Initiative at UIC hosted programs that generated contributions to this anthology. Chicago Access Network Television (CAN TV) provided recordings for transcription.

The Long Term is only possible because of the wider work of a constellation of organizations across the globe that work for

freedom and often explicitly identify as abolitionist—many of them
held down by women of color queer feminists—including: All of
Us or None, Assata's Daughters, Audre Lorde Project, Bent Bars,
Black Lives Matter Chicago, Black and Pink, Black Youth Proj-
ect 100, BreakOUT!, Campaign to End the Death Penalty, Chi-
cago Alliance Against Racism and Political Repression, Chicago
Torture Justice Memorials, Community United Against Violence,
Creative Interventions, Critical Resistance, People Against Prisons
Aotearoa, FIERCE!, INCITE! Women, Gender Non-Conforming,
and Trans people of Color Against Violence, Justice Now!, Mijente,
Moms United Against Violence and Incarceration, National Bail
Out, Organized Communities Against Deportation, Philly Stands
Up/Philly's Pissed, Prisoner Correspondence Project, Project NIA,
RAPP (Release Aging People in Prison), Resist Reimagine Re-
build Coalition, Sisters Inside, Sista II Sista, Southerners On New
Ground, Storytelling and Organizing Project, Stella, Sylvia Rivera
Law Project, Transgender, Gender Variant, and Intersex Justice Proj-
ect, Transformative Justice Law Project, Undercurrents. *And more.*

Within these networks, we name and elevate the particular importance of currently and formerly incarcerated people to shape our
collective thinking and labor—including Marissa Alexander, Kevin
Cooper, David Gilbert, Mumia Abu-Jamal, Oscar López Rivera,
CeCe McDonald, Vickie Roach, Kemba Smith, and more.

We offer this list of organizations and these names recognizing that it's not exhaustive and that many came before us—from
the Combahee River Collective to Young Women's Empowerment
Project to We Charge Genocide, from Marilyn Buck to Audre
Lorde to Troy Davis and Marsha P. Johnson—who also worked for
our freedom, *for the long term.*

*Any proceeds from this project will support organizing for people serving
long-term sentences through the Prison+Neighborhood Arts Project. To
learn more about P+NAP's work, please visit p-nap.org.*

Notes

Introduction

1. Beth E. Richie, *Arrested Justice: Black Women, Violence, and America's Prison Nation* (New York: New York University Press, 2012).
2. According to 2016 U.S. Census Bureau, "State and County Quickfacts: Illinois," www.census.gov/quickfacts/IL.
3. Josh Zeitz, "How Trump Is Recycling Nixon's 'Law and Order' Playbook," *Politico*, July 18, 2016, www.politico.com/magazine/story/2016 /07/donald-trump-law-and-order-richard-nixon-crime-race-214066.
4. Naomi Murakawa, *The First Civil Right: How Liberals Built Prison America* (New York: Oxford University Press, 2014).
5. Peter Wagner and Bernadette Rabuy, "Mass Incarceration: The Whole Pie," Prison Policy Initiative, March 14, 2017, www.prisonpolicy.org /reports/pie2017.html.
6. Angela Caputo, "Cell Blocks," *Chicago Reporter*, March 1, 2013.
7. Gillian Harkins and Erica R. Meiners, "Teaching Publics in the American Penalscape," *American Quarterly* 68, no. 2 (2016) 405–8.
8. Ibid.
9. John Maki, "Monitoring Tour of Stateville Correctional Center," John Howard Association of Illinois, September 14, 2010, p. 6–7, www.thejha.org/sites/default/files/Stateville%20Report.pdf.
10. Marge Piercy, "To Be of Use," in *Circles on the Water* (New York: Alfred A. Knopf, 1982), 106.
11. "Gender Violence and the Prison Industrial Complex," INCITE! Critical Resistance statement, 2001, www.incite-national.org /page/incite-critical-resistance-statement.
12. Lance Kelly Esteban, "Philly Stands Up: Inside the Politics and Poetics of Transformative Justice and Community." *Social Justice* 37, no. 4 (2012): 44-57.
13. Kimberlé Crenshaw, "Mapping the Margins: Intersectionality, Identity Politics, and Violence against Women of Color," in *The Public Nature of Private Violence*, ed. M. A. Fineman and R. Mykituk (New York: Routledge, 1994), 93–118.
14. See, for example, "Abolition," Critical Resistance, http:// criticalresistance.org/about/not-so-common-language.

15. Marie Gottschalk, *Caught: The Prison State and the Lockdown of American Politics* (Princeton, NJ: Princeton University Press, 2015).

16. Marc Mauer and Nazgol Ghandnoosh, *Fewer Prisoners, Less Crime: A Tale of Three States*, The Sentencing Project, July 23, 2014, www.sentencingproject.org/publications/Fewer-Prisoners-Less -Crime-A-Tale-of-Three-States.

17. Wagner and Rabuy, "Mass Incarceration: The Whole Pie 2017."

18. Angela Y. Davis, *The Meaning of Freedom: And Other Difficult Dialogues* (San Francisco: City Lights Books, 2012), 51.

19. Maya Schenwar, "Your Home Is Your Prison," op-ed, *Truthout*, January 19, 2015, www.truth-out.org/news/item/28609-your-home-is-your-prison.

20. Karlene Faith, "Reflections on Inside/Out Organizing," *Social Justice* 27, no. 3 (2000): 158–67.

21. Keeanga-Yamahtta Taylor, *From #BlackLivesMatter to Black Liberation* (Chicago: Haymarket Books, 2016), 144–46, 148–51.

22. Angela Y. Davis, *Are Prisons Obsolete?* (New York: Seven Stories Press, 2003); Marc Mauer, *Race to Incarcerate* (New York: New Press, 1999); Ruth Wilson Gilmore, *Golden Gulag: Prisons, Surplus, Crisis, and Opposition in Globalizing California* (Berkeley: University of California Press, 2007); Mumia Abu-Jamal, *Jailhouse Lawyers: Prisoners Defending Prisoners v. the USA* (San Francisco: City Lights Books, 2009); Joy James, *Imprisoned Intellectuals: America's Political Prisoners Write on Life, Liberation, and Rebellion* (Lanham, MD: Rowman and Littlefield, 2003); Bettina Aptheker and Angela Y. Davis, eds., *If They Come in the Morning: Voices of Resistance* (New York: Third Press, 1971).

23. Michelle Alexander, *The New Jim Crow: Mass Incarceration in the Age of Colorblindness* (New York: New Press, 2010).

24. Nelson Mandela, *Long Walk to Freedom: The Autobiography of Nelson Mandela* (New York: Little, Brown, 2009), 624.

25. Saidiya Hartman, *Scenes of Subjection: Terror, Slavery, and Self-Making in Nineteenth-Century American* (New York: Oxford University Press, 1997), 6.

26. Richard Fausset, "Will 1,500 Street Cameras Be a Wet Blanket in New Orleans?," *New York Times*, January 30, 2018.

27. Khaled A. Beydoun and Justin Hansford, "The F.B.I.'s Dangerous Crackdown on 'Black Identity Extremists,'" *New York Times*, November 15, 2017.

28. Alan Pyke, "Chicago Leaders: City Can Afford Shiny, New Police Academy, Just Not Schools or Community Services," ThinkProgress, November 9, 2017, https://thinkprogress.org /rahm-emanuel-cop-academy-chicago-565014ca2135.

29.   Paula X. Rojas, "Are the Cops in Our Heads and Hearts?," in *The Revolution Will Not Be Funded: Beyond the Non-profit Industrial Complex*, ed. INCITE! Women of Color Against Violence (Cambridge, MA: South End Press, 2007), 197–214.
30.   Davis, *Meaning of Freedom*, 50.

We Are Alive

1.   Assata Shakur and Joanne Chesimard, "Women in Prison: How It Is with Us," *Black Scholar* (April 1978): 12.
2.   Lyle May, "Why We Must Educate Our Prisoners," *Scalawag*, November 29, 2016, www.scalawagmagazine.org/2016/11/letter-from-death-row-why-we-must-educate-our-prisoners.

Prison Is Not Just a Place

1.   The Northern Reception and Classification Center is an adjacent processing and intake center for people sentenced to state prisons.
2.   Frederick Douglass, *Narrative Life of Frederick Douglass* (New York: Millennium Publications, 1945), 83.
3.   Ibid., 104.

Larger Than Life

1.   Ashley Nellis, "Still Life: America's Increasing Use of Life and Long-Term Sentences," Sentencing Project, 2017, www.sentencingproject.org/wp-content/uploads/2017/05/Still-Life.pdf.

Time after Time

1.   *National Transgender Discrimination Survey*, National Center for Transgender Equality, 2016, www.transequality.org/issues/national-transgender-discrimination-survey.
2.   "SB-310: Name and Gender Change: Prisons and County Jails," California Legislature, October 16, 2017, leginfo.legislature.ca.gov/faces/billNavClient.xhtml?bill_id=201720180SB310.

A Living Chance

1.   Interview with Tracee Ward, Central California Women's Facility, August 2014.

2. The majority of women sentenced to LWOP were convicted due to their proximity to the crimes of their abusive partners or were convicted of killing their abusive partners. Prior to 1992, evidence of domestic violence was not allowed in one's trial. Furthermore, prosecutors often cast the women codefendants as "black widows" or "femme fatales" who used their sexuality to manipulate male codefendants into committing crimes. Many trans and gender-nonconforming people are labeled as "violent" or "aggressive." LWOP sentencing impacts people of color and poor people disproportionately. LWOPs are discriminated against inside prison because the administration restricts their access to certain educational programs and job placements. The higher-paying jobs and more comprehensive educational programs are reserved for people with parole-eligible sentences.

3. The Joint Venture Program is a center that provides technology training and low-paying work to people inside. The California Prison Industry Authority is a state-operated agency that employs people in prison with higher-paying work assignments upon successful completion of coursework in areas such as carpentry, welding, and electronics. The California Department of Corrections and Rehabilitation (CDCR) bars LWOPs from accessing both of these opportunities.

4. In California the felony murder rule doctrine significantly broadens criminal liability for a homicide to include people who did not commit murder themselves but may have participated in a felony during which a murder took place. Many people in women's prisons with LWOP were sentenced under felony murder rule because they were present during the crimes of their abusers and were unable to prevent a murder from happening due to fear for their own lives.

5. "Vocations" refers to certificates of completion from vocational programs offered by the CDCR.

Lock 'Em Up and Throw Away the Key

1. Ashley Nellis, "Still Life: American's Increasing Use of Life and Long-Term Sentences," Sentencing Project, 2017, www.sentencingproject.org/wp-content/uploads/2017/05/Still-Life.pdf.
2. Nicole Flatow, "Top European Human Rights Court Deems Life in Prison without Parole Inhuman and Degrading," ThinkProgress, July 10, 2013, https://thinkprogress.org/top-european-human-rights-court-deems-life-in-prison-without-parole-inhuman-and-degrading-d615fc306396.
3. Urban Institute, "A Matter of Time: The Causes and Consequences of

Rising Time Served in America's Prisons," July 2017, http://apps.urban
.org/features/long-prison-terms/a_matter_of_time_print_version.pdf.

4. This is not to say that political backlash against the social movements of
    the 1960s and 1970s is the complete explanation for the emergence of
    mass incarceration, perhaps just the most relevant in an examination of
    the rise of harsh sentencing. The restructuring of the political economy
    along neoliberal lines also played a huge part, precipitating a series of
    economic and social crises that transformed much of the poorer layers
    of the working class into surplus labor ripe for imprisonment. For a
    detailed examination of this, see Ruth Wilson Gilmore's classic, *The
    Golden Gulag: Prisons, Surplus, Crisis, and Opposition in Globalizing
    California* (Berkeley: University of California Press, 2007). Angela Davis
    talks about how mass incarceration is part of a strategy of dealing with
    surplus populations of color, as "disposable" both in the United States
    and the global South. Davis, *Freedom Is a Constant Struggle: Ferguson,
    Palestine, and the Foundations of a Movement* (Chicago: Haymarket
    Books, 2016), 107. A survey of the explanations for the rise of mass
    incarceration appears in James William Kilgore, *Understanding Mass
    Incarceration: A People's Guide to the Key Civil Rights Struggle of Our Time*
    (New York: New Press, 2015), chapter 1.

5. I define the era of mass incarceration as that spanning 1980 to the
    present. Clearly, though, as people like Elizabeth Hinton have pointed
    out, the roots go back much further. See Hinton, *From the War on
    Poverty to the War on Crime: The Making of Mass Incarceration in America*
    (Cambridge, MA: Harvard University Press, 2016).

6. See, for example, Robert C. Cottrell, *Sex, Drugs, and Rock 'n' Roll:
    The Rise of America's 1960s Counterculture* (New York: Rowman and
    Littlefield, 2015).

7. ABC News, "War Resisters Remain in Canada with No Regrets,"
    November 19, 2005, http://abcnews.go.com/WNT/story?id=1325339.

8. Todd Gitlin, *The Sixties: Year of Hope, Days of Rage* (New York: Bantam
    Books, 1987), 342 and 401.

9. Cited in Eric Cummins, *The Rise and Fall of the California's Radical
    Prison Movement* (Stanford, CA: Stanford University Press, 1994), 203.

10. Quoted in Process Editors, "Organizing the Prisons in the 1960s and
    1970s: Part One, Building Movements," *Process: A Blog for American
    History*, September 20, 2016, www.processhistory.org/prisoners-rights-1.

11. Elliott "L. D." Barkley, video of speech in Attica prison,
    www.youtube.com/watch?v=VJ0gWUNTru8.

12. The committee focused on preventing the state from prosecuting those

who had taken part in the rebellion. Over the years, they had great success. Their story is chronicled in detail in Heather Ann Thompson's marvelous account of the Attica uprising, *Blood in the Water: The Attica Uprising of 1971 and Its Legacy* (New York: Pantheon, 2016).

13. Brian Mann, "The Drug Laws That Changed How We Punish," National Public Radio, February 14, 2013, www.npr.org/2013/02/14 /171822608/the-drug-laws-that-changed-how-we-punish.

14. Pratt spent twenty-seven years in prison after being framed on a murder charge. He was released in 1997 and died in Tanzania in 2011. Abu-Jamal has been in prison since 1982, Peltier since 1977. Both were convicted of killing law enforcement officers in separate incidents, and both proclaim their innocence.

15. Quoted in Sarah Childress, "Michelle Alexander: 'A System of Racial and Social Control,'" *Frontline*, April 29, 2014, www.pbs.org/wgbh/frontline /article/michelle-alexander-a-system-of-racial-and-social-control.

16. Robert Farley, "Bill Clinton and the 1994 Crime Bill," FactCheck.org, April 12, 2016, www.factcheck.org/2016/04/bill-clinton-and-the-1994 -crime-bill.

17. US Department of Justice, "State Sentencing Law Changes Linked to Increasing Time Served in State Prisons," media release, January 10, 1999, www.bjs.gov/content/pub/press/tssp.pr.

18. Cited in "California Proposition 184, Three Strikes Sentencing Initiative," *BallotPedia*, https://ballotpedia.org/California_Proposition _184,_Three_Strikes_Sentencing_Initiative_(1994).

19. Vincent Schiraldi, Jason Coburn, and Eric Lotke, "Three Strikes and You're Out: An Examination of the Impact of 3-Strike Laws 10 Years after Their Enactment," policy brief, Justice Policy Institute, September 10, 2004.

20. "Juvenile Justice," *Frontline*, n.d., www.pbs.org/wgbh/pages/frontline /shows/juvenile/stats/states.html.

21. Camille Augustin, "Once Rikers Island Took Kalief Browder's Life, His Siblings Knew Their Mother Was Next," *Vibe*, March 1, 2017, www.vibe.com/featured/kalief-browder-siblings-interview-spike-tv.

22. "US: End Life without Parole for Juvenile Offenders: Amicus Curiae Brief Filed with the Supreme Court," Human Rights Watch, January 26, 2012, www.hrw.org/news/2012/01/26/us-end-life-without-parole -juvenile-offenders.

23   Josh Rovner, "Juvenile Life without Parole: An Overview," Sentencing Project, May 5, 2017, www.sentencing project.org/publications/juvenile -life-without-parole.

24. Editorial Board, "Justice at Last for the Youngest Inmates?," editorial,

New York Times, November 20, 2017, www.nytimes.com/2017/11/20 /opinion/life-sentence-youth-parole.html?clickSource=story-heading.

25. Rovner, "Juvenile Life without Parole."
26. From *60 Minutes*, CBS TV, June 21, 2009. See "Supermax: A Clean Version of Hell," CBSNews.com, October 11, 2007, www.cbsnews.com /news/supermax-a-clean-version-of-hell.
27. Solitary Watch, "FAQ," n.d., http://solitarywatch.com/facts/faq.
28. Death Penalty Information Center, "Execution List 2016," https://deathpenaltyinfo.org/execution-list-2016.
29. Urban Institute, "Matter of Time."
30. E. Ann Carson and Elizabeth Anderson, "Prisoners in 2015," US Department of Justice, Bureau of Justice Statistics, December 29, 2016, www.bjs.gov/index.cfm?ty=pbdetail&iid=5869.
31. US Sentencing Commission, Special Report to the Congress, *Mandatory Minimum Penalties in the Federal Criminal Justice System*, August 1991, p. ii, www.ussc.gov/sites/default/files/pdf/news/congressional-testimony-and -reports/mandatory-minimum-penalties/1991_Mand_Min_Report.pdf.
32. Urban Institute, "Matter of Time."
33. Carson and Anderson, "Prisoners in 2015."
34. Ibid.
35. Amnesty International, *United States of America: Death by Discrimination—The Continuing Role of Race in Capital Cases*, April 23, 2003, www.amnesty.org/en/documents/AMR51/046/2003/en.
36. Sentencing Project, "Fact Sheet: Incarcerated Women and Girls," November 2015, www.sentencingproject.org/wp-content/uploads /2016/02/Incarcerated-Women-and-Girls.pdf.
37. Saneta deVuono-Powell, Chris Schweidler, Alicia Walters, and Azadeh Zohrabi, *Who Pays? The True Cost of Incarceration on Families* (Oakland, CA: Ella Baker Center, Forward Together, and Research Action Design, 2015), 13.
38. Ibid., 12.
39. Ibid., 27.
40. Jennifer Gonnerman, "Million-Dollar Blocks," *Village Voice*, November 9, 2004, www.villagevoice.com/2004/11/09/million-dollar-blocks.
41. Ashley Nellis, *Life Goes On: The Rise in Life Sentences in America*, Sentencing Project, September 18, 2013, www.sentencingproject.org /publications/life-goes-on-the-historic-rise-in-life-sentences-in-america.
42. Lambda Legal, "Transgender Incarcerated People in Crisis," n.d., p. 1, www.lambdalegal.org/sites/default/files/2015_transgender-incarcerated -people-in-crisis-fs-v5-singlepages.pdf.

43. Sylvia Rivera Project, "Flow Chart: Disproportionate Incarceration," n.d., https://srlp.org/Resources/Flow-Chart-Disproportionate-Incarceration.

44. Ed Pilkington, "'Prison within Prison': A Transgender Inmate's Years-Long Battle for Treatment," *The Guardian*, July 26, 2015, www.theguardian.com/us-news/2015/jul/26/transgender-woman-inmate-prison-michelle-norsworthy.

45. Alexes Harris, "The Cruel Poverty of Monetary Sanctions," The Society Pages, March 4, 2014, http://depts.washington.edu/wcpc/sites/default/files/wcpc/The%20Cruel%20Poverty%20of%20Monetary%20Sanctions%20_%20The%20Society%20Pages%202014.pdf.

46. "Five Things about Deterrence," National Institute of Justice, modified June 6, 2016, https://nij.gov/five-things/Pages/deterrence.aspx.

47. Eric Holder, "Department Policy on Charging Mandatory Minimum Sentences and Recidivist Enhancements in Certain Drug Cases," memorandum, August 12, 2013, www.justice.gov/sites/default/files/oip/legacy/2014/07/23/ag-memo-department-policypon-charging-mandatory-minimum-sentences-recidivist-enhancements-in-certain-drugcases.pdf.

48. Mark W. Bennett, "How Mandatory Minimums Forced Me to Send More Than 1,000 Nonviolent Drug Offenders to Federal Prison," editorial, *The Nation*, October 24, 2012, www.thenation.com/article/how-mandatory-minimums-forced-me-send-more-1000-nonviolent-drug-offenders-federal-pri.

49. Families Against Mandatory Minimums, "Recent State-Level Reforms to Mandatory Minimums Laws," June 1, 2016, http://famm.org/wp-content/uploads/2013/08/Recent-State-Reforms-June-2016.pdf.

50. Nicole D. Porter, "State Advances in Criminal Justice Reform, 2016," policy brief, Sentencing Project, January 2017, www.sentencingproject.org/wp-content/uploads/2017/01/State-Advances-in-Criminal-Justice-Reform-2016-1.pdf.

51. Jennifer Peltz, "NYC Marijuana Arrests Drop Moderately under New Mayor," *New York Law Journal*, May 14, 2014, www.newyorklawjournal.com/id/1202655114797/nyc-marijuana-arrests-drop-moderately-under-new-mayor.

Rethinking Truth-in-Sentencing in Illinois

1. This article is an edited combination of two pieces on truth-in-sentencing by the author. For full articles, see Joseph Dole, "Rethinking Truth-in-Sentencing in Illinois," Praxis Center, July 21, 2015, www.kzoo.edu

/praxis/rethinking-tis-illinois, and Joseph Rodney Dole, "Preliminary Findings Concerning the Financial Costs of Implementing Illinois' Truth-in-Sentencing Laws (2002–2004)," Real Cost of Prisons, January 11, 2011, www.realcostofprisons.org/materials/dole-preliminary -findings.pdf.

2. *West's Illinois Criminal Law and Procedure*, 2004 ed. (Eagan, MN: West Publishing, 2004).

3. Ibid.

4. Planning and Research Unit, "Statistical Presentation 2003," Illinois Department of Corrections Springfield, Illinois, August 30, 2004, 11, table 4, www2.illinois.gov/idoc/reportsandstatistics/Documents /2003StatisticalPresentation.pdf. "Class X" refers to various serious felony charges punishable by 6–30 years imprisonment, including but not limited to aggravated battery, aggravated kidnapping, and home invasion.

5. Paula M. Ditton and Doris James Wilson, "Truth in Sentencing in State Prisons," special report (NCJ170032), US Department of Justice, Bureau of Justice Statistics, January 1999, https://bjs.gov/content/pub/pdf/tssp.pdf.

6. Ibid.

7. Ashley Gilpin, "The Impact of Mandatory Minimum and Truth-in-Sentencing Laws and Their Relation to English Sentencing Polices," *Arizona Journal of International and Comparative Law* 29 (2012), http:// arizonajournal.org/wp-content/uploads/2015/10/05_29_1_GilpinV2.pdf.

8. Planning and Research Unit, "Statistical Presentation 2002," Illinois Department of Corrections, Springfield, Illinois, July 31, 2003, 126, www2.illinois.gov/idoc/reportsandstatistics/Documents /2002statisticalpresentation.pdf.

9. US Department of Justice, Violent Crime Control and Law Enforcement Act of 1993, fact sheet (NCJ FS000067), www.ncjrs.gov/ txtfiles/billfs.txt.

10. Nancy G. LaVigne, Cynthia A. Mammalian, with Jeremy Travis and Christy Visher, *A Portrait of Prisoner Reentry in Illinois*, research report, Urban Institute, Justice Policy Center, April 2003.

11. Planning and Research Unit, "Statistical Presentation 2004," Illinois Department of Corrections, Springfield, Illinois, October 7, 2005, www2.illinois.gov/idoc/reportsandstatistics/Documents/Statistical %20Presentation%202004.pdf. In 1998 the legislature reenacted TIS preemptively because the state would soon rule (in 1999) that Public Act 89-404 violated the single-subject rule, which requires that legislation address only one question or issue.

12. David Olsen, Magnus Seng, Jordan Boulger, and Mellissa McClure, *The*

Impact of Illinois' Truth-in-Sentencing Law on Sentence Lengths, Time to Serve, and Disciplinary Incidents of Convicted Murderers and Sex Offenders, Loyola University of Chicago. Prepared for the Illinois Criminal Justice Information Authority, June 2009; William J. Sabol, Katherine Rosich, Kamala Mallik Kane, David P. Kirk, and Glenn Dubin, *The Influences of Truth-In-Sentencing Reforms on Changes in States' Sentencing Practices and Prison Populations*, research report, US Department of Justice, National Institute of Justice, Office of Justice Programs, April 2002.

13.   Olsen et al., "Impact of Illinois' Truth-In-Sentencing Law."

14.   Dole, "Preliminary Findings."

15.   Jessica Pupovac, "Guarding Grandpa," *Chicago Reader*, January 6, 2011, www.chicagoreader.com/chicago/illinois-prisons-budget-elderly-old-inmates/Content?oid=3013140.

16.   Christian Henrichson, Joshua Rinaldi, and Ruth Delaney, *The Price of Jails: Measuring the Taxpayer Cost of Local Incarceration*, Vera Institute of Justice, New York, May 2015, https://storage.googleapis.com/vera-web-assets/downloads/Publications/the-price-of-jails-measuring-the-taxpayer-cost-of-local-incarceration/legacy_downloads/price-of-jails.pdf.

17.   The Illinois Department of Corrections considers fifty years of age to be elderly.

18.   Pew Center on the States, *One in 31: The Long Reach of American Corrections*, Pew Charitable Trusts, Washington, DC, March 2009, www.pewtrusts.org/~/media/assets/2009/03/02/pspp_1in31_report_final_web_32609.pdf.

A Kinder, Gentler System?

1.   "Parole Board of Canada," Government of Canada, modified November 21, 2017, www.canada.ca/en/parole-board.html.

2.   Office of the Correctional Investigator, "Roles and Responsibilities," Government of Canada, modified September 16, 2013, www.oci-bec.gc.ca/cnt/roles-eng.aspx.

3.   Bill C-10, Safe Streets and Communities Act, 1st sess., 41st Parliament, 2012, http://laws-lois.justice.gc.ca/PDF/2012_1.pdf; "Truth in Sentencing Act," S.C. 2009, c. 29, Justice Laws Website, Government of Canada, modified January 24, 2018, http://laws-lois.justice.gc.ca/eng/annualstatutes/2009_29/page-1.html; Damian Rogers, "Enhanced Credit for Pre-Trial Custody: Leave Denied to Seek It Retroactively," *CanLII Connects*, Canadian Legal Information Institute, February 2, 2016, http://canliiconnects.org/en/commentaries/40064.

4.   Judy Hemming, "The Supreme Court Clarifies Sentencing Rules: *R. v Summers*," *CanLII Connects*, Canadian Legal Information Institute, November 9, 2014, http://canliiconnects.org/en/commentaries/30660.

5.   *R. v. Summers*, [2014] 1 SCR 575 at para. 67, 2014 SCC 26 (CanLII), www.canlii.org/en/ca/scc/doc/2014/2014scc26/2014scc26.html.

6.   Lindsay Porter and Donna Calverley, "Trends in the Use of Remand in Canada," *Juristat*, May 17, 2011, www.statcan.gc.ca/pub/85-002-x /2011001/article/11440-eng.pdf.

7.   Kathleen Harris, "Supreme Court Strikes Down 2 Conservative Sentencing Reforms," CBC News, Canadian Broadcasting Company, April 15, 2016, www.cbc.ca/news/politics/supreme-court-sentencing -mandatory-minumums-1.3537150.

8.   *R. v. Lyons*, [1987] 2 SCR 309 at para. 22, https://scc-csc.lexum.com /scc-csc/scc-csc/en/item/248/index.do; Mary Thibodeau, "A Decrease of Judicial Discretion in Action: *R. v. Szostak*," *CanLII Connects*, Canadian Legal Information Institute, September 15, 2015, http://canliiconnects .org/en/commentaries/38604.

9.   "CSC Statistics—Key Facts and Figures," Correctional Service of Canada, updated June 2017, www.csc-scc.gc.ca/publications/005007 -3024-eng.shtml; Correctional Service of Canada, "CSC and Long Term Supervision Orders (LTSO)," 2013, http://publications.gc.ca /collections/collection_2014/scc-csc/PS84-15-2013 cng.pdf.

10. Shelley Trevethan, Nicole Crutcher, and John-Patrick Moore, "A Profile of Federal Offenders Designated as Dangerous Offenders or Serving Long-Term Supervision Orders," Research Branch–Correctional Service of Canada, December 2002, www.csc-scc.gc.ca/research/r125-eng .shtml#Toc8026210.

11. Bill C-2, Tackling Violent Crime Act, 2nd sess., 39th Parliament, 2008, http://laws-lois.justice.gc.ca/eng/AnnualStatutes/2008_6/page-5 .html#docCont.

12. *R. v. Lyons*, [1987] 2 SCR 309 at para. 13, https://scc-csc.lexum.com /scc-csc/scc-csc/en/item/248/index.do.

13. Marian Botsford Fraser, "Forgotten Woman: The Bleak Prison Life of Renée Acoby," *The Walrus*, Walrus Foundation, November 5, 2013, https://thewalrus.ca/forgotten-woman.

14. Jim Bronskill, "Supreme Court Upholds Dangerous Offender Provisions in Criminal Code," CTV News, December 21, 2017, www.ctvnews.ca /politics/supreme-court-upholds-dangerous-offender-provisions-in -criminal-code-1.3731167.

15. *R. v. Boutilier*, [2017] SCC 64, December 21, 2017, https://scc-csc

.lexum.com/scc-csc/scc-csc/en/item/16921/index.do.

Football Numbers

1.   "Criminal Justice Facts," The Sentencing Project, www.sentencingproject
      .org/criminal-justice-facts.

Two Terms

1.   Truth in Sentencing (TIS) is a federal law introduced in the 1990s by
      President Bill Clinton that required people to serve 85 percent of their
      sentence. Thirty-five states adopted the law, which also made them
      eligible for incentive grants to expand state prisons. In Illinois, TIS
      legislation was adopted in August 1995 (state fiscal year 1996) that
      required those convicted of murder to serve 100 percent of their sentence,
      those convicted of criminal sexual assault to serve at least 85 percent of
      their sentence, and those sentenced to prison for other violent crimes
      involving great bodily harm to also serve at least 85 percent of their
      sentence. Prior to the implementation of TIS in Illinois, those sentenced
      to prison for murder and criminal sexual assault served, on average, less
      than 40 percent of their sentences as a result of the various reductions
      under the provisions of Good Conduct Credit (GCC), Meritorious Good
      Time (MGT), and Supplemental Meritorious Good Time (SMGT).
      David Olsen, Magnus Seng, Jordan Boulger, and Mellissa McClure,
      "The Impact of Illinois' Truth-in-Sentencing Law on Sentence Lengths,
      Time to Serve, and Disciplinary Incidents of Convicted Murderers and
      Sex Offenders," Loyola University of Chicago. Prepared for the Illinois
      Criminal Justice Information Authority, June 2009).
2.   Officers are instructed to not drink the prison's water; instead they bring
      in bottled water. At least once a month, I notice that toilet water comes
      out brown for hours at a time.
3.   There are many clothing restrictions at the prison; holes in jeans is one
      of them.
4.   My mom and brother visited from Texas and noticed that the "Big AZ
      Breakfast" sandwich cost only $2.50 at the gas station but $6.00 in the
      Stateville vending machine.
5.   Bruce Rauner, "In Name of Justice, I'm Closing Stateville's F House,"
      Chicago Sun Times, October 14, 2016, https://chicago.suntimes.com
      /opinion/gov-rauner-in-name-of-justice-im-closing-statevilles-f-house.

Concentrating Punishment

1.   Robert J. Sampson, *Great American City: Chicago and the Enduring Neighborhood Effect* (Chicago: University of Chicago Press, 2012), 113.

2.   Analyses derived from Cook County Circuit Court data made available by Chicago Justice Project, "Convicted in Cook," http://convictions .smartchicagoapps.org.

3.   Robert J. Sampson and Charles Loeffler, "Punishment's Place: The Local Concentration of Mass Incarceration," *Daedalus* 139, no. 3 (2010): 20–31.

4.   Todd R. Clear et al. *Predicting Crime through Incarceration: The Impact of Rates of Prison Cycling on Rates of Crime in Communities*, National Institute of Justice, Document no. 247318, May 27, 2014, www.ncjrs .gov/pdffiles1/nij/grants/247318.pdf.

5.   Wagner and Rabuy, "Mass Incarceration: The Whole Pie 2017," Prison Policy Initiative, March 14, 2017, www.prisonpolicy.org/reports /pie2017.html.

6.   Mark L. Hatzenbuehler et al. "The Collateral Damage of Mass Incarceration: Risk of Psychiatric Morbidity among Nonincarcerated Residents of High-Incarceration Neighborhoods," *American Journal of Public Health* 105, no. 1 (2015): 138–43.

7.   Authors' analyses derived from the 2010 American Community Survey five-year estimates and Cook County Circuit Court data made available by the Chicago Justice Project. See Chicago Justice Project, "Convicted in Cook."

8.   William J. Sabol and James P. Lynch, "Assessing the Longer-Run Effects of Incarceration: Impact on Families and Employment," in *Crime Control and Social Justice: The Delicate Balance*, ed. Darnell Hawkins, Samuel Myers Jr., and Randolph Stine (Westport, CT: Greenwood, 2003), 3–26.

9.   William M. Rohe, "Reexamining the Social Benefits of Homeownership after the Housing Crisis," in *Homeownership Built to Last: Lessons from the Housing Crisis on Sustaining Homeownership for Low-Income and Minority Families*, ed. Eric S. Belsky, Christopher E. Herbert, and Jennifer H. Molinsky (Washington, DC: Brookings Institution Press, 2014), 99–142.

10. Bruce Western, *Punishment and Inequality in America* (New York: Russell Sage Foundation, 2006).

11. Authors' calculations, using data from Circuit Court of Cook County convictions and global incarceration rate comparisons from the International Centre for Prison Studies. "World Prison Brief,"

International Centre for Prison Studies, www.prisonstudies.org. For more on international data, see Michelle Ye Hee Lee, "Yes, U.S. Locks People Up at a Higher Rate Than Any Other Country," *Washington Post*, July 7, 2015, www.washingtonpost.com/news/fact-checker/wp/2015/07 /07/yes-u-s-locks-people-up-at-a-higher-rate-than-any-other-country /?utm_term=.3a134443f8ff.

12. Lise McKean and Jody Raphael, "Drugs, Crime, and Consequences: Arrest and Incarceration in North Lawndale," *North Lawndale Employment Network Report*, October 2002, www.nlen.org/wp-content /uploads/2014/06/Drugs-Crime-and-Consequences.pdf.

13. Circuit Court of Cook County convictions between 2005 and 2009; "Incarcerated Women and Girls," fact sheet, Sentencing Project, November 30, 2015, www.sentencingproject.org/publications/incarcerated -women-and-girls.

14. Matthew Desmond, *Evicted: Poverty and Profit in the American City* (New York: Crown Publishers, 2016).

15. Christopher Muller and Christopher Wildeman, "Geographic Variation in the Cumulative Risk of Imprisonment and Parental Imprisonment in the United States," *Demography* 53, no. 5 (2016): 1499–1509.

16. Sampson and Loeffler, "Punishment's Place," 20–31. As a technical term, "concentrated disadvantage" is a marker of relative poverty across neighborhoods and is taken as a composite variable of "welfare receipt, poverty, unemployment, female-headed households, racial composition . . . and density of children." See Sampson, *Great American City*. Relatedly, "cumulative disadvantage theory emphasizes how early advantage or disadvantage is critical to how cohorts become differentiated over time. Not only do the early risk factors shape trajectories in the short-term outcomes but in the long-term outcomes as well. The effects of risk factors accumulate over the life course, thereby increasing heterogeneity in later life." Kenneth F. Ferraro and Jessica A. Kelley-Moore, "Cumulative Disadvantage and Health: Long-Term Consequences of Obesity?," *American Sociology Review* 68, no. 5 (2003): 707, 708.

17. As Christopher Muller writes, "criminal offending cannot be measured directly." Muller, "Northward Migration and the Rise of Racial Disparity in American Incarceration," *American Journal of Sociology* 118, no. 2 (2012): 283.

18. Elizabeth Hinton, *From the War on Poverty to the War on Crime: The Making of Mass Incarceration in America* (Cambridge, MA: Harvard University Press, 2016).

19. Sampson, *Great American City*.

20. Todd R. Clear, *Imprisoning Communities: How Mass Incarceration Makes Disadvantaged Neighborhoods Worse* (New York: Oxford University Press, 2009).

21. Douglas Perkins et al., "Participation and the Social and Physical Environment of Residential Blocks: Crime and Community Context," *American Journal of Community Psychology* 18, no. 1 (1990): 83–115.

22. Jacob S. Rugh and Douglas S. Massey, "Racial Segregation and the American Foreclosure Crisis," *American Sociological Review* 75, no. 5 (2011): 629–51.

23. Daniel Immergluck, *Foreclosed: High-Risk Lending, Deregulation, and the Undermining of America's Mortgage Market* (Ithaca, NY: Cornell University Press, 2009).

24. Anne E. Brodsky, Patricia J. Campo, and Robert E. Aronson, "PSOC in Community Context: Multi-Level Correlates of a Measure of Psychological Sense of Community in Low-Income, Urban Neighborhoods," *Journal of Community Psychology* 27, no. 6 (1999): 659–79.

25. Clear et al., *Predicting Crime*.

26. Kim Manturuk, Mark Lindblad, and Roberto Quercia, "Friends and Neighborhoods: Homeownership and Social Capital among Low- to Moderate-Income Families," *Journal of Urban Affairs* 32, no. 4 (2010): 471–88.

27. Analyses derived from Cook County Circuit Court data made available by Chicago Justice Project, "Convicted in Cook."

28. Clear, *Imprisoning Communities*.

29. Loïc Wacquant, *Deadly Symbiosis: Race and the Rise of Neoliberal Penalty* (Oxford, UK: Polity, 2004; Chichester, UK: John Wiley & Sons, 2015).

30. Cyndi Banks, *Criminal Justice Ethics: Theory and Practice* (Los Angeles: Sage, 2017).

31. Retribution is rooted in vengeance. It is a moral position that says punishment provides an end all by itself. From the lens of retribution, incarceration creates pain for offenders by isolating them from everyone and everything they know and love. In contrast, incapacitation, deterrence, and rehabilitation are more practical positions, claiming that incarceration can prevent future wrongdoing. If someone is no longer allowed in society, then they can no longer pose a threat, their absence will serve as a warning to others, and their time away may be instructive for them. See Robert Nozick, *Philosophical Explanations* (Cambridge, MA: Harvard University Press, 1983), 366–68.

32. Artist Jay Z has spoken out about this phenomena in the bail bonds industry. He writes, "If you're from neighborhoods like the Brooklyn

one I grew up in, if you're unable to afford a private attorney, then you can be disappeared into our jail system simply because you can't afford bail." See Shawn Carter, "Jay Z: For Father's Day, I'm Taking on the Exploitative Bail Industry," *Time*, June 16, 2017, http://time.com /4821547/jay-z-racism-bail-bonds.

33.	Alicia R. Riley, "Neighborhood Disadvantage, Residential Segregation, and Beyond—Lessons for Studying Structural Racism and Health," *Journal of Racial and Ethnic Health Disparities* 5, no. 2 (357–65). Yet detailed sociological accounts of neighborhoods like Chicago's Austin neighborhood often fail to capture the structural racism at play. Far too often, systemic racial bias is ignored and explained away through an ahistorical concept called "neighborhood disadvantage." This concept functions as a catchall description of existing conditions referring to the predominance of dark-skinned residents, single-parent households, high unemployment, and/or low educational attainment. These characteristics are associated with low levels of human, social, or fiscal capital. While they include a long list of characteristics, most definitions of neighborhood disadvantage are ahistorical and fail to capture how many of these characteristics are a product of policy choices and structural violence rather than chance, culture, or behavior.

34.	To see the local concentration of incarceration across cities, see the Justice Atlas, which reveals the "place-based dimension of incarceration, re-entry, and community supervision in states around the country." "Justice Atlas of Sentencing and Corrections," Justice Mapping Center, www.justiceatlas.org.

35.	Aaron Marks, "These 5 Neighborhoods Supply over a Third of NYC's Prisoners," *Gothamist*, May 1, 2013, http://gothamist.com/2013/05/01 /these_interactive_charts_show_you_w.php.

36.	Matthew R. Durose, Alexia D. Cooper, and Howard N. Snyder, "Recidivism of Prisoners Released in 30 States in 2005: Patterns from 2005 to 2010," special report, US Department of Justice, Bureau of Justice Statistics, April 2014, www.bjs.gov/content/pub/pdf/ rprts05p0510.pdf.

Suspension

1	Playwright and cofounder of the Let Us Breathe Collective Kristiana Rae Colón originally presented a reading of "Suspension" at the Geographies of Justice Seminar hosted by the Social Justice Initiative at the University of Illinois at Chicago in January 2017.

"Mass Incarceration" as Misnomer

1. Steven R. Donziger, ed., *The Real War on Crime: The Report of the National Criminal Justice Commission* (New York: HarperCollins, 1996).

2. Marc Mauer and Meda Chesney-Lind, eds., *Invisible Punishment: The Collateral Consequences of Mass Imprisonment* (New York: New Press, 2002); Michelle Alexander, *The New Jim Crow: Mass Incarceration in the Age of Colorblindness* (New York: New Press, 2010).

3. "Eric Holder's Keynote Address: Shifting Law Enforcement Goals to Reduce Mass Incarceration," Brennan Center for Justice, September 23, 2014, www.brennancenter.org/analysis/keynote-address-shifting-law -enforcement-goals-to-reduce-mass-incarceration. See also Jacob Sullum, "Eric Holder Condemns Mass Incarceration (Again)," editorial, *Forbes*, November 22, 2013, www.forbes.com/sites/jacobsullum/2013 /11/22/eric-holder-condemns-mass-incarceration-again.

4. Sam Frizell, "Hillary Clinton Calls for an End to 'Mass Incarceration,'" *Time*, April 29, 2015, http://time.com/3839892/hillary-clinton-calls -for-an-end-to-mass-incarceration. Full video of the speech is available at Columbia University's YouTube channel, "Hillary Clinton Keynote Speech – 18th Annual Dinkins Forum," www.youtube.com/watch?v =NnGAy5nIwlo (accessed August 2015).

5. "Remarks by the President at the NAACP Conference," Obama White House archives, July 14, 2015, www.whitehouse.gov/the-press-office/2015 /07/14/remarks-president-naacp-conference. Full video of the speech is available at https://youtu.be/UBkFE3sErE8 (accessed August 2015).

6. Ibid.

On Being Human

1. Jesse Wegman, "False Hope and a Needless Death behind Bars," editorial, *New York Times*, September 6, 2016, www.nytimes.com/2016 /09/06/opinion/false-hope-and-a-needless-death-behind-bars.html.

2. "We" refers to members of the group Release Aging People in Prison (RAPP).

3. "Remarks by the President at the NAACP Conference."

"Do We Want Justice, or Do We Want Punishment?"

1. Lila Abu-Lughod, *Do Muslim Women Need Saving?* (Cambridge, MA: Harvard University Press, 2015).

Against Carceral Feminism

1. Andrea Smith, ed., *Color of Violence: The INCITE! Anthology* (Cambridge, MA: South End Press, 2006).
2. US Department of Justice, Violent Crime Control and Law Enforcement Act of 1993, fact sheet, www.ncjrs.gov/txtfiles/billfs.txt.
3. Jill McCorkel, "Criminally Dependent? Gender, Punishment, and the Rhetoric of Welfare Reform," *Social Politics* 11, no. 3 (2004): 389.
4. Steven Hsieh, "Marissa Alexander Now Faces 60 Years in Prison for Firing a Warning Shot in Self Defense," *The Nation*, March 3, 2014, www.thenation.com/article/marissa-alexander-now-faces-60-years -prison-firing-warning-shot-self-defense. NOTE: 2018 update: Marissa Alexander agreed to a plea deal in 2015, and after serving three years in prison she was released on January 27, 2015, but required to wear an ankle monitor for two years. She continues to be politically active, including in movements to challenge the criminalization of Black women (https://marissaalexander.org).
5. "About AB 593," AB 593/AB 1593, The Sin by Silence Bills, http://legislation.sinbysilence.com/about-ab-593.
6. E. Ann Carson, "Prisoners in 2013," US Department of Justice, Bureau of Justice Statistics, September 2014, www.bjs.gov/content/pub/pdf /p13.pdf; Todd D. Minton and Daniela Golinelli, "Jail Inmates at Midyear 2013: Statistical Tables," US Department of Justice, Bureau of Justice Statistics, revised August 12, 2014, www.bjs.gov/content/pub /pdf/jim13st.pdf
7. INCITE!, "INCITE! Critical Resistance Statement," n.d., www.incite -national.org/page/incite-critical-resistance-statement.
8. The zine was later expanded into a book. See Ching-In Chen, Jai Dulani, and Leah Lakshmi Piepzna-Samarasinha, eds., *The Revolution Starts at Home: Confronting Partner Abuse in Activist Communities* (New York: South End Press, 2011). Also at http://criticalresistance.org /wp-content/uploads/2014/05/Revolution-starts-at-home-zine.pdf.
9. Ibid., 91.
10. Natalie J. Sokoloff and Ida Dupont, "Domestic Violence at the Intersections of Race, Class, and Gender: Challenges and Contributions to Understanding Violence against Marginalized Women in Diverse Communities," *Violence Against Women* 11, no. 1 (2005): 38–64, http://journals.sagepub.com/doi/abs/10.1177/1077801204271476.

Circles of Grief, Circles of Healing

1. Pew Charitable Trusts, *Collateral Costs: Incarcercation's Effect on Economic Mobility*, 2010, www.pewtrusts.org/~/media/legacy/uploadedfiles/pcs _assets/2010/collateralcosts1pdf.pdf.

2. Saneta deVuono-Powell, Chris Schweidler, Alicia Walters, and Azadeh Zohrabi, *Who Pays? The True Cost of Incarceration on Families* (Oakland, CA: Ella Baker Center, Forward Together, Research Action Design, 2015), 7, http://ellabakercenter.org/sites/default/files/downloads/who-pays.pdf.

3. Solomon Northrup, *Twelve Years a Slave: Narrative of Solomon Northup, a Citizen of New-York* . . . (New York: Miller, Orton and Mulligan, 1855), 81–82.

4. Dorothy E. Roberts, "Prison, Foster Care, and the Systemic Punishment of Black Mothers," *UCLA Law Review* 59 (2012): 1476–1500, www.uclalawreview.org/pdf/59-6-2.pdf.

5. Connie Chung, *The Politics of (Un)Mothering: A Literature Review on Homeless Mothers* (Saarbrücken, Germany: Lambert Academic Publishing, 2011).

6. Beth E. Richie, *Arrested Justice: Black Women, Violence, and America's Prison Nation* (New York: NYU Press, 2012).

7. "In the Wake: A Salon in Honor of Christina Sharpe," Barnard College, February 2, 2017, https://vimeo.com/203012536.

Fund Black Futures as an Abolitionist Demand

1. Black Youth Project 100, "Agenda to Build Black Futures," n.d., http://agendatobuildblackfutures.org/wp-content/uploads /2016/01/BYP_AgendaBlackFutures_booklet_web.pdf.

Meditations on Abolitionist Practices, Reformist Movements

1. "What Is the PIC? What Is Abolition?," Critical Resistance, n.d., http://criticalresistance.org/about/not-so-common-language.

2. Mission statement, Critical Resistance, n.d., http://criticalresistance.org /about.

3. Questions in this dialogue were asked by the editors of *Upping the Anti: A Journal of Theory and Action.*

4. See "The Oakland Power Projects," Critical Resistance, n.d., http:// criticalresistance.org/chapters/cr-oakland/the-oakland-power-projects.

5. See "LA for Youth—1% Campaign," Youth Justice Coalition/Take Action, n.d., www.youth4justice.org/take-action/ la-for-youth-1-campaign.

6. For more information, see Malcolm X Grassroots Movement, https:// mxgm.org.

By Any Means Necessary

1. The incident occurred on May 16, 2010. See Elisha Anderson, "Grandmother Says She Watched Police Kill 7-Year-Old," *USA Today*, June 10, 2013, www.usatoday.com/story/news/nation/2013/06/10 /detroit-police-girl-killed/2408763.

Schooling and the Prison-Industrial Complex

1. "About Free Write Arts and Literacy," www.freewriteartsliteracy.org/about.
2. Antonia Darder, *Reinventing Paulo Freire: A Pedagogy of Love* (New York: Routledge, 2017).
3. Angel Pantoja, "Trust," *Best Practice #2: A Sense of Trust*, video performance, https://education.psych.uic.edu/research/urban-youth -trauma-center/public-awareness/youth-videos/youth-violence -prevention-spoken-word-videos.
4. Michelle Alexander, *The New Jim Crow: Mass Incarceration in the Age of Colorblindness* (New York: New Press, 2012).
5. Michelle Mbekeani-Wiley, *Handcuffs in the Hallways: The State of Policing in Chicago Public Schools*, Sargent Shriver National Center on Poverty Law, February 2017, http://povertylaw.org/files/docs/handcuffs -in-hallways-final.pdf.
6. Kasey Henricks, Amanda E. Lewis, Iván Arenas, and Deana G. Lewis, *A Tale of Three Cities: The State of Racial Justice in Chicago Report*, Institute for Research on Race and Public Policy (Chicago: University of Illinois at Chicago, 2017), 98, http://stateofracialjusticechicago.com/wp -content/uploads/IRRPP_StateOfRacialJusticeReport.pdf.
7. Sentencing Project, "Fact Sheet: Incarcerated Women and Girls," 2017, p. 4, www.sentencingproject.org/publications/incarcerated-women-and- girls.
8. Joshua Rovner, *Racial Disparities in Youth Commitments and Arrests*, April 1, 2016, www.sentencingproject.org/publications/racial-disparities -in-youth-commitments-and-arrests.
9. Crystal T. Laura, *Being Bad: My Baby Brother and the School-to-Prison Pipeline* (New York: Teachers College Press, 2014).
10. Free Write Arts and Literacy, *Evidence: Free Write Anthology*, vol. 7 (Chicago: Free Write Arts and Literacy, 2016), 62, http:// freewriteartsliteracy.org/wp-content/uploads/2016/12/free-write -anthology_2016.pdf.
11. National Research Council, *The Growth of Incarceration in the United States: Exploring Causes and Consequences* (Washington, DC: National

Academies Press, 2014), www.nap.edu/read/18613/chapter/1.

12. Barry Holman and Jason Ziedenberg, *Dangers of Detention: The Impact of Incarcerating Youth in Detention and Other Secure Facilities*, Justice Policy Institute, 2013, p. 8, www.ncjrs.gov/App/Publications/abstract .aspx?ID=269394.

13. Free Write, *Means of Survival: Free Write Anthology*, vol. 3 (Chicago: Free Write Arts and Literacy, n.d.), 7, http://freewriteartsliteracy.org /wp-content/uploads/2016/04/Antholgy-03-Means-Of-Survival.pdf.

14. Quoted in National Research Council, *Growth of Incarceration*, 176.

Ban the Box and the Impact of Organizing by Formerly Incarcerated People

1. This article is largely derived from two pieces on Ban the Box by the author, with edits. For full reports, see Linda Evans, *Ban the Box in Housing, Education, and Voting: A Grassroots History*, Critical Resistance http://criticalresistance.org/wp-content/uploads/2014/04/B2B2_Final. pdf, and Linda Evans, *Ban the Box in Employment: A Grassroots History*, Legal Services for Prisoners with Children, www.prisonerswithchildren. org/wp-content/uploads/2016/10/BTB-Employment-History-Report-2016.pdf.

2. Author's note: Having been in prison myself, I have chosen at times to use the term "we" when referring to people who have been formerly incarcerated or convicted. With very few exceptions, I have used the names of organizations but not individuals. I knew it would be impossible to find out all the names of the people who organized for Ban the Box around the country. Rather than include some individuals and exclude others whose work is just as important, I decided to mention only organizations in order to emphasize the collective nature of our accomplishments.

3. Editors' note: Linda Evans, author of this article, was a founding member of All of Us or None.

4. In 2013 All of Us or None worked with the Lawyers' Committee on Human Rights, National Employment Law Project, Community Housing Partnership, and the San Francisco Human Rights Commission to pass the Fair Chance Ordinance, governing housing providers and all public and private employers with twenty or more employees. "Fair Chance Implementation Strategies for Government Employees," by Zoë Polk and Michelle Natividad Rodríguez is an excellent resource on implementing and enforcing ban the box policies:

www.nelp.org/publication/fair-chance-implementation-case-studies-for
-government-agencies.

5. "Enough Is Enough: The Story of All of Us or None," video, November
3, 2015, https://www.youtube.com/watch?v=_ka_nokbvHs; "Locked Up,
Locked Out," video, November 3, 2015, www.youtube.com/watch
?v=uwl0xbndVHs. Both produced and edited by Eve Goldberg.

6. These states are Connecticut, Hawaii, Illinois, Massachusetts,
Minnesota, New Jersey, Oregon, Rhode Island, Vermont, and
Washington, DC.

7. Beth Avery and Phil Hernandez, "Ban the Box: US Cities, Counties,
and States Adopt Fair Hiring Policies," toolkit, National Employment
Law Project, January 1, 2018, www.nelp.org/publication/ban-the-box
-fair-chance-hiring-state-and-local-guide.

8. Formerly Incarcerated, Convicted People and Families Movement,
https://ficpmovement.wordpress.com.

9. Barack Obama, Fair Chance Business Pledge, November 2, 2015,
https://obamawhitehouse.archives.gov/issues/criminal-justice/fair
-chance-pledge.

10. Cindy Chang, "Louisiana Is the World's Prison Capital," *New Orleans
Times-Picayune,* May 13, 2012, updated April 6, 2016, www.nola.com
/crime/index.ssf/2012/05/louisiana_is_the_worlds_prison.html.

11. Voice of the Ex-Offender, *Communities, Evictions, and Criminal
Convictions: Public Housing and Disparate Impact: A Model Policy,* 2013,
https://ficpmovement.files.wordpress.com/2013/04/communities
-evictions-criminal-convictions.pdf. Voice of the Ex-Offender later
changed its name to Voice of the Experienced.

12. Eli Hager, "From Prison to PhD: The Redemption and Rejection of
Michelle Jones," *New York Times*, September 13, 2017, www.nytimes
.com/2017/09/13/us/harvard-nyu-prison-michelle-jones.html.

13. Natalie Swaby, "Supreme Court Rules Law Student Who Turned Life
around Can Take Bar Exam," King 5 News, www.king5.com/article/news
/local/seattle/supreme-court-rules-law-student-who-turned-life-around
-can-take-bar-exam/492493596.

14. Center for Community Alternatives, *The Use of Criminal History Records
in College Admissions Reconsidered*, 2010, www.communityalternatives.org
/pdf/Reconsidered-criminal-hist-recs-in-college-admissions.pdf; Center
for Community Alternatives, *Boxed Out: Criminal History Screening and
College Application Attrition*, 2015, www.communityalternatives.org/pdf
/publications/BoxedOut_FullReport.pdf.

15. Education from the Inside Out Coalition, "EIO Coalition tells SUNY to

#Banthebox," March 9, 2016, www.youtube.com/watch?v=xE0lJ-SvpsQ.

16. SUNY Albany Graduate Student Association, Equity and Inclusion Committee, "Ban the Box Resolution," March 7, 2016, http://sunysa.org /wp-content/uploads/2015/10/1516-110BantheBoxResolution.pdf.

17. Christopher Uggen, Ryan Larson, and Sarah Shannon, *Six Million Lost Voters: State-Level Estimates of Felony Disenfranchisement*, 2016, Sentencing Project, 2016, p. 3, www.sentencingproject.org /publications/6-million-lost-voters-state-level-estimates-felony -disenfranchisement-2016.

18. "Criminal disenfranchisement" is also known as "felony disenfranchisement." The former term is used here for clarity, because several states also disenfranchise people with misdemeanors.

19. CCRC Staff, "Felony Disenfranchisement, Rights State by State," October 26, 2016, Collateral Consequences Resource Center, http:// ccresourcecenter.org/2016/10/26/felony-voting-rights-state-by-state.

20. See National Council for Incarcerated and Formerly Incarcerated Women and Girls, http://nationalcouncil.us.

#CLOSErikers

1. JustLeadershipUSA, "About Us," www.justleadershipusa.org/about-us.

A Mother Confronts Chicago Police Torture

1. Mary L. Johnson, "A Mother Confronts Police Torture in Chicago," November 30, 2015, Praxis Center, www.kzoo.edu/praxis/a-mother -confronts-police-torture-in-chicago.

Pelican Bay Hunger Strike

1. Todd Ashker, "Moving Forward with Our Fight to End Solitary Confinement, *San Francisco Bay View*, May 20, 2015 http://sfbayview .com/2015/05/moving-forward-with-our-fight-to-end-solitary -confinement.

2. Todd Ashker, "Agreement to End Hostilities," August 12, 2012, https://toddashker.org/agreement-to-end-hostilities.

3. Quoted in Kijani Tashiri Askari and Akili Castlin, "We Can't Breathe! Thoughts on Our Agreement to End Hostilities, *San Francisco Bay View*, July 25, 2015, *http://sfbayview.com/2015/07/we-cant-breathe- thoughts-on-our-agreement-to-end-hostilities.*

4. Ibid.

5.   Letter from April Harris, California Institution for Women, March 21,
      2015.
6.   Todd Ashker, "Moving Forward: With Our Fight to End Solitary
      Confinement [SHU/Ad.-Seg.]," March 30, 2015, https://
      prisonerhungerstrikesolidarity.files.wordpress.com/2015/04/todd
      -ashker-3-30-15-treatise-on-shu-torture-and-call-to-action.pdf.
7.   "Step Down Program (SDP)," California Department of Correction
      and Rehabilitation, www.cdcr.ca.gov/rehabilitation/SDP.html.
8.   Mutope Duguma, "Four Years since Our Hunger Strikes Began, None of
      Our Core Demands Have Yet Been Met: Our Protracted Struggle Must
      Continue," *San Francisco Bay View*, June 21, 2015, http://sfbayview.com
      /2015/06/four-years-since-our-hunger-strikes-began-none-of-our-core
      -demands-have-yet-been-met-our-protracted-struggle-must-continue.
9.   Ibid.
10.   H. Rap Brown, "Free Huey Rally, February 1968," The Pacifica Radio/
      UC Berkeley Social Activism Sound Recording Project, www.lib
      .berkeley.edu/MRC/rapbrown.html.
11.   "Power Concedes Nothing: A Discussion on CDCr's Insidious
      Maintenance of SHU Torture Units," Prisoner News, March 25, 2014,
      http://freedomarchives.org/pipermail/ppnews_freedomarchives
      .org/2014-March/005377.html.
12.   Todd Ashker et al., "Prisoners' Demands," Prisoner Hunger Strike
      Solidarity, April 3, 2011, https://prisonerhungerstrikesolidarity
      .wordpress.com/education/the-prisoners-demands-2.

The Lil' Paralegal Who Could and the Birth of a New Law

1.   Through discovery and in trial testimony, I learned this person had been
      paid this exact amount.
2.   My lawyer then told me I could request the pictures with an additional
      court order.
3.   Maura Kelly, "Aiming for a Bigger Bullet Database, Proposal Would
      Make Gunmakers Help," *Chicago Tribune*, April 21, 2000.

Litanies for Survival

1.   "FICPM National Platform," Formerly Incarcerated, Convicted People
      and Families Movement, https://ficpmovement.wordpress.com.

Breaking Walls

1. Anthony Holmes, "Violent Victim Impact Statement," Case Number 2007R00712, Chicago Torture Justice Memorials website, https:// chicagotorture.org/files/2012/03/17/Holmes_sentencing_statement.pdf.

2. Alice Kim and Joey Mogul's forthcoming book (Beacon Press) about the struggles for justice in the Burge torture cases discusses the city of Chicago's culpability and transformation.

3. See Vickie Casanova Willis and Standish E. Willis, "Black People Against Police Torture: The Importance of Building a People-Centered Human Rights Movement," *Public Interest Law Reporter* 21 (2015): 235, via Race, Racism, and the Law, http://racism.org/index.php/articles/law -and-justice/criminal-justice-and-racism/134-police-brutality-and -lynchings/2006-black-people-against-police-torture.

4. Joey Mogul, "Lawyer for Chicago Torture Victims: A Model for Responding to Police Torture," *Time*, May 12, 2015, http://time.com /3852431/lawyer-for-chicago-torture-victims-a-lesson-for-responding -to-police-brutality.

5. Mariame Kaba, "We Must Love Each Other: Lessons in Struggle and Justice from Chicago," *Prison Culture*, February 15, 2015, www.usprisonculture.com/blog/2015/02/15/we-must-love-each-other -lessons-in-struggle-and-justice-from-chicago.

6. See http://criticalresistance.org and http://www.incite-national.org.

7. Holmes, "Violent Victim Impact Statement."

8. F. Amanda Tugade, "Chicago Police Tortured Dozens of Black Men. Now, Victims Are Demanding Reparations," *In These Times*, December 17, 2014, http://inthesetimes.com/article/17468/chicago_torture_reparations_bill.

9. "Torture Survivors: A Roundtable," Chicago Access Network Television, December 14, 2011, www.youtube.com/watch?v=e58CbI19KCA.

10. See G. Flint Taylor, "The Chicago Police Torture Scandal: A Legal and Political History," *CUNY Law Review* 17 (2013): 329–81. www.cunylawreview.org/wp-content/uploads/2015/02/04-Chicago -Police-Torture.pdf.

11. "Survivor Darrell Cannon Says 'Never Again' to Chicago Torture," Amnesty International USA, June 26, 2014, www.youtube.com /watch?v=-grucHqsOnU.

12. Joan Parkin, "Justice for the Death Row Ten," *New Abolitionist*, no. 5 (November 1998), www.nodeathpenalty.org/new_abolitionist /november-1998-issue-5/justice-death-row-ten.

Formerly Incarcerated, Convicted People and Families Movement Platform

1. National Organizations of the FICPFM, https://ficpmovement
   .wordpress.com/about/national-organizations-of-the-ficpm.
2. "FICPM National Platform," Formerly Incarcerated, Convicted People
   & Families Movement, https://ficpmovement.wordpress.com/about
   /ficpm-national-platform.

Permissions

We are thankful to the authors and original publishers for granting permission to include the following writings in *The Long Term*:

"Affirmation." Reprinted with permission from Eve L. Ewing, *Electric Arches* (Chicago: Haymarket Books, 2017).

"Against Carceral Feminism." Reprinted with permission from Victoria Law, "Against Carceral Feminism," *Jacobin* (October 17, 2014). www.jacobinmag.com/2014/10/against-carceral-feminism.

"Breaking Walls: Lessons from Chicago." Originally published in a slightly different form as "Breaking Walls, Making History: Lessons from Chicago," *The Abolitionist* (Summer 2016). https://abolitionistpaper.files.wordpress.com/2017/04/the-abolitionist-issue-26.pdf. Reprinted with permission from Alice Kim.

"By Any Means Necessary: Reflections on Malcolm X's Birthday— What If What's Necessary Is Awe-Inspiring, Unconditional, Militant Love?" Reprinted with permission from adrienne maree brown and the publisher, "By Any Means Necessary: Reflections on Malcolm X's Birthday," *YES!* (May 20, 2010). www.yesmagazine.org/peace-justice/by-any-means-necessary.

Formerly Incarcerated, Convicted People and Families Movement Platform. Reprinted with permission from Formerly Incarcerated, Convicted People and Families Movement, 2011. https://ficpmovement.wordpress.com/about/ficpm-national-platform.

"It Do What It Do (Me & Homer Talk Poetry)." Reprinted with permission from Krista Franklin, *Study of Love & Black Body* (Detroit: Willow Books, 2012).

"'Mass Incarceration' as Misnomer." Originally published in a

357

slightly different form on *The Abolitionist* (Summer 2016). https:// abolitionistpaper.files.wordpress.com/2017/04/the-abolitionist -issue-26.pdf. Reprinted with permission from Dylan Rodríguez.

"Meditations on Abolitionist Practices, Reformist Moments." Excerpted from "Abolitionist Practices, Reformist Moments" in *Upping the Anti* 19 (2017). http://uppingtheanti.org/journal /article/19-abolitionist-practices-reformist-moments. Reprinted with permission from Rachel Herzing and Erica R. Meiners.

"A Mother Confronts Chicago Police Torture." Originally published in a slightly different form on Praxis Center (November 30, 2015). www.kzoo.edu/praxis/a-mother-confronts-police-torture-in-chicago. Reprinted with permission from Mary L. Johnson and the publisher.

"On Leaving Prison." Reprinted with permission from Monica Cosby and the publisher, *Truthout* (May 23, 2017). www.truth-out. org/opinion/item/40679-on-leaving-prison-a-reflection-on- entering-and-exiting-communities.

"Pelican Bay Hunger Strike: Building Unity behind Bars." Originally published as "Pelican Bay Hunger Strike: Four Years and Still Fighting," *Counterpunch* (July 9, 2015). www.counterpunch.org /2015/07/09/pelican-bay-hunger-strike-four-years-and-still-fighting. Reprinted with permission from Claude Marks and Isaac Ontiveros.

"Ten Strategies for Cultivating Community Accountability." Originally published in a slightly different form on *Prison Culture* (September 16, 2013). www.usprisonculture.com/blog/2013/09/16 /guest-post-strategies-for-cultivating-community-accountability -by-ann-russo. Reprinted with permission from Ann Russo.

"Uprooting the Punitive Practices of New York's Parole Board." Originally published as "N.Y. Must Lift Punitive Practices of State's Parole Board," *Times Union* (May 9, 2017). www.timesunion.com /tuplus-opinion/article/N-Y-must-lift-punitive-practices-of- state-s-11133297.php. Reprinted with permission from Mujahid Farid.

"Whole Foods, Black Wall Street, and My 13-Inch Flat-Screen TV." Reprinted with permission from Andre Patterson and the publisher, Praxis Center (January 11, 2017). www.kzoo.edu/praxis/ whole-foods-black-wall-street.

Contributors

Efrain Alcaraz is the son of two beautiful parents. His family grew up working hard in the fields sowing seeds, pulling weeds, and gathering. No matter what they earned, they made do with what they had. Efrain is wrongfully convicted and has strong memories of the days he spent in the fields when he didn't have much but was happy.

Tara Betts is the author of *Break the Habit* (Trio House Press, 2016) and *Arc & Hue* (Aquarius Press, 2009). She is also coeditor of *The Beiging of America: Personal Narratives about Being Mixed Race in the 21st Century* (2Leaf Press, 2017). Her work has appeared in *Poetry, American Poetry Review, Essence, Nylon,* and numerous anthologies. Betts holds a PhD in English from Binghamton University and an MFA in creative writing from New England College. She teaches at University of Illinois–Chicago and as part of the MFA faculty at Chicago State University. She has led writing workshops at Cook County Jail, Cook County Juvenile Detention Center, and Stateville Correctional Center.

Cookie Bivens is a Black, trans, formerly incarcerated woman based in San Francisco. During her time inside, she successfully advocated for better conditions for transgender women. Paroled in 2016, she is currently working to end the prison-industrial complex. She mentors women inside and out of lockup and has spoken at numerous rallies, schools, and senators' offices, and she mentors women inside and out of lockup. She is a legal assistant at TGI Justice Project, a group of transgender, gender variant, and intersex people—inside and outside of prisons, jails, and detention centers—creating a united family in the struggle for survival and freedom.

Tammy Bond was born and raised in Decatur, Illinois, before joining the US Army after high school in 1986. She is the mother of a thirty-three-year-old daughter. Before her conviction, she spent five wonderful years teaching. She currently works with a nonprofit organization that assists formerly incarcerated individuals with reentry needs.

Janaé E. Bonsu is an activist-scholar and organizer based in Chicago. Her political home is with Black Youth Project 100 (BYP100), a national member-led organization of eighteen-to-thirty-five-year-olds dedicated to creating justice and freedom through a Black queer feminist lens. Janaé coauthored BYP100's public policy agendas—the *Agenda to Keep Us Safe* and the *Agenda to Build Black Futures*—and served on the Movement for Black Lives (M4BL) Policy Table. Janaé is also a PhD student at Jane Addams College of Social Work, where her work focuses on state violence against Black women and alternatives to state intervention.

David Booth is the founder of the Sex Law and Policy Center, an organization working to break down stigmas surrounding people on the sex crimes registry, especially registrants who identify as queer or transgendered. He advocates for inclusive reforms that acknowledge harms while also ensuring dignity and respect for criminalized people.

Kathy Boudin is codirector/cofounder of the Center for Justice at Columbia University and an adjunct lecturer at the Columbia School of Social Work. She served twenty-two years in prison in New York. Since returning home, a key area of her work is focused on long-termers, including challenging the exclusion of people with violent crimes from criminal justice reform; building consciousness about aging people being kept in prison by parole policies; and creating a restorative practice program for long-termers inside New York State prisons.

Carlthel, Damien, and **Elizabeth Brent** are coping with the absence of their eldest brother, Larry Jr., who has been wrongfully imprisoned for twenty-five years. Over this time, they have sustained and forged even stronger relationships with each other. Artistic expression has been both an outlet for Larry to connect to the outside world, as well as a conduit for family members to brave his long absence. Throughout the family's journey amid this struggle, they have not lost faith, as God continues to be their guiding light.

Chester "Chuck" Brost was born in Chicago in 1965. Since his incarceration he has become a writer. He wrote *No More! The Complete Guide to Preventing, Ending and Responding to Sexual Violence* (Gravity Press, 2015), which won the NABE Pinnacle Achievement Award. He is also an artist and is currently painting murals at Stateville Prison.

adrienne maree brown is the author of *Emergent Strategy: Shaping Change, Changing Worlds* (AK Press, 2017) and coeditor of *Octavia's Brood: Science Fiction from Social Justice Movements* (AK Press, 2015). She is a facilitator with the Emergent Strategy Ideation Institute, a doula/healer with Healing By Choice, and a trainer with generative somatics/Black Organizing for Leadership and Dignity (BOLD). adrienne is on the board of the Ruckus Society.

Rachel Caïdor has spent her life learning about feminisms, people-of-color liberation, antiviolence against women, death penalty abolition, and prisoner support. She is a member of Chicago's INCITE! chapter and was a founding member of the Pink Bloque. She works with Love & Protect and the Just Practice Collaborative. She lives in Chicago with a turtle and probably too many plants.

Roger Viet Chung is the lead instructor and curriculum developer for the ROOTS (Restoring Our Original True Selves) Program at San Quentin and Solano State Prisons. He is a core member of the Asian Prisoner Support Committee. He also directs the Restoring Our Communities Reentry program for formerly incarcerated students at Laney Community College of Oakland, where he is a faculty member of the Department of Ethnic Studies.

Kristiana Rae Colón is a poet, playwright, actor, educator, Cave Canem Fellow, creator of #BlackSexMatters and cofounder of the #LetUsBreathe Collective. She was named 2017 Best Black Playwright by the Black Mall. Her plays have premiered in Chicago, New York, London, and other cities. Kristiana's writing, producing, and organizing work to radically reimagine power structures, our complicity in strive, and visions for liberation.

Daniel Cooper is the executive director of the Center for Equitable Cities at Adler University in Chicago. His work focuses on intersecting forms of urban inequality that create and remake disadvantaged communities. He has worked with coalitions and organizations on issues including violence prevention, justice system reform, community and economic development, youth development, and coalition building. He has a PhD in community research and action from Vanderbilt University and a master of urban planning and policy degree from the University of Illinois at Chicago.

Monica Cosby is a mother, grandmother, activist, organizer, restorative justice and peace circle keeper, poet, person of the theater, and a lover of books, music, cats, dogs, and the earth. Her life and work have been shaped and informed by the communities she has belonged to, including the community of artists, scholars, and mothers with whom she was incarcerated for twenty years and whose survival was and is an act of resistance against a system that would dispose of them.

Jermond "JFresh" Davis is an independent songwriter, hip-hop artist, community organizer, and creativity expressionist/entertainer. He graduated from Sidewalk High (the streets) and Blacks University (prison) with an undergrad in manifesting dreams. His contribution, "Loving Inward," is a sharing of his discovery of intimacy and its transformative potential while in California State Prison. He developed his self-taught artistry in Los Angeles.

Joseph Dole has won numerous awards for his writing, including first place in the 2017 *Columbia Journal*'s annual writing contest. He is the author of *A Costly American Hatred* (Midnight Express Books, 2015) and *Control Units and Supermaxes: A National Security Threat* (CreateSpace, 2016). He is currently serving a life without parole sentence at Stateville Correctional Center and spent a decade of his life in isolation at the notorious Tamms Supermax Prison. More of Joe's work is available on his Facebook page: www.facebook.com/JosephDoleIncerateratedWriter.

Raul Dorado is an incarcerated writer serving time at Stateville Correctional Center in Joliet, Illinois. He has published poetry and essays with the Prison + Neighborhood Arts Project (P+NAP), including "The Presumption of Justice: Capitalism and Alchemists." He is currently working toward a bachelor's degree. He can be contacted at Raul Dorado, K53842 Stateville C.C., Joliet, IL 60434.

In the 1960s, **Linda Evans** organized to end the US war against Vietnam with Students for a Democratic Society and the Weathermen. She was active in the women's liberation movement and a leader of the John Brown Anti-Klan Committee, which fought against white supremacy and the KKK. In 1985 she was sentenced to forty years in federal prison for actions protesting US government policies. After her release from prison in 2001, she organized All of Us or None with other formerly incarcerated people and their families. Together they initiated the Ban the Box campaign to fight discrimination based on conviction history in employment, voting rights, education, and housing.

Eve L. Ewing is a sociologist of education and a writer from Chicago. She is author of *Electric Arches* (Haymarket Books, 2017) and *Ghosts in the Schoolyard: Racism and School Closings on Chicago's South Side* (University of Chicago Press, forthcoming 2018), and a scholar at the University of Chicago School of Social Service Administration.

Mujahid Farid is the lead organizer of the Release Aging People in Prison campaign, which works to accelerate the release rate of elderly people in New York prisons. Confined for thirty-three years in New York, Farid earned four college degrees, including two master's, during his incarceration. He was awarded a joint New York State legislative commendation for his community work and was a 2013 Soros Justice Fellow.

Krista Franklin is a writer and visual artist whose poems and visual art have appeared in *Poetry*, *Callaloo*, *BOMB Magazine*, *The Encyclopedia Project*, and *The BreakBeat Poets: New American Poetry in the Age of Hip-Hop* (Haymarket Books, 2015). She holds an MFA in Interdisciplinary Arts–Book and Paper from Columbia College Chicago.

Thea Gahr is a queer bilingual printmaker and educator working in both Oregon and Mexico City. She is a member of the Justseeds artists' cooperative, Escuela de Cultura Popular Martires del 68. Through teaching young people, building community, printmaking, and farming across cultures, she strives to empower ideas of social and environmental justice.

George Gomez has been incarcerated since 2006. While in prison, he found art and music to be his passion. He spends his free time perfecting his art skills, and dreams of having his own tattoo shop one day. When he is not creating art, he likes to "escape" via his music, motivated by his daughter and family.

Phil Hartsfield is a father and a writer. He is currently incarcerated in Illinois (#R46473) serving what amounts to a life sentence and is pursuing his bachelor's degree with a special interest in psychology and law. His writings and artwork can be found on his Facebook page, https://www.facebook.com/phil.hartsfield.7.

Shira Hassan is the former director of Young Women's Empowerment Project, the founder of Just Practice, and a Chicago-based organizer, educator, and social justice leader.

Andres L. Hernandez, a native Chicagoan, is an interdisciplinary, creative practitioner who researches and produces critical readings and alternative imaginings of the physical, social, and cultural environments we inhabit. Working both independently and collaboratively, he explores ways in which private and public spaces are used to promote and sustain injustice, and advocates for the equitable planning, usage, and stewardship of public spaces for the benefit of all. He is an associate professor of art education at the School of the Art Institute of Chicago and is a cofounder of the Revival Arts Collective, a network of citizen activists committed to using arts and cultre as a catalyst for community redevelopment in Chicago.

Rachel Herzing lives and works in Oakland, California, where she fights the violence of policing and imprisonment. She is the codirector of the Center for Political Education, a cofounder of Critical Resistance, and the codirector of the StoryTelling & Organizing Project, a community resource for sharing stories of interventions to interpersonal harm that do not rely on policing, imprisonment, or traditional social services.

Mary L. Johnson is a mother, truth-teller, and pioneer in the struggle against Chicago police torture. She was one of the first people to file a complaint against now-disgraced former commander Jon Burge for allegations of torture and abuse of her son Michael Johnson. For over forty years, she has been tireless in her efforts for justice for Chicago police torture survivors, death row prisoners, and those confined in Illinois's supermax prisons.

Mariame Kaba is an organizer and educator who is active in numerous social movements for prison abolition and racial, gender, and transformative justice. She is the founder and director of Project NIA, a grassroots organization with a vision to end youth incarceration, and a cofounder of numerous organizations, including the Chicago Freedom School, Love and Protect, and most recently Survived & Punished.

James Kilgore is an educator, activist, and writer based at the University of Illinois in Urbana. He is the author of *Understanding Mass Incarceration: A People's Guide to the Key Civil Rights Struggle of Our Time* (New Press, 2015). He has four published novels, all of which were drafted during his six and a half years in federal and state prison. He is currently active in his community as codirector of First Followers Reentry Program and as a member of the anti-prison group Build Programs, Not Jails.

Alice Kim is an organizer, educator, and writer based in Chicago. She is a cofounder of Chicago Torture Justice Memorials and teaches with P+NAP. She is also the director of human rights practice at University of Chicago's Pozen Family Center for Human Rights.

Victoria Law is a freelance journalist focusing on intersections of incarceration, gender, and resistance and the author of *Resistance Behind Bars: The Struggles of Incarcerated Women* (PM Press, 2009). With Maya Schenwar, she is currently cowriting *Your Home Is Your Prison*, which critically examines proposed "alternatives" to incarceration and explores creative solutions that truly end mass incarceration.

David Lee is a cofounder of One Hood United and a founding member of the Coalition to Abolish Death by Incarceration. He is a prolific writer, mentor, and friend to many on both sides of the prison walls. He is also part of the LifeLines Project and serves on Decarcerate PA's Inside Advisory Board. Originally from Philadelphia, he has been serving a death-by-incarceration sentence for the last thirty years.

Deana G. Lewis is a Black feminist, prison abolitionist, and scholar-activist whose scholarly and activist work focuses on tran/cis Black women and girls who have experienced state violence. She is the assistant director and clinical lecturer of gender and women's studies and a doctoral candidate in educational policy studies at the University of Illinois at Chicago.

A Living Chance: Storytelling to End Life Without Parole is an ongoing project initiated in 2014 by the California Coalition for Women Prisoners (CCWP). This project emerged from conversations with longtime CCWP members serving life without parole (LWOP) at the California Institution for Women in Corona, California, and the Central California Women's Facility in Chowchilla. Interviews with Ellen Richardson, Kelly Savage, Amber Bray, Rae Harris, Barbara Chavez, Judith Barnett, Mary Elizabeth Stroder, Stacey Dyer, Natalie DeMola, and Laverne DeJohnette are featured in *The Long Term*.

Damon Locks is a visual artist, musician, sound artist, deejay, and educator. He is currently an artist-in-residence with the Museum of Contemporary Art Chicago's SPACE (School Partnership for Art and Civic Engagement) program. Damon earned his BFA at the School of the Art Institute of Chicago. He organizes and teaches with P+NAP.

Ryan Lugalia-Hollon is the executive director for the P16Plus Council of Greater Bexar County. Before moving to Texas, he codeveloped the YMCA of Metropolitan Chicago's Youth Safety and Violence Prevention programs and was a Justice Fellow for the Institute on Public Safety and Social Justice at Adler University in Chicago. He is coauthor of *The War on Neighborhoods: Policing, Prison, and Punishment in a Divided City* (Beacon Press, 2018).

Boneta-Marie Mabo (Neta-Rie), an Aboriginal and Torres Strait Islander woman of the Piadram clan of Mer Torres Straits and Munbarra clan of Palm Island, is a sugar slave descendant, an angry Black woman, and a lover of fashion and art. She leads the Sisters Inside Young Indigenous Art Group. The inaugural artist-in-residence for the State Library of Queensland's kuril dhagun Indigenous Knowledge Center, she won the People's Choice Award and the National Aboriginal and Torres Strait Islander Art Award for her art celebrating the life of her activist grandfather, the late Eddie Koiki Mabo.

Meenakshi Mannoe is a woman of color living on the unceded and occupied homelands of the Musqueam, Squamish, and Tsleil-Waututh nations in so-called Canada. She is a member of the Stark Raven media collective and the Vancouver Prison Justice Day Committee.

Claude Marks is the director of the Freedom Archives, an educational media archive located in San Francisco dedicated to the preservation and dissemination of historical audio, video, and documents about progressive movements and culture from the 1960s to the present. He is also a former US-held political prisoner.

Janos Marton is the director of policy and campaigns at JustLeadershipUSA, where he launched and managed the #CLOSErikers campaign. A born and raised New Yorker, Janos worked on political campaigns and organized in Mississippi before attending law school. As an attorney, Janos has worked for a civil rights firm and a police oversight body and served as special counsel to an anti-corruption commission.

Erica Meiners writes, teaches, and organizes around access to education for people inside prison and after release, abolition, queer lives, and other liberation movements. The author of *For the Children? Protecting Innocence in a Carceral State* (University of Minnesota Press,

2016), she teaches classes in justice studies, education, and gender and sexuality studies at Northeastern Illinois University.

Toshio Meronek is a writer focusing on the San Francisco Bay Area, housing, and prisons. He covers queer issues for *Truthout* and has reported for *Al Jazeera*, *In These Times*, and *The Nation*. His work also appears in anthologies including *Captive Genders: Trans Embodiment and the Prison Industrial Complex* (AK Press, 2016) and *Trap Door: Trans Cultural Production and the Politics of Visibility* (MIT Press, 2017).

Layne Mullett is founding member of Decarcerate PA and the Coalition to Abolish Death by Incarceration, and is also a cocreator of Life Lines: Voices Against the Other Death Penalty. Layne has been active in social justice movements for over a decade, including organizing against gentrification, austerity, and the prison-industrial complex, and working for the freedom of political prisoners.

Jason Muñoz was born and raised in the Humboldt Park neighborhood of Chicago, Illinois. He aspires to become a published author, writing about life, love, spirituality, and freedom. Now a Christian, he has devoted his life to simplicity in the pursuit of godliness.

Isaac Ontiveros is codirector of the Center for Political Education. During the 2011–13 California hunger strikes, Isaac worked as a media strategist and spokesperson with the Short Corridor Collective at Pelican Bay State Prison and their solidarity network on the outside.

Andre Patterson desires to overcome the stigma of his past through positive acts in the present. He aspires to find purpose and redemption through his writings.

People's Education Movement Chicago is a collective of community educators, K-12 classroom teachers, students, parents, and university professors committed to educational justice in K-20 classrooms using a decolonial lens. As a movement rooted in the struggle against global white supremacy, we work in solidarity with the People's Education Movement Los Angeles and People's Education Movement Bay Area (California). The People's Education Movement Chicago coauthors of "Schooling and the Prison-Industrial Complex" are Erica Davila, Mathilda de Dios, Valentina Gamboa-Turner, Angel Pantoja, Isaura Pulido, Ananka Shony, and David Stovall.

Audrey Petty is a writer and educator based in Chicago. A member of the P+NAP teaching collective, she writes fiction, poetry, and creative nonfiction. Her work has been featured in such publications as *Callaloo, Columbia Journal, Massachusetts Review, ColorLines, Saveur,* the *Oxford American,* and *African American Review.* She also is the editor of *High Rise Stories: Voices from Chicago Public Housing* (Voice of Witness/McSweeney's Books, 2013).

Jill Petty has worked in progressive media for more than fifteen years. She is an editor with Northwestern University Press and previously directed communications/community engagement efforts for Equal Justice Initiative, a nonprofit headed by Bryan Stevenson that provides legal representation to poor people; and for Partners In Health, an NGO that provides health care and socioeconomic services in Latin America, Africa, and the United States. She is a member of P+NAP and lives in Chicago.

Patrick Pursley was wrongfully convicted and spent twenty-four years locked up in Illinois prisons. From prison he fought his case, in part, by helping to create a new law around ballistics testing that eventually won him a new trial. He is currently out on bond as he awaits his trial. Before and since his release from Stateville, he has been organizing a website and youth empowerment project. See the I Am Kid Culture website for more information: https://www.iamkidculture.org.

Beth E. Richie, author of *Arrested Justice: Black Women, Violence, and America's Prison Nation* (NYU Press, 2012), is an activist and academic whose work has focused on gender violence toward Black women and the role that the carceral state plays in the mass criminalization of marginalized groups. She teaches at University of Illinois at Chicago and is part of the P+NAP collective.

Benny "Don Juan" Rios was born and raised in the Pilsen community of Chicago and in Cicero, Illinois. He is forty years old, has been in prison for sixteen years, and is serving a forty-five-year sentence. He is a man who has been transformed by God's saving grace.

Adrienne Skye Roberts is a longtime volunteer member of the California Coalition for Women Prisoners (CCWP). She collaborates with incarcerated CCWP members serving life without parole (LWOP) on the ongoing storytelling project and campaign "A Living Chance: Storytelling to End Life Without Parole." This project is aimed at educating the public about LWOP, developing individual freedom campaigns, and, ultimately, ending LWOP. Adrienne is also a restorative justice facilitator who works with families and community to heal harm.

Dylan Rodríguez is a professor in the Department of Media and Cultural Studies at the University of California, Riverside. He served as chair of the Department of Ethnic Studies from 2009 to 2016 and was elected chair of the UC Riverside Academic Senate by his faculty peers in 2016. Rodríguez is the author of two books: *Forced Passages: Imprisoned Radical Intellectuals and the U.S. Prison Regime* (University of Minnesota Press, 2006) and *Suspended Apocalypse: White Supremacy, Genocide, and the Filipino Condition* (University of Minnesota Press, 2009). His writing and public intellectual works, which include more than four dozen published articles and book chapters, have appeared in a wide cross-section of scholarly and popular venues.

Felix Rosado is a restorative justice practitioner, peace builder, and mentor from behind the walls. Among other things he is a member of Right 2 Redemption and the Coalition to Abolish Death by Incarceration, co-coordinator of the Alternatives to Violence Project, and cofounder of Let's Circle Up. He is also part of the Lifelines Project and serves on Decarcerate PA's Inside Advisory Board. Originally from Reading, Pennsylvania, he's been serving a death-by-incarceration sentence at SCI Graterford for the last twenty-one years.

Sarah Ross is an educator and artist whose work uses narrative and the body to address spatial concerns as they relate to access, segregation, anxiety, and activism. She cofounded P+NAP, a cultural project that brings together artists, writers, and scholars in and outside Stateville prison to create public projects concerning segregation, criminalization, and incarceration.

Ann Russo teaches in women's and gender studies and LGBTQ studies at DePaul University. Her work focuses on queer antiracist feminist abolitionist strategies to cultivate collective healing, intervention, accountability, and transformation in response to violence. Her current book project is *Building Communities to End Violence—A Praxis of Accountability*.

Maya Schenwar is the author of the book *Locked Down, Locked Out: Why Prison Doesn't Work and How We Can Do Better* (Berrett-Koehler Publishers, 2014) and the coeditor of *Who Do You Serve, Who Do You Protect? Police Violence and Resistance in the United States* (Haymarket Books, 2016). She is the editor in chief of *Truthout*. She has written about the prison-industrial complex for *Truthout*, the *New York Times*, *The Guardian*, *The Nation*, *Salon*, *Ms. Magazine*, and others. Maya organizes with Love & Protect and the Chicago Community Bond Fund.

Daniel Scott was born in Illinois and raised in Los Angeles, California. He is a father of three children and the author of three books. He's also a prison litigator who practices civil and criminal law at both state and federal levels. He was wrongfully convicted at the age of nineteen and is pushing for resentencing and exoneration for crimes he did not commit.

Harrison Seuga is currently the director of reentry and core member of Asian Prisoner Support Committee. A former juvenile lifer who spent twenty-one years incarcerated, he now advocates for the currently incarcerated as well as being of service for those reentering the community. He conceptualizes social justice issues as a living being where all its parts contribute to its overall health, and enjoys thinking of new approaches to address the issues of mass incarceration, immigration, and reentry.

Damon Williams is codirector of the #LetUsBreathe Collective, an alliance of artists and activists organizing through a creative lens to imagine a world without prisons and police. He is also a performer and is a cohost of *AirGo*, a radio show and podcast showcasing the voices from Chicago and beyond reshaping culture.

Elton Williams is an incarcerated artist at Stateville Correctional Center in Illinois. He is the proud father of three adult sons and a grandfather of two beautiful granddaughters. When Elton is not working on gaining his freedom, he paints, reads, writes, draws, and dreams. Faith, family, and art keep him grounded in struggle.

Albert Woodfox spent forty-three years in solitary confinement in a Louisiana prison—more than any other person in the United States. Albert, Herman Wallace, and Robert King were members of the Black Panther Party and became known as the "Angola Three" after they were charged with the murder of a prison guard in Angola Prison in 1972. Albert's conviction was overturned three separate times by judges before he was released from solitary confinement in 2016. His memoir, *Solitary*, will be released in March 2019.

Index

shootings in, 112
South Side, 165, 217–19, 292–94,
  309, 311
Strategic Subject List, 230
Uptown, 19, 34
West Garfield Park, 122
West Side, 122–25, 128, 131
Woodfox in, 59–60, 72
Chicago Alliance Against Racism
  and Political Repression, 310,
Chicago Alliance Against Sexual
  Exploitation, 164
Chicago Area Black Lung
  Association, 35
Chicago City Colleges, 311
Chicago City Council, 309
Chicago Committee to Free Black
  Political Prisoners, 60
Chicago Community Bond Fund,
  212, 371
Chicago Legal Advocacy for
  Incarcerated Mothers, 12
Chicago Light Brigade, 310
Chicago Public Schools, 230, 236, 310
Chicago Reader, 104
Chicago Reporter, 3
Chicago Torture Justice Memorials,
  310–13
Chicago Tribune, 224, 277
Chung, Connie, 190
CIA, 225
Cincinnati, Ohio, 247–48
civil rights movement, 2
Civil War, 260
Clark, Mark, 90
Clear, Todd R., 126
Cleaver, Eldridge, 218
Clement, Frank, 270
Clements, Mark, 313
Cleveland, Ohio, 319

Clinton, Bill, 2, 91, 179
Clinton, Hillary, 150, 151
Coalition to Abolish Death by
  Incarceration (CADBI), 25, 26
COINTELPRO, 15, 90, 212
College and Community Fellowship,
  254, 289, 319
Colón, Kristiana, 219–20
Colorado, 94
Columbia University, 150
Combahee River Collective, 7
Communist Party USA, 90
Communities, Evictions, and Criminal
  Convictions, 251
Connecticut, 179, 245, 254, 307
Conservative Party of Canada, 108, 110
Cook County Jail, 36, 37, 39, 70, 314
Corcoran prison, 270
Correctional Service of Canada, 108,
  109, 341
Cosby, Monica, 19
Council 4994, 319
Council on Crime and Justice, 319
Creative Interventions, 181, 183, 205
Crenshaw, Kimberlé, 7
Crime Act. See 1994 Violent Crime
  Control and Law Enforcement
  Act
Criminal Code of Canada (CCC), 109
Critical Resistance, 7–8, 12, 160, 181,
  195, 199, 203, 312
Cuomo, Andrew, 238

Dallas, Texas, 130
Davis, Angela, 8, 10, 17, 219
  Are Prisons Obsolete?, 11
  If They Come in the Morning, 11
Davis, Jordan, 189
Davis, Troy, 11
death penalty, 19, 327

About Haymarket Books

Haymarket Books is a radical, independent, nonprofit book publisher based in Chicago.

Our mission is to publish books that contribute to struggles for social and economic justice. We strive to make our books a vibrant and organic part of social movements and the education and development of a critical, engaged, international left.

We take inspiration and courage from our namesakes, the Haymarket martyrs, who gave their lives fighting for a better world. Their 1886 struggle for the eight-hour day—which gave us May Day, the international workers' holiday—reminds workers around the world that ordinary people can organize and struggle for their own liberation. These struggles continue today across the globe—struggles against oppression, exploitation, poverty, and war.

Since our founding in 2001, Haymarket Books has published more than five hundred titles. Radically independent, we seek to drive a wedge into the risk-averse world of corporate book publishing. Our authors include Noam Chomsky, Arundhati Roy, Rebecca Solnit, Angela Y. Davis, Howard Zinn, Amy Goodman, Wallace Shawn, Mike Davis, Winona LaDuke, Ilan Pappé, Richard Wolff, Dave Zirin, Keeanga-Yamahtta Taylor, Nick Turse, Dahr Jamail, David Barsamian, Elizabeth Laird, Amira Hass, Mark Steel, Avi Lewis, Naomi Klein, and Neil Davidson. We are also the trade publishers of the acclaimed Historical Materialism Book Series and of Dispatch Books.

Also Available from Haymarket Books

Electric Arches | Eve L. Ewing

Exoneree Diaries: The Fight for Innocence, Independence, and Identity | Alison Flowers

Feminist Freedom Warriors: Genealogies, Justice, Politics, and Hope
Edited by Linda E. Carty and Chandra Talpade Mohanty

Freedom Is a Constant Struggle: Ferguson, Palestine, and the Foundations of a Movement | Angela Y. Davis, edited by Frank Barat, preface by Cornel West

From #BlackLivesMatter to Black Liberation
Keeanga-Yamahtta Taylor

I Am Troy Davis | Troy Davis, Martina Davis-Correia, and Jen Marlowe, foreword by Helen Prejean

How We Get Free: Black Feminism and the Combahee River Collective
Edited by Keeanga-Yamahtta Taylor

Six by Ten: Stories from Solitary
Edited by Mateo Hoke and Taylor Pendergrass

A Time to Die: The Attica Prison Revolt | Tom Wicker

The Torture Machine: Racism and Police Violence in Chicago
Flint Taylor

Who Do You Serve, Who Do You Protect?: Police Violence and Resistance in the United States | Edited by Joe Macaré, Maya Schenwar, and Alana Yu-lan Price, foreword by Alicia Garza